I0172064

SUPER POWER

THE POWER FORMULAS
Part Two

Our Father in Heaven,
His Son, Jesus Christ,
and Their Power Formulas

THE POWER FORMULAS
Part Three

Jesus Christ,
The Church of Jesus Christ
and The Power Formulas

And

SUPER POWER

Copyright February 10, 2010
Revised November 6, 2012
Craig A. McManama

From the Cover:
*adapted from
writings of
L. Ron Hubbard

DEDICATION PAGE

These books are dedicated to my parents, LaRae and Robert McManama. I thank you both for your love through the years. Thank you for your confidence in me, and your continuing words of encouragement.

Thank you Dad for your time and patience in helping me improve this manuscript. Thank you Mom for your words of testimony and faith that helped me choose to be a missionary. That decision has made all the difference in my life.

Thank you Mom and Dad for your teachings and examples, which have introduced me to and instructed me in God's Power Formula: The Gospel of Jesus Christ.

ACKNOWLEDGMENTS

I wish to acknowledge and thank my wife, Karla, and my daughters, Cassandra, Sarah, Megan, and my son Joseph for their love and support. Also, thank you to my father, Robert McManama, who reviewed the manuscript, and who made helpful suggestions.

Thank you, also, to Jack Higley, my friend and former missionary companion, for reviewing the manuscript.

A special acknowledgement is given to L. Ron Hubbard, who was the originator of the **Power** and **Power Change Formulas**, and of the idea of the **Conditions**. Without his work, these books would have never been possible.

A special thanks to Kay Williams for editing and for making these manuscripts into a book, and to Kris Humphries for her helpful suggestions.

Thanks to Makayla Robinson for designing and creating the Cover for the Book.

Also, thanks to Philip Wayman who has done the electronic book editing for **Super Power**.

I also wish to acknowledge all who have shared God's **Power Formula** with others. Their actions have changed the world, and they have changed me.

A special thank you goes to our Father in Heaven, to His Son, Jesus Christ, and to the Holy Ghost. They are the Sources of God's **Power Formula**, which is also Their Great Plan of Happiness.

Super Power Change from the Father to the Son
and from the Son to Us

Jesus Christ said:

Behold. I stand at the door and knock. If any man hear my voice, and open the door, I will come in to him, and will sup with him and he with me. **To him that overcometh will I grant to sit with me in my throne, even as I also overcame, and am set down with my Father in his throne.** (*New Test. Revelation* 3:20-21, emphasis added),

<hr>

Also,
"...ye shall be even as I am and I am even as the Father"
(The Book of Mormon, 3 Nephi 28:10)

<hr>

And

God's Commandments and Teachings are His <u>Super Power Formula</u> for us. Keeping His Commandments and Following His Teachings is doing <u>Super Power Change</u> with God.

Contents

THE POWER FORMULAS

PART TWO

Our Father in Heaven,
His Son, Jesus Christ,
and Their Power Formulas

Introduction and Review of Part One of the Power Formulas

In *The Power Formulas Part One, The Book of Mormon and the Power Formulas,* we first reviewed some of the definitions of *Power.* Below are the conclusions as to the meaning of the word *Power* as it is used in these books.

> Power (pou'er), n. 1) Ability to do or act; capability of doing or accomplishing something...12) Often powers of deity; divinity...23) to give power; to make powerful (*Random House Dictionary of the English Language,* 2nd Edition, New York, 1987, page 1516).

What do we think of when we hear or read the word *power?* Many images come to mind; some of these images are positive and some are not. Of the 32 definitions of power in the dictionary, these three define power as it is used in this book.

Definition 23 speaks of transferring or giving power to someone else. The **Power Formula** is a list of actions for transferring power to others. Here is where the first definition comes in, because the **Power Formula** is actually a formula for transferring 'the ability to do or act' and 'the capability of doing or accomplishing something,' to others.

The **Power Formula** can be applied to any type of activity. One example would be a transfer of leadership within in a business organization. However, the powers we are most interested in understanding are the "powers of deity..." mentioned in definition 12 above. The Lord's powers encompass and supercede all other powers.

We are narrowing down the meaning of power as used in these books. We will focus upon the "powers of deity," and upon how His abilities or powers can be transferred to us (*The Power Formulas, Part One, The Book of Mormon and the Power Formulas,* Craig A. McManama, see page 7, hereafter referred to as *Part One*).

Next, in Part One, we examined evidence that God has inspired men to "make a record" for His children. Actually, God has caused there to be more than one Record. One of these records is the *The Book of Mormon.* In *Part One,* we also looked at how God's scriptural records are examples of something called the **Power Formula**.

A Review of Part One of the Power Formulas

The **Power Formula** is among the **Conditions Formulas** identified by, and taught to others by the American author, L. Ron Hubbard. In *Part One*, we reviewed examples in *The Book of Mormon* of individuals and groups who were in these various conditions or operating states. Also, we reviewed how the prophets of ancient America, whom God used to make *The Book of Mormon* record, used actions like those taught in these **Condition Formulas**, in an effort to help their people.

Although it is recommended that you first read *Part One* and *The Book of Mormon* before reading these books, you can start with *Part Two and Part Three* and Super Power, if you prefer. It is my plan to make *Part One* available on the Internet.

For those who do not have access to *Part One*, here is a brief introduction of the **Condition Formulas** and *The Book of Mormon*. This information comes mostly from *The Power Formulas Part One*.

L. Ron Hubbard and the Conditions Formulas

The title for *The Power Formulas*, comes from the writings of L. Ron Hubbard. He was a very prolific writer and lecturer. He wrote many books of science fiction. He also wrote a great deal about other topics including the human mind, survival, ethics, behavior and management. His most widely known work is the book *Dianetics: The Modern Science of Mental Health*. He also founded the Church of Scientology International.

My first experience with his writings occurred in 1988 while taking a business course titled *Management by Statistics*. The content of this course came from L. Ron Hubbard's writings. Specifically, the topics of this course were the **Conditions Formulas**.

In 1988, while re-reading *The Book of Mormon* and studying the **Condition Formulas**, it became apparent to me that principles like those of the **Condition Formulas** were being used by the prophet record keepers who wrote *The Book of Mormon*.

The Conditions

L. Ron Hubbard identified a number of conditions, or operating states, which could be applied to individuals and groups. Here is a list of these conditions:

Power
Power Change
Affluence
Normal
Emergency
Danger
Non Existence
Liability
Doubt
Enemy
Treason
Confusion

(Adapted from L. Ron Hubbard, *Introduction to Scientology Ethics,* Los Angeles, Bridge Publications, 1989, p. 38)

The determination of which Condition an individual or a group is in, can be made by looking at a graph of their statistical trends. However, these Conditions are not just related to statistics. L. Ron Hubbard taught that these Conditions represent levels of ethics as well. (L. Ron Hubbard, *Management Technology Defined*, Los Angeles, Bridge Publications, 1976, see *Condition*, p. 99).

The Condition of any group, or individual determines their present potential for survival. Actions, which produce a condition of high survival ability for oneself and others, are considered ethical. Those actions, which endanger survival, are considered unethical. L. Ron Hubbard defined ethics in this way:

The reason and contemplation of optimum survival (Ibid, see *Ethics*, p. 179).

For instance, a declining statistical trend would indicate that one is in a **Liability Condition,** in terms of survivability. An increasing trend indicates an **Affluence Condition** and a good potential for survival. A trend, which is nearly level, but slightly increasing, is called a **Normal Condition.**

The survival potential of an organization in **Normal Condition** is better than that of one in a **Liability Condition.** Also, the survival potential of an organization, which is operating in a **Normal Condition**, is not as good as one whose statistical performance would indicate a **Condition of Affluence.** Within the group, each individual also has his own personal Condition level related to how well he or she is carrying out their responsibilities to the group.

Starting with **Non-Existence** and above, these Conditions are positive in that something good and of value is being accomplished. **Non-Existence** really means beginning to exist or function in a new position or calling. It means *coming out* of a non-existent state in that position.

For example, as a person begins a new job, he/she starts by learning his/her duties as defined by the policies of the organization the person is working for. Next, the person begins to perform these duties. As this person learns the job, he/she begins to perform better. His/her Condition is upgraded to **Danger**. This next Condition is called **Danger** because it is still below the **Normal Operating Condition** and further improvement is still needed through **Emergency** and then into the **Normal Condition**. The higher on this scale the individual goes, the greater his/her potential for survival as an employee of the organization.

Those Conditions below **Non Existence** are negative, in that, the actions of people or groups or nations in these Conditions are counter-productive and counter-survival. For example, if someone were to accept a position, but never really learns or decides to do his/her job, then the person would become a **Liability** to the organization. Furthermore, if this person then fails to accept responsibility and to make the needed corrections, he/she will begin to have a **Doubt** about the organization. If that person still fails to make changes, he/she would begin to consciously oppose the purposes of the group. This opposition can either be open (**Enemy**), or covert (**Treason**).

L. Ron Hubbard taught that each of these Conditions has a set of actions or **Formulas** for improving up to the next Condition. We could review the examples of actions like each of these **Condition Formulas** in *The Book of Mormon* and the *Bible*. However, the Conditions we are most interested discussing are those at the top of the scale: **Power Change** and **Power**. Most of our attention in *Part One* was focused on the principles of **Power Change and Power Formulas** as they relate to *The Book of Mormon*.

The Power Change Formula

In order to achieve the **Condition of Power**, one must have learned and followed the steps of the **Power Change Formula**. Here is that Formula:

> The **Formula** for the **Power Change Condition** is: when taking over a new post, *Change nothing* until you are thoroughly familiar with your new zone of Power...you just *don't Change anything*...go through the exact same routine every day as your predecessor went through. Sign nothing that he wouldn't sign. *Don't change a single order...* (L. Ron Hubbard, *Modern Management Technology Defined,* Los Angeles, Bridge Publications, 1976 see Power Change, page. 400, emphasis added).

Also, in order to follow the predecessor's actions, and "...don't change anything...", it is necessary to have a record of what the predecessor is doing. This is where the **Power Formula** comes in.

The Power Formula

The highest Condition discussed in The Management by Statistics course was one called **Power**. When one achieves this Condition, he or she has an obligation to prepare and train their successors. L. Ron Hubbard identified a series of steps one can use to help others to achieve this condition of **Power**. He named these steps, **The Power Formula**.

The steps of the Power Formula are listed below.

1. The first law of the condition of Power is, don't disconnect. You can't just deny your connections, you have to take ownership and responsibility for your connections...[Maintain communication with those you work with, live with or serve with].

2. The first thing you've got to do is **make a record** of all its lines and that is the only way you will ever be able to disconnect. So on a condition of Power, the first thing you have to do, is to **write up your whole post**. You have made it possible for the next fellow to assume the state of **Power Change**. If you don't write up the whole post, you are going to be stuck with a piece of that post since time immemorial, and a year or so later someone will still be coming to you and asking you about the post which you occupied.

3. The responsibility is to **write the thing up and get it into the hands of the guy whose going to take care of it**.

4. Do all you can to make the post occupiable (L. Ron Hubbard, *Modern Management Technology Defined*, Los Angeles: Bridge Publications, 1976, 401 emphasis added).

God's Power Formula Records

In *Part Two of the Power Formulas*, we will review another portion of God's **Power Formula** record for us. This is *The Holy Bible*. In *The Holy Bible* we will see descriptions of the relationship between Jesus Christ and His Father. In Their relationship, we shall again see the elements of **The Power** and **The Power Change Formulas.**

In *Part Three* of the **Power Formulas**, the plan is to review the relationship between Jesus Christ and His apostles and His other followers who make up His Church. In these relationships, we shall see the elements of **The Power** and **The Power Change Formulas**. We will also consider God's modern **Power Formula** scriptural records: *The Doctrine and Covenants* and *The Pearl of Price*.

As we review these relationships between our Father in Heaven and His son Jesus Christ, and between Jesus Christ and His followers, we will see that there are twelve main elements. These elements are listed below.

1. Our Father in Heaven has all Power and He is God, the Father of our spirits. We are literally His spirit offspring and family.

2. Our Father in Heaven does not hoard His Power. It is His desire to share it with His Son Jesus Christ and with us.

3. Therefore, Our Father in Heaven has done a **Power Formula** for His Son, Jesus Christ, thus training Him to be our Savior and our God, and in this way, Jesus Christ was prepared to receive "all power" (*Matthew 28:18*).

4. The Son has followed in the Father's path, thereby accomplishing **Power Change,** and He is, therefore, God the Son. In doing so, Jesus Christ has overcome sin, death and

Satan, the enemy of our souls.

5. While He was living in mortality, The Son established His Church. He called twelve apostles as the foundation of His Church organization, with Jesus Christ Himself "being the chief corner stone" (*New Test. Ephesians* 2:19-21). The Savior taught His gospel principles, or His **Power Formula**, to His twelve apostles so they, and His other disciples could become like Him.

6. Although His ancient Church was lost from the earth with the death of His apostles and prophets, the Savior has restored His Church to the earth, complete with new apostles and prophets. These apostles and prophets of Jesus Christ teach the gospel **Power Formula** to the members of Christ's Church including local Church leaders and fathers and mothers of families.

7. These members of His Church, including parents, do **Power Change** with the Savior, by following the example of Jesus Christ and by following the teachings of His apostles and prophets and their local leaders. In this way they can do **Power Change** with the Savior, and eventually also receive all power and become like Him and like the Father (see *The Book of Mormon: 3 Nephi 27:27, 3 Nephi 28:10, New Test; Matthew* 5:48 and *Revelation* 3:20-21, also *The Doctrine and Covenants* 132:20-23. *The Doctrine and Covenants* is a book of revelations received by the Prophet Joseph Smith).

8. The parents of eternal families teach the gospel **Power Formula** to their children so that these children can learn to do **Power Change** with the Savior by following His prophets and apostles, local Church leaders and their parents. The Lord has also provided missionaries to teach His gospel **Power Formula** to those who are not taught it by their parents.

9. **Super Power** means receiving all of God's Power, and it can be received by doing **Super Power Change** with God.

10. The Father and the Son have established Their Temples as the places where Their **Super Power Formula** is taught, and where we can learn to do **Super Power Change** with Them.

11. God's Temples are the places where marriages and family relationships can be made eternal, instead of just "until death do ye part".

12. Because They are Beings of perfect love, and perfect fairness, our Father in Heaven, and His Son, Jesus Christ have made it possible for every person, including those who died before having an adequate opportunity to do so on the earth, to receive every blessing that is available. This includes blessings of receiving Their **Super Power** to do good by helping others. The living can help those who have passed on to progress through receiving vicarious temple ordinances in their behalf.

The first four of these elements will be the subject of *Part Two of The Power Formulas*. The second four will be reviewed in *Part Three of the Power Formulas*. The final four elements will be among the subjects of the concluding book of this series: *Super Power.*

Common Ground Between Scientologists and Latter-day Saints

It is my hope that all individuals will come to believe in, and follow God's **Power Formula,** which is the gospel of Jesus Christ. This book has special implications for those who believe in, and follow the teachings of L. Ron Hubbard. It is my hope that when members of the Church of Scientology International see God's truths in *The Holy Bible* and in *The Book of Mormon*, they will come to believe in and follow Jesus Christ.

In *Part One*, we reviewed how the **Power Formula** references in *The Book of Mormon* provide a link between the beliefs of the members of the Church of Scientology International and the beliefs of the members of The Church of Jesus Christ of Latter-day Saints.

In *Part Two*, we will consider how *The Holy Bible* is also a record of God's **Power Formula** for us, and how *The Holy Bible* also contains teachings, which provide common ground between Scientologists and Latter-day Saints.

In *Part Three*, and in *Super Power*, we will consider teachings found in two modern books of scripture: *The Doctrine and Covenants* and *The Pearl of Great Price.* In these teachings, we will again see the elements of the Lord's **Power Change** and **Power Formulas,** which also provide a bridge between our faiths.

We will now look at these twelve elements in greater detail, starting with **The Power Formula** and **Power Change** relationship between our Father in Heaven and His Son Jesus Christ.

Chapter One

God the Father Has All Power, and He desires to Share His Power with His Son Jesus Christ and with Us

Our Father in Heaven has all Power. This is a fundamental belief of the Judeo-Christian world, and probably of most of the world religions. The *Old and New Testament prophets taught* this principle. Among the *Holy Bible* prophets who have testified of God omnipotence, are the following: Moses *(Genesis 17:1: 18:14);* Samuel *(1st Samuel 14:6;* Jeremiah *(Jeremiah 32:17);* and John *(Revelation 4:8. and 19:6).*

God, our Father in Heaven, is also eternal. He is "without beginning of days or end of years" (*The Pearl of Great Price, Moses* 1:3).

Prior to the creation of this earth, God did not exist alone. Jesus Christ and each of one of us existed with our Father in Heaven prior to this earth life. We were all spirit children of our Father in Heaven. *This is why He is called our Father in Heaven.* Since we are the spirit children or "offspring" of our Heavenly Father, it only makes sense that we also have a Heavenly Mother.

Our Heavenly Mother

A famous Latter-day Saint Hymn also teaches this profound truth:

In the Heavens, are parents single? No, the thought makes reason stare. Truth is reason, truth eternal, tells me I've a Mother there...When I leave this frail existence, when I lay this mortal by, Father, Mother, may I meet you in your royal courts on high? Then, at length, when I've completed all you sent me forth to do, with your mutual approbation let me come and dwell with you. (*Hymns of The Church of Jesus Christ of Latter-day Saints*, 1985, Deseret Book Company, Salt Lake City, Utah, "Oh My Father", page 292).

"Heavenly Parents"

In a document titled "The Family A Proclamation to the World", Read by President Gordon B Hinckley as part of his message at the General Relief Society [the church's organization for women] meeting held September 23, 1995, in Salt Lake City, Utah, the prophet of the Church taught:

> We, THE FIRST PRESIDENCY and the Council of the Twelve Apostles of the Church of Jesus Christ of Latter-day Saints, solemnly proclaim that marriage between a man and a women is ordained of God and that the family is central to the Creator's plan for the eternal destiny of His children.
>
> ALL HUMAN BEINGS – male and female – are created in the image of God. Each is a beloved spirit son or daughter of *Heavenly Parents*, and, as such, each has a divine nature and destiny. Gender is an essential characteristic of individual premortal, mortal, and eternal identity and purpose... (emphasis added).

Jesus Christ, Our Elder Brother

Jesus Christ was the Firstborn spirit child of our Heavenly Parents. Because of His surpassing goodness and intelligence, He volunteered, and our Father in Heaven selected and trained Him to be our Savior. This means that Jesus Christ was the One who was assigned, trained and empowered to lead us through our mortal life and back to the presence of our Heavenly Parents. Jesus Christ was, and is, a God. He is also the older Brother of each of the spirit children of our Heavenly Parents (see Matthew 25:40).

The Godhead—Three Gods, or One?

There are many in the Judeo-Christian world who believe that there is only one God. While it is true that we have only one Father in Heaven, there are other Gods. The prophet Joseph Smith taught that the evidence for the existence for more than one God:

> *...is as prominent in the Bible as any other doctrine. It is all over the face of the Bible.* It stands beyond the power of controversy (*The Teachings of the Prophet Joseph Smith*, compiled by Joseph Fielding Smith, Salt Lake City, Deseret Book, 1976, p. 370, Hereafter referred to as *Teachings*, emphasis added).

In fact, one cannot even get through the very first chapter in the *Holy Bible* before seeing plain evidence that God was not alone in the creation:

> And God said, let *us* make man in *our* image, after *our* likeness *(Genesis 1:26*, emphasis added*)*.

We may ask: who was God the Father speaking to when He said: "...let us make man in our image...?" This question was answered by two apostles of Jesus Christ. First, John identified Jesus Christ as "The Word" who was with the Father in the beginning (see *New Test. John 1:1-3 and*

14). Second, Paul taught that it was through Jesus Christ that the Father "...made the world" (see *New Test. Hebrews 1:1-3)*.

Jesus Christ is the Creator of our world, He is our Elder Brother, our Savior and our God. Our Father in Heaven has directed us to follow Jesus Christ (see *New Test. Matthew 17:1-5)*.

The Holy Ghost is the Third Member of the Godhead

In addition to our Father in Heaven, and His Son Jesus Christ, there is a third member of the Godhead. He is the Holy Ghost. We will consider His role in *Part Two*, Chapter Four, under the Heading of John Chapter 14. Through the prophet Joseph Smith, God has revealed this information about the three members of the Godhead, Who are the Presiding Council of the Heavens:

> The Father has a body of flesh and bones as tangible as man's; the Son also; but the Holy Ghost has not a body of flesh and bones, but is a personage of Spirit. Were it not so, the Holy Ghost could not dwell in us (see *The Doctrine and Covenants* 130:22).

This information about the Godhead is essential to our understanding of the scriptures. It is also essential to understanding of the eighth dynamic. For more information about the eight dynamics discovered by L. Ron Hubbard, see *The Power Formulas* Part One, Chapter 4. Also, more information about this topic is included in *Super Power*.

Intelligence and Power in the Universe

Every person who has lived, or who will ever live upon this earth, has already been through a series of steps or progressions. Each of us is an eternal being. The process of progression is ongoing. Below is a brief overview of these steps in our progression:

1. We first existed as intelligences, and intelligences are uncreated and eternal.

2. God the Father gave us an opportunity to progress and to become perfected beings, such as He is. It is my belief that we were given the opportunity to choose to become one of His spirit children, or not, and then Our intelligences were placed in spirit bodies, which were the offspring of our Heavenly Father and our Heavenly Mother. We are all Their spirit children.

3. After a long and sufficient period of preparation, we were given the choice of receiving a physical, mortal body, or not. To do so, we had to leave the presence of our Heavenly Parents.

4. We came to this earth to be born of earthly parents, so we could receive the precious gift of a physical body; we also came to be tested.

5. After death, which is a separation of the spirit from the body, our spirits reside in the spirit world, which has two divisions: paradise and the spirit prison, which is

also known as hell.

6.   Eventually, we will be resurrected, and if we have made the right choices in life, we will reside with our Heavenly Parents again, becoming as They are. Those who choose not to follow the Savior and thereby not do **Power Change** with God, will still receive perfect resurrected physical bodies, but even though they will live forever in a beautiful glorified world, they will not reside with, nor will they be like, their Heavenly Parents.

The Savior, "One Like Unto God"

As our Father in Heaven surveyed the intelligences that wished to progress, He recognized those with special capabilities. The Intelligence that was most like Our Father was selected to become His Firstborn Spirit Son. This Being became Jehovah, and He is also known as Jesus Christ.

Although He was most like our Father, Jesus Christ did not yet have a physical body. In contrast, Our Father in Heaven has a Spirit and a perfected, immortal, physical body.

Jesus Christ was the Firstborn of our Father and Mother in Heaven's spirit children. Therefore, He is our Elder Brother (see *New Test. Colossians 1:15*).

The Father's great "Plan of Happiness (*The Book of Mormon: Alma 42:8*)" required that a Savior sacrifice His life to atone for our sins. Therefore, the Savior would need to possess a *mortal body*. Because our Father in Heaven has an *immortal* physical body, it was necessary for the Father to choose and to prepare a worthy volunteer from among His children, to become our Savior. He chose the Intelligence that was most "like unto God": Jesus Christ. Our Savior, would be sent to earth by the Father, to lead the Father's other willing children back to Him.

Thus, we see that the Savior, who was known as Jehovah before His birth, and as Jesus Christ in mortality, was given Power in the pre-existence. He had three main duties in the pre-earth life. First, He supported and sustained His Father's plan for our progression. Second, He accepted and prepared for the mission of being our Savior and God. Third, He became the Creator, or organizer, of our world and others.

Opposition to God's Plan is Ancient

In the pre-mortal existence when the Savior was prepared to be our Savior, we existed with Him. Some of the spirits were in opposition to their Father's plan. The leader of this opposition was a spirit being of great ability and intelligence, known as Lucifer. However, while Lucifer had great intelligence, he lacked compassion. He also had another great weakness: pride. Lucifer believed that his plans were superior to those of the Father. He also desired to have the Father's power for the wrong reason: he wanted to rule over others.

Our Father had already presented the "great plan of happiness." A two-third's majority of our Father in Heaven's spirit children chose to follow the Father's plan. The other one-third of these spirits chose to rebel. Their chief, Lucifer, proposed a different plan. It was a plan of compulsion rather than freedom. His goal was to usurp Power, rather than achieving it through following the Father's **Power Formula**. Lucifer rebelled and started "...a war in heaven..."(see *New Testament Revelation* 12:7-9, *The Book of Mormon, Alma* 42:8; and *Pearl of Great Price, Abraham* 3:22-27).

John Taylor, the third prophet and president of The Church of Jesus Christ of Latter-day Saints, wrote concerning the great council in heaven and the actions of our Father in Heaven, Jesus Christ and Lucifer in this way:

> For in view of the creation of the world and the placing of man upon it, whereby it would be possible for them to obtain tabernacles [physical bodies], and in those tabernacles obey laws of life and with them again be exalted among the gods, we are told, at that time 'The morning stars sang together, and the sons of God shouted for joy' (*Old Test. Job* 38:7)."
>
> The question then arose, how and upon what principle should salvation, exaltation and eternal glory of God's sons be brought about? It is evident that at the council, certain plans had been proposed and discussed and after a full discussion of those principles and the declaration of the Father's will pertaining to His design, Lucifer came before the Father with a plan of His own, saying, 'Behold [here am] I. Send me, I will be thy son and will redeem all mankind, that one soul shall not be lost and surely I will do it; wherefore, give me thine honor.' But Jesus on hearing this statement made by Lucifer said: 'Father thy will be done and the glory be thine forever.' From these remarks made by the well-beloved Son, we should naturally infer that in the discussion of this subject, the Father had made known His plan and design pertaining to these matters, and all that His well-beloved Son wanted to do was carry out the will of His Father as it would appear had been before expressed. He also wished the glory to be given to His Father, who as God the Father and the originator and designator of the plan had the right to all the honor and glory. But, Lucifer wanted to introduce a plan contrary to the will of His Father and then wanted His honor and said: 'I will save every soul of man, wherefore give me thine honor.' He wanted to, contrary to the will of His Father, and presumptuously sought, to deprive man of His free agency [freedom of choice], thus making him a serf and *placing him in a position in which it was impossible for him to obtain that exaltation which God designed should be man's, through obedience to the laws* which He has suggested; and again Lucifer wanted the honor and Power of His Father to enable him to carry out principles which were contrary to the Father's wish.

President John Taylor also taught:

> It is consistent to believe that at this Council in the heavens, the plan that should be adopted, in relation to the sons of God who were then spirits and had not yet obtained a tabernacles [bodies], was duly considered. One third of the spirits in the pre-existence also rebelled with Lucifer and followed him.

These spirits failed their first estate [meaning their first test]. Therefore, they were denied the opportunity of receiving bodies upon the earth. They, with Lucifer, were cast out from the presence of the Father. These spirits are now upon the earth. They have organized and have formed a force in opposition to the will of our Father in Heaven. Their purpose is to make us all as miserable as they themselves are [for further information on this topic, see *The Book of Mormon, 2nd Nephi* 2:18 and 27], John Taylor, *Mediation and Atonement*, pages 93 and 94 as quoted in *Jesus the Christ*, James E. Talmage, Deseret Book, Salt Lake City, 1973, pages 15 and 16).

Why did Lucifer Choose to be the Enemy of Our Souls?

Lucifer, who became Satan, has made himself the enemy of our souls. By doing so he has also made himself the enemy of God. Why does Satan do the things he does?

In *The Power Formula Part 1,* chapter 9, we reviewed some of the reasons why Satan acts the way he does. Under the heading, *Enemy of our souls,* it was noted that

> ...he became the adversary during the pre-mortal life. His condition fell to **Enemy** and **Treason** when he rebelled against our Father in Heaven. The soul includes the body and the spirit (see *Doctrine and Covenants* 88:15).

Therefore, as the enemy of our souls, it is Satan's purpose to both destroy our physical bodies (counter survival intention) and to destroy us spiritually, meaning separating us from our Father in Heaven. Satan's intentions are counter to happiness and progression. His intention is to promote unhappiness and death.

The purposes of Satan are exactly opposite from those of God the Father and His son Jesus Christ. The Savior's intentions are to promote life both in the health and survival of our bodies, and to promote our optimum survival and our ultimate happiness by bringing us back into the presence of our Father in Heaven. Living with and like our Father in Heaven does is the definition of Eternal Life. Jesus Christ is the friend of our souls (see *New Testament: John* 15:12-15, and *Doctrine and Covenants* 84:63).

Recently, one of the apostles of The Church of Jesus Christ of Latter-day Saints has given new insight into one possible reason for Satan's actions. Perhaps you have wondered why Satan persisted in his evil doing, after having been cast out from being in the presence of the Father. According to President Henry B. Eyring of the Church's First Presidency:

> ...agency [the freedom to choose our own course in life] is the source of...risk. It is so priceless a gift from our Heavenly Father that a war in Heaven was fought and our agency defended. Lucifer sought to take it from us and to take for himself the honor and glory of our Father. The teenager you love may well have been one of the warriors on the side of agency and truth. *Satan seems to feel he can win a double victory by drawing teenagers into sin. He can destroy one of his antagonists and in the process try to prove the Father wrong, prove that the risk of agency was too great.* (A Life Founded in Light and Truth. Henry B. Eyring,

Ensign of the Church of Jesus Christ of Latter-day Saints, July 2001, page 10, emphasis added).

What a remarkable insight! Lucifer does not get it. He still is trying to prove that he is right and the Father was wrong. He views his vanquishment from the pre-mortal world as only a loss of one battle, and not the end of the war. Indeed, a recurring theme in these volumes will be the series of victories of Jesus Christ over Satan. Jesus Christ was victorious over Lucifer and his followers in the pre-mortal life. He was also victorious over Satan's temptations in his mortal ministry. Jesus Christ shall yet have final victories over Satan at His second coming, and at the end of the world.

The 3rd Party

In addition to tempting us, one of the ways that Satan and his followers seek to produce misery in the world is by promoting contention. When Jesus Christ appeared to the people of ancient America, he taught and warned them that:

> ...there shall be no disputations among you, as there have hitherto been... for verily, verily I say unto you, he that hath the spirit of contention is not of me, but is of the devil, who is the father of contention, and he stirreth up the hearts of men to contend with anger, one with another. Behold this is not my doctrine to stir up the hearts of men with anger, one against another, but it is my doctrine that such things should be done away. (*The Book of Mormon, 3rd Nephi* 11:28-30).

In promoting contention among individuals, groups or nations, Satan is an example of something described by L. Ron Hubbard as "the 3rd party law." This law states, in part, that:
> ...While it is commonly believed to take two to make a fight, a third party must exist and must develop it for a conflict to occur (L. Ron Hubbard, *Introduction To Scientology Ethics,* Bridge Publications, 1968 ... 2007, Los Angeles, page 285).

The important thing to realize is that when we begin to feel contention, there is a third party involved. When we feel contention, we should stop, take stock of the situation and realize that we are being influenced by another being, unseen but felt. With this knowledge, we have power to end the contention, thus making it possible to restore affinity and love to our relationships.

The Friend of Our Souls

Our Savior Jesus Christ is victorious over the enemy of our souls. The Father knew that because of our actions, and because of our own free will, each of us would commit sins while here upon the earth. Sins are counter-survival actions. The Father also knew that in order to return to His presence, we would need to become free of the effects of these acts.

This is one reason why the Father prepared Jesus Christ to be our Savior. The Father in His infinite wisdom, knowing the hearts and intents of His spirit children, could determine from the beginning that His Son, Jesus Christ would not fail in His mission as our Savior. The Father also knew that His Son would need training in order to carry out His mission.

The training and experience were sufficient in the pre-existence to prepare the Savior in all things, except one. In order for our Savior to eventually become an Eternal Father, Jesus Christ needed to experience mortal life. He needed to receive a physical body, actually come to an earth, and live. He needed to experience trials, pain and suffering of this life.

He also needed to experience death. It was only through personal experience that He could learn how to succor, or strengthen us, in our sufferings, trials and temptations. Only after experiencing these trials, could Jesus Christ fully empathize with, and help us, His brothers and sisters (see *The Book of Mormon, Alma* 7:11-13). During His life on earth, Jesus experienced the worst that earth life and Satan had to offer.

The Father's preparation of His Son was sufficient to allow the Son to function, not only as our Savior, but also as the Creator of worlds. The Father also prepared His Son to be a Revelator, to the prophets of ancient and modern times. The Father has done very little in the way of speaking or revealing truths through prophets. This has, almost exclusively, been the province of His Son. The exceptions to this are when the Father has spoken to testify of His Son's Authority, Power and Godhood when He revealed that we are to, "Hear ye Him". In doing so the Father completed the final step of the **Power Formula** which is "...make the post occupiable..." for His Son Jesus Christ.

The name by which Jesus was known during his pre-mortal existence, and to the ancient prophets, is the name Jehovah. Although the Savior had not yet experienced mortal life, in the pre-existence He had access to the knowledge, wisdom and experience of His Father. This helped Him to train and teach the prophets. The Savior, Jehovah, was a God, and He has been given "all power" in Heaven and Earth. (See *New Test. Matthew* 28:18).

That Jesus Christ is actually Jehovah is testified in the scriptures. When the Savior appeared to the Nephites, *The Book of Mormon* records that He told them that He was:

...the God of Israel, and the God of the whole earth (see *3 Nephi* 11:14).

Jesus Christ's Power of Resurrection

Because Jesus Christ's body was the offspring of an immortal Father, He inherited the capability of immortality. Also, because His mother was mortal, he inherited the capability of dying. These two characteristics allowed Him to both lay down His life for our sake, and to take it up again in the resurrection

In addition to the Power to resurrect Himself, Jesus Christ has the Power to resurrect each one of us, and He will do so. All of the Father's children who received an earthly body will eventually receive an immortal and perfect body in the resurrection. Thus, Jesus Christ has Power over physical death. He has conquered death through resurrection. The resurrection of our bodies is a free gift from Jesus Christ to all of His brothers and sisters.

The Savior has already exercised the Power to resurrect others on at least two occasions (see

New Test. Matthew 27:52 *and The Book of Mormon 3 Nephi* 23:9). These chapters tell how others were resurrected in both hemispheres, after the Savior's resurrection.

Our Relationship to Jesus Christ

Our relationship to our Savior is one of brother or sister: He being the first or elder Brother of us all in the spirit world. In addition to being our elder Brother, He is also superior to all of us in terms of intelligence and character traits.

In *The Pearl of Great Price* and *The Book of Abraham*, revealed to the prophet Joseph Smith, the Lord speaks about the pre-existent intelligences and the gradations that existed among them. *Abraham* 3:19-25 states:

> And the Lord [the Father] said unto me: These two facts do exist, that there are two spirits, one being more intelligent than the other; there shall be another more intelligent than they, and I, the Lord thy God, am more intelligent than they all. ...My wisdom excelleth them all. For I rule in the Heavens above and in the earth beneath, in all wisdom and prudence, over all intelligences thine eyes have seen from the beginning. I came down in the beginning in the midst of all the intelligences thou hast seen. Now the Lord has shown unto me, Abraham, the intelligences that were organized before the world was; and among those there were many of the noble and great ones; and God saw these souls that they were good. He stood in the midst of them and he said: These will I make my rulers; for he stood among those that were spirits, and he saw that they were good; and he said unto me: Abraham, thou art one of them; thou was chosen before thou wast born. *There stood one among them that was like unto God [the Father],* and he said unto those that were with him: We will go down, for there is space there and we will take of these materials and will make an earth whereon they may dwell; and we will prove them herewith to see if they will do all things whatsoever the Lord their God shall command them.

In these verses, we learn that our Father in Heaven's intelligence is greater than all ours. Although our intelligence is much less than that of the Father, or the Son, we have the potential to increase in intelligence. We have been commanded by Jesus Christ to become "...perfect even as your Father which is in Heaven is perfect." (*New Test. Matthew 5:48*). This commandment does not contain any exclusions, such as become perfect, except in knowledge, love, wisdom or power.

In the verses quoted above from *The Book of Abraham*, please note that, the Father declared that His Son was "... one that was like unto God." The Father could not come to earth and become our Savior because He is immortal. In order to carry out the atoning sacrifice needed to bring about the victory over death and sin, our Savior had to be able to die. He had to be mortal. Therefore, the Father had to have Someone else to carry out His plan, as His Representative.

The Father's Representative would need to be so in tune with Him, and so like Him, that the actions and teachings of the Representative would be the same as though the Father were carrying out the work upon the earth Himself. Only in this way could He insure that the plan would proceed to its ultimate and perfect conclusion. Thus, we see the need for the Father to teach his Son and train him in this most important mission.

Although it is extremely important that we do not become proud or try to compare our present knowledge and wisdom with that of the Father and the Son, we do need to learn to view ourselves as having the potential to become like Them, *for this is how they view us.* They see a much greater potential in us than we see ourselves. In summary, below are three important concepts about our origin and our potential:

1. Our existence and intelligence is eternal. This part of us has always existed.
2. Our spirits are the children of God, and thus we have the potential to become like our Heavenly Parents.
3. Only by following the Savior's gospel plan, which is **His Power Formula**, can we ever hope to come to the lofty heights of Perfection, Knowledge, Wisdom and Power where Jesus Christ and Our Heavenly Parents operate.

The Greatest Cycle of Action

The concept of a cycle of action was also a principle taught by L. Ron Hubbard (L. Ron Hubbard, *Modern Management Technology Defined*, Los Angeles: Bridge Publications, 1976, see Cycle of Action, p. 125.) Our Father in Heaven uses a spiritual creation, physical creation, perfection cycle of action for the progression of His children. The selection of a Savior and His training is the key element to making this cycle succeed.

This training and teaching in the pre-existent life constitutes our Father's Power Formula for his Son, Jesus Christ. We will next consider *how* the Father has done this **Power Formula** for His Son.

CHAPTER TWO

Our Father in Heaven Has Done a Power Formula for His Son, Jesus Christ

Three Possibilities About Jesus Christ

1.   He is the Father in Heaven. If this were true, Jesus Christ would be His own Father. This is the doctrine believed by most Christian churches, but as we shall see, this concept is not scriptural, nor accurate.

2.   He was man only, a great teacher perhaps, but nothing more. This is how most of the non-Christian world views Jesus Christ.

3.   He is the Son of our Father in Heaven, and a separate Being from the Father. Also, He has gone through a period of preparation and progression. In The Book of Mormon, we find references that the Son has been prepared by His Father (see Alma 13:5). In Ether 3:14, the Savior referred to himself in these terms: "Behold I am He who was prepared from the foundation of the world to redeem my people. Behold I am Jesus Christ..."

Also, in other revelations given to the prophet Joseph Smith, the Lord has amplified this explanation of His preparation. The Pearl of Great Price, The Book of Moses, chapter 5 verse 57 refers to the Son's preparation in these words: "...His only begotten Son...was prepared before the foundation of the world" (emphasis added). In a book of revelations received by the Prophet Joseph Smith, titled The Doctrine and Covenants, we learn that Jesus Christ has "finished his preparations" (*Doctrine and Covenants* 19:19).

In order for Him to have been prepared, He must have been prepared by another—The Father! This is the accurate view about our Savior and His relationship to the Eternal Father. This is also the perfect and most lofty example of the Power and Power Change Formulas.

How the Son was Prepared by Our Father in Heaven to be Our Savior

The first principle of the **Power Formula** is "don't disconnect...", meaning, maintain communication with the person or persons for whom you are doing a **Power Formula**. The second step is to "make a record". Next, the record is to be given to the person who is going to be taking the place of the one who is in power. Finally, the person in power is to "do all you can..." to help the one who is doing **Power Change** to succeed. We may then ask, how did the Father's actions fulfill these steps, including how did the Father make a record and get it to His Son to prepare and train Him to be our Savior, and our God?

The Father's Power Formula for His Son, Steps 1-3

Author Truman Madsen has written about this subject. By way of background, Madsen was a philosophy and religion scholar, and a professor at Brigham Young University. He also served as the director of the B.Y.U. Jerusalem Center. He was writing about the first vision given to prophet Joseph Smith. When Joseph was 14, he received a vision, which came in answer to a prayer about which church to join. In the year 1820, the young Joseph Smith went alone to a grove of trees to pray. As he prayed, Joseph saw: "a pillar of light and two personages within this light." Brother Madsen taught:

Having seen the light, he now saw two personages, one of whom said to him, indicating the other: 'This is My Beloved Son'.

In the Wentworth letter [a letter Joseph Smith later wrote to a newspaper publisher named Wentworth summarizing Latter-day Saint beliefs], the Prophet adds, speaking of the Two, that:

They exactly resembled each other in features and likeness (notice They not just resembled, they exactly resembled each other in features and likeness). We speak of a family resemblance 'like father, like son'. The Son looked like his Father. One of Christ's apostles, Phillip once asked Jesus to, 'show us the Father'. The Master replied, I have been so long with you and yet thou has not known me Phillip? He that hath seen me, hath seen the Father'. This is not because they are one and the same, but because they are in appearance as well as in nature exactly similar.

Truman Madsen also taught:

Young Joseph learned in the sacred grove, that to see the Father is to see the Son, and visa versa. A deeper point is the relationship of these two Beings. Joseph taught in 1840 — and I think it was an extension of what he learned in the grove that morning — that the statement of the master about His doing nothing but what he had seen the Father do, has infinite implications.

President Joseph Fielding Smith [one of the Presidents and Prophets of the Church of Jesus Christ of Latter-day Saints], wrote 'the statement of our Lord that he could do nothing but what he had seen the Father do, means simply that it had been revealed to Him [Jesus Christ] what His Father had done *(Doctrines of Salvation 1:32-33)*.'

Again, the relationship is exact. If Christ Himself was uniquely begotten and the Firstborn in spirit, and if He was the Christ not only of this earth, but also as the prophet taught later, of the galaxy, so before Him, **the Father Himself was a Redeemer and had worked out the salvation of the souls of whom He was a brother and not a Father.** This is deep water. The conclusion is drawn by Joseph Smith in his 'King Follett' discourse: **'What did Jesus do? Why; I do the things I saw my Father do when the worlds came rolling into existence.** My Father worked out his kingdom with fear and trembling and I must do the same' (*Teachings of the Prophet Joseph Smith*, page 358). In his final discourse in the Nauvoo grove, Joseph Smith taught: "The Savior said, the work that my Father did so I do also...He took himself a body and laid down His life that He might take it up again... (*Teachings of the Prophet Joseph Smith*, page 382).

What else it may mean, and it is mind boggling, **it means that the Father, by experience, knows exactly what his Son has been through. And the Son, by experience, knows exactly what the Father has been through.** Therefore, when He says 'I and my Father are one', He is not expressing a metaphysical identity. He is speaking in a oneness of spirit, harmonic throbbing of love and insight that can come only in the pattern of eternal redemption. So in the mind of a 14-year-old boy, that seed of insight blossomed and grew (Truman Madsen; *Joseph Smith the Prophet*, pages 12, 13, emphasis added).

Thus, we see that the Father prepared a record of how He had done His work. This record was presented to the Savior in the form of a vision, before the Savior came to earth, and almost certainly again, while the Savior was upon the earth. This re-preparation of the Christ is very possibly what was happening to the Savior during His solitary 40-day fast day in the wilderness, just before he started His teaching mission (see *New Test. Matthew* 4:1-12).

In the book *Jesus The Christ*, apostle James E. Talmage taught that the Savior was receiving further instruction, which we could also define as preparatory training, during His 40 days of fasting and prayer in the wilderness:

Christ's realization that He was the chosen and foreordained Messiah came to Him gradually. As shown by His words to His mother on the occasion of the memorable interview with the doctors in the temple courts, He knew, when but a Boy of twelve years, that in a particular and personal sense He was the Son of God; yet **it is evident that a comprehension of the full purport of His earthly mission developed within Him only as He progressed step by step in wisdom. His acknowledgment by the Father [at the time of His baptism as discussed below], and the continued companionship of the Holy Ghost, opened His soul to the glorious fact of his divinity.** He had much to think about, much that demanded prayer and the communion with God that prayer alone could insure (James E. Talmadge, *Jesus the Christ*, page 120, emphasis added).

In this way, the first three steps of the **Power Formula**, between the Father and His Son were fulfilled, a second time. Just as the Father had maintained communication and connection with His Son, and had prepared and given Jesus Christ a Record of how to fulfill his mission in the pre-mortal life, the Father repeated those steps for the Savior after His birth.

The Father's Power Formula for His Son, Step Four

The 4th step is one of the Father helping the Son to assume the position of being a God and

Savior. One way that the Father has done this, is by bearing witness that Jesus Christ is His "Beloved Son." You can read of this in the *New Testament* of *The Holy Bible, Matthew* 3:13-17:

> Then cometh Jesus from Galilee to Jordan unto John, to be baptized of him. But John forbade him saying, 'I have need to be baptized of thee, comest thou unto me?' And Jesus answering said unto him, 'suffer [allow] it to be so now: for thus it becometh us to fulfill all righteousness.' Then he suffered him. And Jesus, when he was baptized, went up straightway out of the water: and, lo, the heavens were opened unto him, and he saw the Spirit of God descending like a dove, and lighting upon him: And, lo, a voice from heaven saying, *'This is my beloved Son, in whom I am* well pleased' (emphasis added).

The Father confirmed to all, including we, who would later read the record of the event, that His Son's condition is one of **Power**. Also, there are many other instances where the Father has done the same. He bore this same testimony at the Mount of Transfiguration, to Peter James and John. At this time, the Father said: "This is My Beloved Son, in whom I'm well pleased; *hear ye Him*" (see *New Test. Matthew* 17:1-5).

The Father bore the same testimony that Jesus was His beloved Son, to the people of *The Book of Mormon* when the Savior appeared to them following His resurrection. This is found in the 11th chapter of *3rd Nephi* of *The Book of Mormon*. After introducing Jesus Christ as His Beloved Son, the Father again added this phrase, "…Hear ye Him."

Also, when Joseph Smith went into the grove to pray to find out which church to join, the Father appeared with His Son, and bore testimony again that Jesus Christ was His Son, and said: "Hear ye Him."

By instructing us to "Hear ye Him", God the Father has acknowledged to us, that His Beloved Son's Power of Godhood is supreme in our lives. "Hear ye Him," is not a suggestion. Rather, it is an instruction, and a commandment from the Father to us. We are not to try to bypass the Son. We can't achieve our highest potential growth or get back to the Father unless we follow His Son.

We must hear the Savior. The word 'hear' is really akin to "hearken" which means to listen and to obey. The Son speaks for His Father. Therefore, we cannot obey the Father unless we obey the Son.

Jesus specifically testified that we cannot bypass Him and hope to return to our Father in Heaven:

> …I am the way, the truth, and the life; *no man cometh unto the Father but by me* (*New Test. John 14:6,* emphasis added).

We have these recorded testimonies by the Father of His Son Jesus Christ. More importantly, for each of us, the Father is willing to shed forth into our hearts, by the power of the Holy Ghost, that Jesus is the Christ, the Son of God, our Savior, and our God.

The Father helped His Son assume the position of Savior and God. The Father expects each of us to honor His Son as our God. In *John 5:21-23*, the Savior taught:

...for as the Father raiseth up the dead and quickeneth them; even so, the son quickens whom he will. For the Father judges no man, but has committed all judgment unto the Son: *That all men should honor the Son even as they honor the Father. He that honoreth not the Son honoreth not the Father which hath sent him* (emphasis added).

If we feel that we can honor the Father, without also honoring His Son as God, then we are mistaken. For as Jesus Christ taught in the verses above, "he that honoreth not the Son, honoreth not the Father who sent him."

God the Father has prepared his Son, Jesus Christ to become our God and Savior. The Father has borne testimony of this fact to each of us. In this way, the Father has done, and continues to do all He can to make His Son's "post" or position as our Savior and our God "occupiable". By so doing, the Father has completed the 4th step of the **Power Formula** for His Son, Jesus Christ.

How We Can Honor the Father and the Son

The Father expects us to honor His Son and receive Him as God and as our Savior. The way we do this is to honor Jesus Christ's example. This means to follow Jesus Christ's gospel **Power Formula** for us. For just as the Father did a **Power Formula** for His Son, Jesus Christ, the Son has done a **Power Formula** for us. Also, just as the Son has done and is doing **Power Change** with the Father, we can do **Power Change** with Jesus Christ.

We will next look at how Jesus Christ has done, and is doing **Power Change** with The Father.

Chapter Three

Jesus Christ Began Doing Power Change with His Father in Heaven Before His Mortal Life, and He Continued Doing Power Change while he was upon the earth, and After His Resurrection

The essence of the **Power Change Formula** is: that those who are moving into a position of a superior, will do exactly what that person in power has done before them. In doing so, the one doing **Power Change** sacrifices his own will, if it be contrary to the will of the one who has preceded him. In *John* 5:30, Jesus taught that:

> I can of my own self do nothing: as I hear, I judge. And my judgment is just; because I seek not to do my own will, but the will of the Father, which hath sent me.

In *John 6:38* the Savior taught,

> I came down from heaven not to do my own will but the will of him who sent me.

In *John* 7:16, Jesus taught:

> ...my doctrine is not mine but His that sent me.

In *John* 12:49-50, the Savior further taught:

> ...for I have not spoken of myself; but the Father which sent me. *The Father gave me commandment what I should say and what I should speak* [a Power Formula]. *And I know that His commandment is life everlasting; whatsoever I speak therefore,* **even as the Father said unto me, so I speak** [Power Change with the Father] *(*emphasis added).

"...Even as the Father said unto me, so I speak": how could there be a better description of the central principle of **Power Change**, which is "...don't change anything..."? (L. Ron Hubbard, *Modern Management Technology Defined*, Los Angeles, Bridge Publications, 1976, see Power Change, page. 400).

As reviewed in the previous chapter, the Father has done a **Power Formula** for His Son by giving Him the record of His own actions and teachings when He, the Father, was a Savior of another world. This has made it possible for the Son to become our Savior and God by doing

Power Change with His Father. He did so by following His Father's example exactly.

The deeds Jesus did are those that His Father taught Him. In fact, He reported that His deeds were those, which he had *seen* His Father do. Not only did Christ do what He has seen His Father do, He also taught exactly what His Father had instructed Him to teach the people.

As noted previously, Our Father in Heaven prepared Jesus Christ to be our Savior, before the creation of the world. The Father did so by showing His Son, in a vision, how He, the Father, had also been a Savior, and how He had carried out His own eternal redemption of a group of spirit brothers and sisters. While He (our Father) was functioning in the role of Son and Savior, He was doing **Power Change** with His Father. The FATHER of our Father in Heaven is Jesus Christ's, and our Grand Father in Heaven.

How wonderful it is to realize that God's **Power Formula** is eternal, and that the plan has been repeated and will be repeated eternally. The plan works. Therefore, it is used over and over and over again. God's great purposes are to promote life, love, progression, perfection and joy. This is accomplished as intelligent beings follow their Perfect Parents in the greatest cycle of action, which is the **Cycle of the Celestial Power Change and Celestial Power Formulas.** Another name for **Celestial Power** is **Super Power**. **Super Power** is the subject of the final book contained within these pages.

The Result of the Son's Doing Power Change with His Father was That He Received "All Power in Heaven and in Earth"

Because He has done **Power Change** with the Father, Jesus Christ has All Power. Jesus Christ taught, after His resurrection, that:

> ...all power is given unto me in heaven and in earth (*Matthew 28:18,* emphasis added).

The Savior, through following exactly the teachings, example and behavior of His Father, was able to completely and perfectly carry out **Power Change**.

The result of a person carrying out the **Power Change Formula** is that he or she has then comes into a **Condition of Power** him or herself. The Savior has achieved Power equal to that of His Father, for there can't be any more power than "all power". However, this doesn't mean that the Father has given up His Power, for He is also omnipotent.

"All Power" = Super Power

By receiving "all power...in heaven and in earth...', Jesus Christ has pleased His Father immensely (see *John* 8:29 and *Matthew* 3:17). The Father wanted to empower His Son. Also, the Father and the Son want to empower us.

To help us to receive His Power, The Father has directed our attention to His Son, by telling us to "hear Him." By doing so, the Father has verified that He has empowered His Son, Jesus

Christ, to act in His behalf. Indeed, the Father will not accept any who try to by-pass or to go around His Son, in an effort to return to Him, or to try to gain His Power. Again, we must come to the Son to come to the Father. By way of reminder, Jesus Christ taught, "I am the way, the truth and the life, no man cometh to the Father but by me" (*John* 14:6).

Jesus Christ's Earthly Mission

When the Savior came to this earth, He had many important assignments from the Father. The Savior was doing the same things that He had seen His Father do. In this way He accomplished **Power Change** with the Father. Below, we will review some of the elements of the Savior's earthly mission.

1. He was to take upon Himself a body of flesh and bones, and experience difficulties, challenges and the joys of life upon the earth.

2. He was to live and keep the law perfectly Himself. He was to keep all the principles and receive all the ordinances that would be required of us, in order for us to return to the Father. This included the ordinance of baptism, which He sought and received, even though he had no sins, which needed to be cleansed. *The Book of Mormon* teaches that the reason the Savior was baptized was "to fulfill all righteousness." Also, *The Book of Mormon* emphasizes that if the Savior needed to be baptized to "fulfill all righteousness", how much greater need have we, being imperfect, to be baptized. In this wonderful chapter in *The Book of Mormon*, the Savior also taught us the principle of **Power Change** in these words: *"...follow me, and do the things which ye have seen me do"* (*The Book of Mormon, 2nd Nephi* Chapter 31).

3. After being baptized by John the Baptist, the Savior organized His church. He selected, ordained and trained twelve apostles. Jesus prepared these men to lead His church. Jesus Christ taught the apostles what to do and say, thus doing a **Power Formula** for them. The apostles' responsibility was to teach us what they had been taught. In doing so, they were carrying out a **Power Change** with Jesus Christ as the earthly leaders of the Church of Jesus Christ, *and* they were also doing a **Power Formula** for us!

4. The fourth thing the Savior did during His life was to teach the Gospel **Power Formula**, which had been taught to Him by His Father. This plan was to be taught by Him initially to the descendants, or "house" of Israel. Later, His chosen and empowered representatives were inspired to teach the gospel to all who would listen. His gospel plan starts with a spiritual **Non Existence Formula** for those who were not yet members of His Church. As we develop faith in Jesus Christ, repent of our sins, are baptized "...for the remission of sins", and receive "...the gift of the Holy Ghost", our hearts are changed, and we are spiritually born of God. This is the spiritual **Non Existence Formula**.

   This is how we can come out of spiritual **Non Existence** in our relationship to God (see *New Test. Acts* 2: 37-38 and *1st John* 5: 1-4). Those who continue to follow the Savior throughout their lives will eventually receive His **Power Formula** and **Super Power Formula** and be able to do **Power Change** and **Super Power Change** with God. We see the Savior actually taught two separate **Power Formulas** while He was upon the earth—one for Church leadership to the apostles, and the other **Power Formula** was for all His followers. They were to follow Him by living lives of service and love, as He has done (see *The Book of Mormon, 2nd Nephi* 31:16-17).

5. The next portion of the Savior's mission on the earth was to make the atonement for our sins. This would allow us to overcome the negative effects of these anti-survival acts. The *New Testament* refers to the Savior as the Lamb who was "slain from [before] the foundation of the world" (*Revelation* 13: 8). This means that His atoning sacrifice is part of the Father's plan, and Jesus Christ accepted this portion of His mission before coming to earth. In the Garden of Gethsemane, and upon the cross, the Savior took upon Himself the sins of all mankind. He experienced the suffering in our place that is associated with our sins. This was the great service that had to be performed to bring us back into the presence of our Father in Heaven. His atoning sacrifice allows us eventually to become perfect as a result of His help, and our acceptance of Him, and by our following His example.

Even though the Savior's mission, and doing **Power Change** as our Savior was completed with His resurrection, He continues to do His Father's will, and to keep His Father's commandments (see *The Book of Mormon, 3 Nephi* 26:1-2). There will never be a time when the Son is not following the example of His Father, and our Father.

In the next chapter, we will review *New Testament* verses, which show that the Father has done a **Power Formula** for His Son, and the verses that demonstrate that the Son has done **Power Change** with His Father.

Chapter Four

The Savior's Earthly Mission and How He Has Done POWER AND SUPER Power Change with His Father in Heaven

In His role as our God and Savior, Jesus Christ has many responsibilities. L. Ron Hubbard has referred to differing areas of responsibility as wearing different hats. The following is a partial summary of Jesus Christ's "Hats" or areas responsibility for His pre-mortal, mortal and post-mortal periods of His existence.

Among the Pre-mortal "Hats" or Areas of Responsibility of Jesus Christ are These Listed Below

1. The Firstborn spirit child of the Father in the spirit world, and the Heir of the Father.
2. The Creator of Heaven and Earth.
3. He was, and is, Jehovah, the second member of the Godhead.
4. As Jehovah, He was the God of the *Old Testament*, and the revelator to the prophets, including those in the land of Israel, (*The Holy Bible*) and the Israelite prophets who had traveled to ancient America (*The Book of Mormon*).

Among the "Hats" or Areas of Responsibility of Jesus Christ in Mortality are These Listed Below

1. The Son of Mary, and our Father in Heaven, and a member of the family of Mary and Joseph.
2. The Student of the scriptures in preparation for His role as our Savior.
3. The Teacher of the Gospel of Jesus Christ.
4. The Founder of the Church of Jesus Christ.
5. The Healer of the bodies, minds and spirits of men, women, and children.
6. The Victor over Satan and his followers, both in the wilderness after His 40-days fast, and in casting out evil spirits, from men, women, and children upon the earth.
7. The Initiator, Organizer, and Director of the great missionary effort to share His gospel **Power Formula.**
8. God among men and women on the earth, or Immanuel, "God with us".
9. He suffered for our sins and He allowed His life to be taken as a sacrifice for the sins of mankind.
10. The One who brought about the resurrection, including His own body, and of others after

His resurrection. This bodily resurrection will eventually be given to all who have lived upon the earth.

11. The Preparer of the apostles and prophets to carry on His work after His ascension into heaven (Jesus Christ did a **Power Formula** for His apostles, prophets, and for all of His followers).

12. The Second Comforter, meaning that for those individuals who prepare themselves sufficiently during this mortal life, will have:

> ...the Lord Jesus Christ Himself...[to] attend him [or her], or appear unto him from time to time, and even He will manifest the Father unto him...and the visions of the heavens will be opened unto him, and the Lord will teach him face to face... (*The Teachings of the Prophet Joseph Smith* pages 150, 151, and see also John 14:16, 17, 18, 21 and 23).

In fulfilling these responsibilities, Jesus Christ continued doing all things His Father had shown Him, and assigned Him to do, thus continuing to do **Power Change** with His Father.

Among the "Hats" or Post Mortal Areas of Responsibility of Jesus Christ After His Resurrection Are These Listed Below

1. The Deliverer of the spirits of those in the spirit world, by starting the missionary work of teaching the gospel to the spirits of those who were in Paradise, and in sending missionaries to teach those in the spirit prison, or "hell".

2. The Revelator to the apostles, prophets and disciples of His ancient Churches in the Holy Land, and in ancient America.

3. The Restorer of His Church in the modern times, also called "the Latter Days".

4. The Second Comforter (*see above*).

5. The Deliverer of the people of Israel from destruction at the time of His 2nd coming.

6. King and God who will personally reign on the whole earth during the 1,000-year millennium.

7. The Victor over Satan during the final battle at the end of the world.

8. The Judge of the quick and the dead.

9. The Preparator of this earth as a Celestial abode for those who have followed Him, thus doing **Power Change** with God.

10. The Perfecter of these same people.

11. Finally, Christ will become a Father in Heaven, for He will have completed **Power** and **Super Power Change** with God the Father.

12. Jesus Christ will then repeat the great **Power Formula** and **Power Change Cycle of Action**. He will then do a **Power** and **Super Power Formula** to prepare another Savior and God the Son for new worlds. The great cycle of action or "one eternal round" will continue, as it has, forever (see *The Book of Mormon, 1st Nephi* 10:19).

How the Savior Became a Mortal Being

We will spend but a short amount of time reviewing Jesus' birth and childhood. This story is well known to Christians and to many non-Christians throughout the world. Those who are interested in learning about His birth and childhood should read *Luke* chapter 2 for further insights on this. However, we will review a few important points about the Savior's early life.

We need to understand that Jesus Christ, although the son of a mortal woman was not fathered by a mortal man. His Father was God the Eternal Father. From His mother Mary, the Savior inherited the capacity to be mortal (i.e. to die). From His Father, the Savior inherited the capacity to resurrect His body. Both of these powers were necessary in order for Him to be able to suffer and die for us, and to accomplish a resurrection for Himself and for us.

The other point about the Savior's early life that needs to be understood is that by age 12, and probably much sooner than this, the Savior was aware of the fact that God, our Heavenly Father was actually the Father of His physical body as well as of His spirit body. This is illustrated in a story told in *Luke* 2:40-49:

> And the child grew, and waxed strong in spirit, filled with wisdom: and the grace of God was upon Him. Now His parents went to Jerusalem every year at the feast of the Passover. And when He was twelve years old, they went up to Jerusalem after the custom of the feast. During their journey home, the child Jesus tarried behind in Jerusalem; and Joseph and His mother knew not of it. But they, supposing Him to have been in the company, were a day's journey; and they sought Him among their kinfolks and acquaintances. When they found Him not, they turned back again to Jerusalem seeking Him. And it came to pass, that after three days, they found Him in the temple sitting in the midst of the doctors both hearing them and asking them questions. And all that heard Him were astonished at His understanding and answers. And when they saw Him, they were amazed; and his mother said unto Him, "Son, why hast thou thus dealt with us? Behold thy father and I have sought thee sorrowing. And he said unto them, how is it that you have sought me? Wist [know] ye not, that *I must be about my Father's business*? (*Luke* 2:40-49, emphasis added)

Jesus Christ's Stable Datum

L. Ron Hubbard identified and defined the concept of a Stable Datum. He wrote:

> ...2. Anybody of knowledge more particularly and exactly, is built from one datum [a piece of knowledge...] That is its stable datum. Invalidate it and the entire body of knowledge falls apart. A stable datum does not have to be the correct one. It is simply the one that keeps things from being in a confusion and on which others are aligned. 3. a datum which keeps things from being in a confusion and around which other data align.
>
> (L. Ron Hubbard, *Modern Management Technology Defined, Los Angeles: Bridge Publications, 1976. See Stable Datum, p 491)*

As we review the Gospel of John, we can see the Stable Datum, or primary motivating truth in the life of Jesus Christ. Jesus Christ's Stable Datum was His Faith in and His love for His Father. Because of His love for Father, and for us the Savior had a great desire to follow His Father, thus doing Power Change with Him.

His Love for The Father and His Desire to do the Father's Will Are First, Last and Always in the Savior's Life

It is important to note that in His very first recorded words that Jesus spoke at the age of twelve, were about His Father. Jesus Christ knew that His Father was really God the Eternal Father. Also, at age twelve, the Savior had already learned that He was to be doing His Father's will or "business." The answer He gave to his mother's question indicates that He had some understanding of what the Father's will was, and that He was involved in doing His Father's will, as He taught others.

It is also interesting that the Savior's last recorded words in mortality were about His Father and the mission His Father had given Him. From the cross, He cried with a loud voice and said, "It is finished" (*John* 19:30). *Luke* added: " And when Jesus had cried with a loud voice, He said "Father into thy hands I commend my spirit, and having said this, He gave up the ghost." (*Luke* 23:46).

Our attention in this chapter will be directed to what happened to the teachings and actions of the Savior between these first and last utterances. His actions and teachings were all carried out in the framework of His completing the mission His Father had prepared Him to accomplish. Jesus Christ taught:: "...I do always those things that please Him" (John 8:299, emphasis added).

The Savior's mission contained four main elements. These are listed below.

1. Doing **Power** and **Super Power Change** with His Father by doing the things which He had seen His Father do.

2. Teaching the gospel He had learned from the Father, in an effort to raise the spiritual **Condition** of all those who would listen and follow Him back to His Father. His teaching of the gospel was actually a spiritual **Non Existence Formula,** which means a spiritual rebirth through faith, repentance, baptism and receiving the gift of the Holy Ghost, and enduring to the end in following the example of Jesus Christ.

3. A third action of the Savior was to call future leaders of His Church, and train them to do His work after His departure. Jesus did **Power** and **Super Power Formulas,** for His apostles and prophets and established the church organization through which they could eventually share His **Gospel Power** and **Super Formulas** with everyone.

4) Accomplishing His atonement which included two parts: First, suffering and dying as a sacrifice for our sins, and second, overcoming death through the resurrection.

To simplify the coming chapter, we will include both **Power Formula** and **Super Power Formula** under the term **Power Formula.** This is in regards to the relationship between the Father and the Son. This is also true for **Power** and **Super Power Change.** Both are implied when this chapter speaks of **Power Change** between God the Father, and His Son, Jesus Christ.

How Jesus Christ Did Power Change with His Father

The evidence that Jesus Christ followed all of the actions of His Father, thus doing the **Power Change** with the Father, are also written 'all over the face of the *Bible*'. This is a major theme of the *New Testament*.

Rather than trying to find every single reference related to this topic in *The Holy Bible*, we will look at only one book. This is the book of *John*. In John's gospel or testimony of Jesus Christ, we see probably the plainest and most complete presentation of this theme of the **Power Formula—Power Change** relationship between God the Father and His Son Jesus Christ. These references plainly show that the Savior was carrying out **Power Change** with his Father.

JOHN CHAPTER 1

John's gospel begins in this way:

1. In the beginning was the Word, and the Word was with God and the Word was God.
2. The same was in the beginning with God.
3. All things were made by Him; and without Him was not anything made that was made (*John* 1:1-3).

These verses indicate four truths. First, Jesus Christ was present at the beginning, meaning before the creation of this earth. The second truth in these verses is that He was with God the Father. The third truth found in these verses is that Jesus was also a God at that time. Fourth, it was actually Jesus Christ who did the work of the creation.

Some people have mistaken the meanings of these verses thinking that Jesus Christ is our Father in heaven. However, if one reads further in the first chapter of *John*, we find these words:

> And the word was made flesh, and dwelt among us, (and we beheld His glory, the glory as o*f the only begotten of the Father*) full of grace and truth (*John* 1:14, emphasis added).

This verse indicates that Jesus Christ was "the only begotten of the Father." Jesus is not the Father in heaven. He is the Son of the Father. Further, in this chapter, the apostle John, quoted John the Baptist's testimony of the Savior when he said: "And I saw and bear record that this is *the Son of God*" (*John* 1:34, emphasis added).

Chapter 1 of *John* refers to the Savior's calling of His apostles. In calling these apostles, the taught them the essence of the **Power Change Formula** in these few words: "Follow me" (*John* 1:43).

We shall find that these words meant more than just walking behind Him. The apostles were to teach the truths that they learned of Him, and they were to do the things that they saw Him do, just as Jesus was teaching and doing the things He had learned from His Father in Heaven.

JOHN CHAPTER 2

The First Miracle, and Defending the Sanctity of His Father's House, the Temple

In this chapter, the Savior was attending a wedding feast in Canaan. It is here that He performed His first miracle when He turned water into wine. He did so at His mother's request. John 2:11 reads:

> This beginning of miracles did Jesus in Cana of Galilee, and manifested forth His glory; and His disciples believed on Him.

Next, this chapter refers to Jesus going to the Passover in Jerusalem. It was at this time that He first cleansed or drove out the moneychangers from "my Father's house", the temple (verses 13-17). Also, even in this early part of His ministry, Jesus Christ knew and prophesied of His death and His resurrection, which would not occur for three years (see verses 18-23).

JOHN CHAPTER 3

The third chapter of *John* begins with a teaching incident between Jesus Christ and a man named Nicodemus, who was "a leader of the Jews" (*John* 3:1). In these verses, the Savior taught the principles of the new birth that are a spiritual **Non-Existence Formula.** For more information regarding the spiritual **Non-Existence Formula** and being born of God, please see *The Power Formulas Part One.*

Why the Father Sent His Son into the World

Also, in this chapter the Savior first taught the important principle that He had been sent by the Father. In addition, John explained the reason why Jesus had been sent by His Father, in these words:

> For God so loved the world that He gave His only begotten Son that whosoever believeth in Him should not perish, but have everlasting life. For God sent not His Son into the world to condemn the world; but that the world through Him might be saved (*John* 3:16-17).

This is the first presentation of the theme that Jesus Christ was sent by the Father in the *Book of John*. Also, this famous verse teaches that the Father's purpose in sending His Son to the earth was positive. He did so "that the world [meaning His children] might be saved".

Later in this chapter, Jesus was teaching some of the followers of John the Baptist when He said:

> For He whom God hath sent [meaning Himself, Jesus Christ] speaketh the words of God [meaning the Father]: for God giveth not the spirit by measure [partially] unto Him. The Father loveth the Son and hath given all things into his hand (*John* 3:34-35) [The "th" and "ith" endings for "hath", "speaketh", "giveth" and "loveth" are older English for "s"].

In speaking "...the words of God [the Father]...", the Savior was doing **Power Change** ("...don't change anything...") with His Father.

JOHN CHAPTER 4

This chapter begins with a story of how Jesus taught a woman of Samaria when they were together at a well. As He taught this woman, the Savior testified that He was indeed the Messiah, "... which is called the Christ" (see *John* 4:25-26).

Joshua the Messiah

Perhaps now is a good time to consider the meanings of the names and titles of Jesus Christ. The word Christ is actually a title, rather than a name. Apostle James E. Talmage has written the following, regarding the meanings of the word Christ:

> Christ is a sacred title, and not an ordinary appellation, or common name; it is of Greek derivation, and in meaning is identical with its Hebrew equivalent *Messiah*...signifying the Anointed One...[this title is] expressive of the Lord's divine origin and Godship."

Also, regarding the name Jesus, James E. Talmage has written:

> Jesus is the individual name of the Savior, and as thus spelled is of Greek derivation, its Hebrew equivalent was *Yehoshua* or *Yeshua*, or as we render it in English Joshua…meaning 'Help of Jehovah', or 'Savior' (*Jesus the Christ*, pages 35, 36).

Therefore, if our English *Bible* had been translated from Hebrew rather than from Greek, we would refer to our Savior as *Joshua the Messiah*.

The Savior's "Meat"

Later in *John* chapter 4, the Savior's disciples, being concerned about His health, asked Him to eat. He taught them this principle:

> Jesus said unto them, my meat is to do the will of Him that sent me, and to finish His work (*John* 4:34).

Here again, the Savior taught the principle that He was sent by the Father to do the will of the Father and to finish the work that the Father had given Him. His strong desire to do His Father's will was compared to our need for food.

This chapter also tells of the Savior's healing of a child, even though the child was located in a different city. John wrote,

> This is again the second miracle that Jesus did when He came out of Judea into Galilee (*John* 4:54).

JOHN CHAPTER 5

The Savior Testified that the Father had Prepared Him
(Thus Doing a Power Formula for Him)

This chapter of John tells the story of the Savior healing a crippled man on the Sabbath Day at the pool called Bethesda. After He had healed this man, some of the leaders of the Jews

> …sought to slay him because he had done these things on the Sabbath day but *Jesus answered them My Father worketh hitherto [before] and I work."*
> Therefore, the Jews sought the more to kill Him, because He not only had broken the Sabbath, but had also said that God was His Father making Himself equal with God. Then Jesus answered and said unto them:
> Verily, verily, *I say unto you, the Son can do nothing of Himself but what He*

seeth the Father do: for what things soever He [the Father] doeth, these also doeth the Son likewise [Power Change]. For the Father loveth the Son [Power Formula Step 1] and sheweth Him all things that Himself doeth [Power Formula Steps 2, 3] ... for as the Father raiseth up the dead and quickeneth them; even so the Son quickeneth whom He will. For the Father judgeth no man, but hath committed all judgment unto the Son: That all men should honor the Son, even as they honor thy Father [Power Formula Step 4]. He that honoreth not the Son honoreth not the Father which hath sent Him (see John 5:19-23, emphasis added).

These verses contain perhaps the most important exposition in scriptures that the Father has done **Power Formulas** for His Son. Before Jesus was born upon this earth, the Father showed the Son, a record of what He, the Father, had done. This means that the Father must have once lived upon another world and the Father had raised "up the dead" as a Savior, just as the Son would be doing.

Jesus also Testified that He was Doing What the Father had Prepared Him to do (Thus Doing Super Power Change with His Father)

Jesus Christ was following the same principle as taught in the **Power Change Formula**, which is "...don't change anything..." This is evidenced by these words:

> ...The Son can do nothing of Himself, **but what He seeth the Father do.** *For what things soever He [the Father] doeth, these also doeth the Son likewise (John 5:19, emphasis added).*

This verse is a perfect summary of how the Son does **Power Change** with His Father. In verse 30 the Savior taught:

> I can of my own self do nothing, as I hear, I judge, and my judgment is just; because *I seek not mine own will, but the will of the Father which hath sent me.*

Why would the Savior make a distinction between Himself and His Father if they are one and the same person?

Note the Son was doing the will of the Father. By doing so, H did **Power Change** with the Father. Also, the Father and the Son are not the same person. Rather, they are "...two Men..." (see *John* 8:17).

One other point, in addition to not disconnecting from His Son, making a record, and seeing that His Son received it, the Father also completed the final step of the **Power Formula** for His Son. He did so by revealing, through the Savior, that all men should ".... honor the Son as they honor the Father." In this way, the Father was doing all He could "to make the post [of Savior and God] occupiable" for Jesus Christ. This is the final step of the **Power Formula.**

"The Works, Which the Father Hath Given Me to Finish"

In *John* 5:36, the Savior amplified His teachings in this way:

> But I have greater witness than that of John [the Baptist]: for the works which the Father hath given me to finish, the same works that I do, bear witness of me, that the Father hath sent me. *And the Father Himself, which hath sent me, hath borne witness of me* [Power Formula, Step 4]...*Ye have neither heard His voice at any time nor seen His shape* (*John* 5: 36-37, emphasis added).

At that instant, they were both hearing the voice of the Son and seeing Him. This again shows the distinction between the Father and the Son. They were seeing the Son, but they had not yet seen the Father. This is because Jesus Christ is *not* the Father. Rather, He was the Son of the Father.

In John Chapter 5, we see evidences of what the prophet Joseph Smith taught, that the fact that the Father and the Son are separate beings, is: "...written all over the face of the *Bible*..." (*The Teachings of the Prophet Joseph Smith*, page 370). Two other truths are also "...written all over the face of the *Bible*..." These are that the Father has done a **Power Formula** for His Son, Jesus Christ, and that the Son has done **Power Change** with God the Father.

JOHN CHAPTER 6

In *John* chapter 6, the Savior demonstrated His power over the elements that make up this world. First:

> A great multitude followed him and they saw the miracles which He did on them that were diseased (*John* 6:3).

This demonstrated the Savior's power or control of the elements that make up the people's bodies. Second, He fed 5,000 people with only five loaves of bread and two small fish (*John* 6:4-14). This demonstrated the Savior's ability to organize matter.

Third, in this chapter is an account of the Savior walking on the water. This again demonstrated His control over the elements and forces of nature such as by changing liquid water into a solid surface or by showing His control over the force of gravity.

You will recall that in doing these great works, the Savior was doing the works that He had seen His Father do (see *John* 5:19-20).

The Son of Man

Jesus Christ also spoke of Himself and the Father in this way:

> Labor not for the meat which perisheth, but for that meat which endureth unto everlasting life, which *the Son of Man* shall give unto you; for Him hath the Father sealed. (see *John* 6:27, emphasis added).

Perhaps at this time would be good to review what the phrase and title "The Son of Man" means. The Savior used this title in reference to Himself on multiple occasions. Through a revelation to the prophet Enoch, later made known to the prophet Joseph Smith, the Lord has revealed the meaning of this phrase. One of the titles of the Father is "Man of Holiness." His Son is, therefore, the Son of the Man of Holiness, or in brief, the Son of Man. Thus, the Son of Man means the Son of God (see *The Pearl of Great Price, Moses* 7:35).

In *John* Chapter 6 verse 21, the Savior:

> ...said unto them. This is the work of God [the Father, that ye believe on Him whom He hath sent,

again indicating that He, had been sent by the Father. This is a reoccurring theme throughout John's Gospel and *The New Testament*. The Father wanted us to know that He had sent His Son, and we are to believe in Him, hear Him and follow Him. This is another example of the Father doing the 4th step of the **Power Formula** for His Son, Jesus Christ.

Eternal Life is What We Should Hunger For

After having been miraculously fed, some of the 5,000 who were following Jesus were doing so in hopes of getting a free lunch as well as free dinners and breakfasts from then on. They were not following Him to gain the eternal life that He offered. Some of them even asked for an additional sign from Him, even though many had been healed, and they had just been fed miraculously. They said:

> ...what sign showest thou then that we may see and believe thee? What dost thou work? Our fathers did eat manna in the desert as it is written; he gave them bread from heaven to eat. Then Jesus said unto them, Verily, verily I say unto you. Moses gave you not that bread from heaven [it came from God—not Moses]; but my Father giveth you the true bread from heaven. For the bread of God is He who is cometh down from heaven and giveth life unto the world. Then said they unto Him, Lord evermore give us this bread. And Jesus said unto them, I am the bread of life; he that cometh unto Me will never hunger; and he that believeth on Me shall never thirst. *John* 6:30-35, emphasis added).

These verses were an effort by the Savior to teach these people that they should follow Him, not to be fed food, but because they had faith in Him, so they could receive eternal life.

Again, in *John* 6:34, Jesus Christ described God as "...the Father which hath sent me..." Also, in *John* 6:38, the Savior again made a distinction between doing His own will and the will of the Father when He said: "For I came down from Heaven, not to do mine own will, but the will of Him that sent me."

The Savior then used a metaphor comparing the acceptance of Himself, and the living of His doctrine as being like eating His flesh and drinking his blood, again referring to Himself as the bread of life. This metaphor has created confusion in the minds of some Christians. There are who those who believe in a doctrine that is called transubstantiation. This doctrine is a belief that when people partake of the sacrament, the bread and wine actually turn into the flesh and blood of Jesus Christ. This, of course, is not the case.

A modern Apostle, James E. Talmage, explained the meaning of this metaphor in this way:

> There was little excuse for the Jews pretending to understand that our Lord meant an actual eating and drinking of His material flesh and blood. The utterances to which they objected were far more readily understood by them than they are by us on first reading: for the representation of the law and of truth in general as bread and the acceptance thereof as a process of eating and drinking, were figures [metaphors] in every-day use by the Rabbis of that time. Their failure to comprehend the symbolism of Christ's doctrine was an act of will, not the natural consequence of innocent ignorance. *To eat the flesh and drink the blood of Christ was and is to believe in and accept Him as the literal Son of God and Savior of the world, and to obey His commandments. By these means only may the Spirit of God become an abiding part of man's individual being, even as the substance of the food he eats is assimilated within the tissues of His body* (see *Jesus The Christ*, page 342, emphasis added).

In concluding this teaching, the Savior said:

> As the living Father hath sent me, and I live by the Father; so he that eateth me [accepts Him as Savior and follows Him] even he shall live by me. This is that bread which came down from Heaven, not as your Fathers did eat manna and are dead; but he that eateth of this bread shall live forever. (*John* 6:57-58).

"...To Whom Shall We Go...?"

Unfortunately, many of those who heard these teachings, would not accept them, and they chose not to follow Him. They turned away when they found out that He would not continue to give them free food for the rest of their lives.

> From that time, many of his disciples went back and walked no more with Him. Then Jesus said unto the twelve, will ye also go away? **Then Simon Peter answered, Lord, to whom shall we go? Thou hast the words of eternal life. And we believe and are sure thou art the Christ, the Son of the living God** (*John* 6:66-69, emphasis added).

JOHN CHAPTER 7

In *John* chapter 7, we learn that even some of Jesus Christ's family, or "kinsmen" did not believe in Him (See *John* 7:5). It is sad to note the degree of suppression that was going on at this time. The people were even afraid to speak of Jesus because of "the fear of the Jews" [meaning those leaders of the Jews, who opposed Christ and who were seeking His death].

In *John* 7:16, the Savior's words give evidence to both the fact that He was a different Person from the Father, and that He was carrying out the will of the Father. He said:

> My doctrine is not mine, but His that sent me (*John* 7:16).

This is another example of the principle of **Power Change**. Jesus Christ was teaching the people the exact teachings which the Father had taught Him.

Jesus then taught:

> If any man will do his will he shall know of the doctrine, whether it be of God or whether I speak of myself (*John* 7:17).

What a great principle! If we want to know if Jesus' teachings are the true teachings of God the Father, or not, we simply need to live the principles He taught. As we do so, we will learn by our experience, and by the testimony of the Holy Spirit, that the teachings of Jesus Christ are true.

JOHN CHAPTER 8

John 8 may be the greatest chapter in *The Holy Bible*. This chapter is full of many great truths. It powerfully teaches that the Savior's mission is central to the Fathers plan for this earth. The chapter begins with the famous story of the woman apprehended for committing adultery. The leaders of the Jews saw an opportunity to entangle Jesus, and perhaps find an accusation against Him. When they pressed Jesus to pass judgment on this woman, the Savior declined. Here is John's account of this incident:

> Jesus went unto the mount of Olives. And early in the morning he came again into the temple, and all the people came unto him; and he sat down, and taught them. And the scribes and Pharisees brought unto him a woman taken in adultery; and when they had set her in the midst, they say unto him, Master, this woman was taken in adultery, in the very act. Now Moses in the law commanded us, that such should be stoned: but what sayest thou? This they said, tempting him that they might have to accuse him. But Jesus stooped down, and with his finger wrote on the ground, as though he heard them not. So when they continued asking him, he lifted up himself, and said unto them, He that is without sin among you, let him first cast a stone at her. And again he stooped down, and wrote on the ground. And they which heard it, being convicted by their own conscience, went out one by one, beginning at the eldest, even unto the last: and Jesus was left alone, and the woman standing in the midst. When Jesus had lifted up himself, and saw none but the woman, he said unto her, Woman, where are those thine accusers? hath no man condemned thee? She said, no man, Lord. And Jesus said unto her, neither do I condemn thee: go, and sin no more (see *John* 8:1-11).

Before we consider the Savior's teachings on this occasion, we will first look at the setting and the circumstances associated with this story. John gives us details, but doesn't always explain their meaning. First, in verse one, we learn that the Savior "...went unto the Mount of Olives, and early in the morning He came again to the Temple..." The Mount of Olives is about 1/2 mile away, and the path to it from the Temple Mount passes through the Garden of Gethsemane. Why did He go to the Mount of Olives? John is silent on this question. However, to my understanding, whenever the Savior went somewhere by Himself, it was always so He could be alone to pray to His Father.

The next details mentioned by John were that the Savior did this early in the morning, and that after visiting the Mount of Olives, He went to the Temple to teach the people there. Modern apostle, James E. Talmage speaks of the Temple as being His 'usual place of resort'—where He went to teach and to interact with others.

When He was accosted by the Pharisees, who demanded a decision—a judgment from Him, He did not respond, until He was ready. L. Ron Hubbard cautioned against responding to a demand for a decision until you have obtained and considered all the information needed to make a *correct* decision. The Savior's next actions are instructive. He did not immediately respond, or even acknowledge their question, which, in reality, was a temptation. Here is what He did instead:

> But Jesus stooped down, and with his finger wrote on the ground, as though he heard them not. So when they continued asking him, he lifted up himself, and said unto them, He that is without sin among you, let him first cast a stone at her. And again he stooped down, and wrote on the ground (see *John* 8:6-8).

Before we consider His magnificent response to this trap, we will look at another detail. He "...stooped down, and with His finger wrote on the ground, as though He heard them not" (verse 6). What did He write? John, again was silent on this, but he thought it important enough to mention that the Savior did it twice. Later in our review of *John* chapter 8, we will consider what He may have written on the ground with His finger.

These accusers knew they were not without sin. However, there was One without sin, there at that time. It was the Savior Himself. Even though He could have condemned her, He did not do so. Rather, He said: "...neither do I condemn thee. Go, and sin no more" (verse 11).

This story gives us great hope, for we are all sinners. Even though we have all sinned, the Savior and the Father continue to love us. They have a "great plan of happiness" for us. This plan includes faith in Jesus Christ and repentance. The last step in repentance is to "sin no more."

"...Two Men..."

The Savior then began to teach the people other great lessons. He taught them who He was, and how He was related to their God. He also taught, as plainly as possible, that He and the Father were not one, but two:

It is also written in the law, that **the testimony of two men is true. I am one that beareth witness of myself, and the Father that sent me beareth witness of me** (*John* 8:17-18) "…written all over the face of the Bible…" page 71.

"…Written All Over The Face of the Bible…"

Perhaps it was verses like the above which lead the Prophet Joseph Smith to say that the fact that the Father and the Son are separate individuals, is "…written all over the face of the *Bible.*" It simply cannot be denied. Also, it is written all over the face of *The Holy Bible* that the Son was following in the footsteps of His Father. Jesus Christ did His Father's will, and taught His Father's doctrine. Thus, the Savior carried out **Power Change** with His Father.

Power Formula and Power Change Between the Father and the Son

Regarding His relationship with His Father, the Savior taught some of His strongest evidence in these verses:

> I have many things to say and to judge of you: but He that sent me is true; and *I speak to the world those things, which I have heard of him.* They understood not that he spake unto them, when ye have lifted up the Son of Man, then ye shall know that *I am He* [their Messiah, and if they would allow it, their Savior] *and that I do nothing of myself; but as my Father has taught me I speak these things.* And He that sent me is with me: the Father has not left me alone; for I do always those things that please Him (*John* 8:26-29, emphasis added).

These verses provide more great examples of how the Father had done **Power Formula** for the Jesus Christ, and how the Son was doing **Power Change** with the **Father**. When He taught them: "… I do nothing of myself, but as my Father has taught me", this was evidence that the Father had given the Savior His **Power Formula**. Also, when Jesus Christ then said: "I speak these things", He was doing **Power Change** with His Father, for He was teaching the things He had learned for the Father, changing nothing.

How to Avoid the Condemnation of 'Dying in Our Sins'

Jesus Christ also explained why failure to accept Him would keep them from being able to return to our Father in Heaven. By rejecting the Savior, these scribes and Pharisees, exposed themselves to judgment for their sins. He taught them:

> I said therefore unto you that ye shall die in your sins for ye if believe not that I

am He, ye shall die in your sins (verse 24).

The Savior's atoning sacrifice makes repentance and forgiveness possible. By rejecting the Savior and His atoning sacrifice, people cut themselves off from the only means of forgiveness. Thus, such individuals are exposed to the whole penalties of the law of God. In effect, such individuals decide to suffer rather than allowing the Savior's suffering to pay the penalties for their sins.

As noted earlier, the Savior did not condemn the woman who was brought to Him. The truth is this: it is we who condemn ourselves. The way we do so is by rejecting the only One who can save us from condemnation!

The Cure for Addiction to Sin

Jesus Christ then taught the people how they could become free from the addiction of sin:

> ... **If ye continue in my word [believing in Him and following Him by keeping His commandments] then ye are my disciples indeed and ye shall know** *the truth and the truth shall make you free*. They answered him, 'We be Abraham's seed, and are never in bondage to any man: how sayest thou, ye shall be made free?' **Jesus answered them, Verily, verily I say unto you, whosoever committeth a sin is the servant of sin.** And the servant abideth not in the house forever: but the Son abideth forever. **If the Son therefore shall make you free, ye shall be free indeed** (verses 31-36).

It is the Son who can free us from the addiction of sin. He is "the truth", who can make us free. As He later taught:

> *I am the way, the truth and the life...* (see *John* 14:6, emphasis added).

From these verses we learn two very important truths: 1) Committing sins leads to addiction: "...whosoever committeth a sin is the servant of sin," and 2) the cure for sin and addiction is coming unto the Savior. This occurs through the spiritual **Non Existence Formula**, which is: Faith in Jesus Christ, repentance from sins, baptism, receiving the gift of the Holy Ghost, and enduring to the end of our lives, in following the Savior's example.

These actions lead to spiritual rebirth, which includes not only the forgiveness for past sins, but also the strength to overcome the addicting power of sin, so we don't repeat our mistakes in the future. A scripture which explains how the Savior can free us from addiction is found in *The Book of Mormon*.

Benjamin, a prophet and a king had been teaching his people his final message. This message was about the Savior. When he had finished teaching them, Benjamin surveyed the people to learn what had been the effect of his teachings. This was the result:

And now it came to pass that when king Benjamin had thus spoken to his people, he sent among them, desiring to know of his people if they believed the words which he had spoken unto them. And they all cried with one voice, saying: Yea, we believe all the words which thou hast spoken unto us; and also, we know of their surety and truth because of *the Spirit of the Lord Omnipotent, which has wrought a mighty change in us, or in our hearts, that we have no more disposition to do evil, but to do good continually* (*Mosiah* 5:1-2, emphasis added).

Jesus Christ Used the Principle of Repetition in His Teachings

He then, again, testified that the things He taught them did not originate with Him. Jesus revealed in Verse 38 that He received a visual record, **Power Formula**, from His Father and that the Father "was with" His Son, while the Savior saw this record:

I speak that which I have seen with my Father... (Verse 38).

In verse 37, Jesus revealed that He not only saw the Father's **Power Formula Record**, He also "...heard" it [from God the Father].

Also, in *John* 8:37 He testified that He knew of their intentions to kill Him. He repeated this in verse 40:

But now *ye seek to kill me*, a man that hath told you the truth, which I have heard of God: this did not Abraham (emphasis added).

In verse 40 Jesus also repeated an earlier teaching originating from His Father (see verse 28).

But now ye seek to kill me, *a man that hath told you the truth which I have heard of God*...(emphasis added).

In verse 42, the Savior repeated for the fourth time, in this chapter alone, that He had been sent by the Father. He taught:

And yet if I judge, my judgment is true: for I am not alone, but I and *the Father that sent me* (verse 16, emphasis added).

I have many things to say and to judge of you: but *he that sent me is true*; and *I speak to the world those things which I have heard of him* (verse 26, emphasis added).

And he that sent me is with me: the Father hath not left me alone; for I do always those things that please him (verse 29, emphasis added).

Jesus said unto them, If God were your Father, ye would love me: for *I *proceeded forth and came from God; neither came I of myself, but he sent me* (verse 42, emphasis added).

And I seek not mine own glory...I honor my Father....(verses 49-50)

In other places, Jesus also used repetition to stress vital topics. An example of this is seen in His commandment for us to "love one another". He repeated this teaching at least five times personally (see *John* 13:34, 15:2 and 17). Also, He taught this same principle through His prophets at least three more times (see *2ⁿᵈ John* 1:5; *Doctrine and Covenants* 88:123; and *Moses* 7:33)

L. Ron Hubbard Also Taught that Repetition in Teaching is Important

L. Ron Hubbard taught:

HOW TO ISSUE INSTRUCTIONS TO PERSONNEL
1. Have a definite clear-cut and correct estimate of the situation.
2. Make a precise, properly communicative statement in writing of exactly what you want done.
3. Reissue 2.
4. Reissue 2.
5. Reissue 2.
There are no other steps..."
(L. Ron Hubbard Basic Staff Volume, Bridge Publications, Los Angeles, 1986, pages 542 and 543).

"I Am"

Eventually they got around to asking Him a question that they would later use to try to condemn Him:

Art thou greater than our Father Abraham, which is dead? And the prophets are dead; whom makest thou thyself?" (John 8:53). [Jesus answered], "If I honor myself, my honor is nothing. It is my Father that honoreth me of whom ye say that

He is your God (verse 54) It is my Father honoureth me of whom ye say, that he is your God.

These simple words put to rest forever the claims of those who say: 'but He never said He was the Son of God'. Furthermore, He taught the people that not only was God His Father, but that He, Himself, was a God as well:

Your father Abraham rejoiced to see my day and he saw it and was glad. Then said the Jews unto Him. Thou art not yet fifty years old, and hast thou seen Abraham? Jesus said unto them: Verily, verily I say unto you, before Abraham was, *I am!* Then took they of stones to cast at Him. But Jesus hid Himself and went out of the temple into the midst of them and so passed by (*John* 8:54-59, emphasis added).

Why did the people become so angry when Jesus taught that "before Abraham was *I am*"? In his commentary about these verses Apostle James E. Talmage wrote:

> This was an unequivocal and unambiguous declaration of our Lord's eternal Godship. By the awful [profound] title of "I am" He had made Himself known to Moses and thereafter was so known in Israel... It is the equivalent of "Yahveh" or "Jahveh", now rendered "Jehovah," and signifies "The Self-Existent One," "The Eternal," "The First and the Last..." (see *Jesus the Christ*, page. 411).

The Savior was teaching these people two great truths. First, that He was senior to (and greater in authority than) Abraham, and second, that He is their Savior and God, Jehovah, or "I am".

Written by the Finger of the Lord

Earlier in our examination of the 8th chapter of John, we considered the fact that Jesus stooped over and wrote something on the ground while He was being interrogated by the Pharisees. Now that we have learned that Jesus Christ is also "I Am", or Jehovah, we may have some insight unto what He wrote. Is it not possible that while these Pharisees were quoting the Law of Moses to the One who gave Moses the Law, that the Savior was recalling something He had written many years before—with His Finger on stone plates? Perhaps He was re-writing one of His original commandments upon which the Law of Moses (or really the Law of Jehovah) in the *Old Testament* was based. That commandment was:

"Thou shalt not commit adultery" (see *Exodus* 20:14).

How sad it was that these Pharisees were trying to use Jehovah's own law to find a reason to condemn Jehovah Himself! How hard it must have been for the Savior to hear these words. How it must have hurt His tender and loving heart. We will consider this further in the last book of this series: *Super Power.*

Truths Learned from John Chapter 8

In conclusion, among the truths taught by the Savior, in the eighth chapter of *John*, are these:

1. Jesus Christ did not condemn the sinner, the Savior encouraged her to "sin no more," thus

giving hope to her and to all of us that we can be forgiven and accepted by our God.

2.   He and the Father are not the same person, rather they are "two Men".

3.   He had been sent by the Father.

4.   He came, not seeking His own glory, but He came to honor the Father.

5.   He did nothing of Himself, rather He *did* what His Father had taught Him to do, and *taught* the teachings that the Father's **Power Formula** had instructed Him to teach, both visually and verbally.

6.   He taught the people the teachings His Father had given Him, thus doing **Power Change** with God the Father.

7.   Jesus Christ taught that our acceptance of Him as our Savior, and as the Son of God is essential, if we do not want to: "... to die in your sins."

8.   That committing sins leads to addiction.

9.   Furthermore, He taught that in order to free ourselves from the bondage of addiction to sin, we need to accept Him as our Savior and come unto Him, for He is "the Truth" Who can make us free.

10.   By rejecting Christ, and by seeking to murder Him, these scribes and Pharisees were also rejecting their Father in Heaven, and instead, they were choosing to follow another 'father'— 'the devil' (verses 39-44).

11.   Jesus testified unequivocally that He is the Son of God: "it is my Father that honoreth me; of whom ye say that He is your God" (*John* 8:54).

12.   Jesus Christ also taught that He is the God Jehovah, or "I am", who had taught the prophets anciently, and thus He is senior to Abraham, and to all the prophets.

The Savior's Compassion

One last thought about John Chapter 8. Imagine, for a minute, yourself watching as the leaders of the people forcibly brought the adulteress before Jesus with malice in their hearts. Can you see, or better still, can you feel how sad the Savior must have been when some of His spirit brothers confronted Him, with no love for Him or for the woman who was their sister and His sister?

In contrast, Jesus Christ was, and is, a Being of perfect love and compassion. The meaning of compassion is:

> ...suffering with another, perfect sympathy...*a mixed passion compounded of love and sorrow*...(Noah Webster, *American Dictionary of the English Language*, 1828, published in Facsimile by the Foundation of American Christian Education, San Francisco, 1967, emphasis added).

The suffering that Jesus Christ experienced for our sins did not begin with His atonement in Gethsemane. Nor did His suffering end with His death upon the cross. He, and His Father are saddened when we commit sins, and when we refuse to repent, for They want *all* of us to return to Them. They don't want to lose even a single soul, for we are Their family, and They love all of us with total and perfect love.

Now that we have reviewed the wonderful truths contained in this chapter, perhaps you can see why *John* Chapter 8 is, possibly, the greatest chapter in *The Holy Bible*. As mentioned previously, we will also have more to consider about *John* Chapter 8 in the final book of this series: *Super Power*, under the heading *"God is [tough] Love"*.

JOHN CHAPTER 9

In *John* 9, the Savior healed a man who had been born blind. This miracle was performed on the Sabbath day. His enemies again used this to accuse Him. "Therefore said some of the Pharisees, this man is not of God because He keepeth not the Sabbath day"(verse 16). These Pharisees questioned the formerly blind man in an effort to find evidence to use against the Savior. However, the man who had been healed, confounded all their attempts. They became so frustrated, that they: "...said unto Him, Thou wast altogether born in sin, and dost thou teach us? And they cast him out" (*John* 9:34). To be cast out is equivalent to being excommunicated from the Jewish faith.

In Search of One Sheep

Verses 35-36 tell of the Savior's great love for every individual: "Jesus heard that they had cast him out; and *when He had found him...*" [indicating that the Savior went looking for the man who had been cast out].

When Jesus found this man, He taught him the gospel. The Savior was doing the same thing as the shepherd described in the parable He taught about the lost sheep. In this parable, a shepherd goes out to search for one lost sheep of his flock, (see *Matthew* 18:11-14). *Jesus took the time to look for a single person, and to help comfort and teach him the gospel. What greater example could there be of God's love for all people.* The Savior healed not only a man's eyes, but his soul as well.

JOHN CHAPTER 10

In *John* chapter 10, the Savior taught that He was in fact, "...the good shepherd." He also speaks of His relationship to the Father in terms of His mission, and specifically that He had been sent to "lay down my life" (*John* 10:17).

The Forgotten Father

Because of their confusion about the Godhead, much of the Christian world has, *in effect*, forgotten God the Father. This is because they have the mistaken idea that Jesus *is* the Father. When they think of Jesus as also being the Father, there is no real need to consider or revere the Father as a separate Being. An example of this is seen when such a person speaks of 'going to be with Jesus', after this life. What about going to be with the Father?

Although many Christians have, in effect, forgotten the Father, this is something the Savior *never* did. Nothing was on the Savior's mind more than His Father and doing His Father's will. In fact, in this one chapter, *John* 10, Jesus

Christ mentioned His Father twelve times!

Verse 32 is particularly interesting. In this verse, when the Jewish leaders were again taking up stones with which to stone Him, Jesus asked them a question: "Many good works have I showed you from my Father; for which of those works do you stone me?" The meaning of the phrase "good works which I have showed you *from my Father*" is that Christ was actually doing *the same works* He had seen his Father do during His pre-mortal, **Power Formula,** training to become our Savior.

Also it is likely that the Savior was trained again, by the Father, during His 40-day fast in the wilderness, before He started His teaching ministry.

As we have reviewed earlier, Christ taught, "I have done nothing save that which I have seen my Father do." This is a great example of Principle 2 of the **Power Formula**, which the Father performed for His Son. Heavenly Father made a record for the Son of His own works that He had performed during His mortal life on another world, where He was fulfilling the role of God the Son and Savior. In speaking of doing the works, which He had learned from His Father, Jesus Christ was also demonstrating the principle of **Power Change** with God the Father, i.e. "...don't change anything".

It is also interesting to note that the Savior referred to his Father in these terms: "My Father, which gave them [His followers to] me, is greater than all; and no man is able to pluck them out of my Father's hand" (*John* 10:29). Jesus Christ later said, "My Father is greater than I" (*John* 14:28). This verse alone is enough to establish two facts. **These are: first, that Jesus Christ is not the Father and second, that the Father was, at that time, greater than He**. This verse demonstrated that the Father was senior to the Son. *This is why the Father could do a **Power Formula** for His Son Jesus Christ.* Also, this is why the Son had to do **Power Change** to become as great as His Father!

Sheep and The Shepherd

In *John* 10, Jesus Christ taught:

> I am the good Shepherd: the good Shepherd giveth his life for the sheep. I am the good Shepherd and know my sheep and am known of mine...and as the Father knoweth me, even so know I the Father: and I lay down my life for the sheep (verses 11, 14, & 15).

These verses teach many important lessons. Among them are those listed below.

1. We are to follow Christ even as sheep listen to and follow the voice of their Shepherd.
2. Not everyone who hears Christ will listen and obey. The Savior referred to those who will follow Him as "my sheep." There is a good example of this in verses 19 and 20: "There was division therefore among the Jews for these sayings. And many of them said, He hath the devil, and is mad; why hear ye him? Others said, These are not the words of him that hath the devil. Can the devil open the eyes of the blind?" Here we can see a distinction between His sheep and those who are not His sheep.

As we reviewed in previous chapters, we all lived prior to coming to this earth life. It was during this pre-mortal existence, that we first listened to, and had the opportunity to obey the Father and the Son. Evidently, not all of our Father's spirit children give their full attention to His words. Some of the spirits there felt more love for the Savior and more loyalty to Him than others. Some have better prepared themselves prior to this life so that when they came to this earth, and heard the gospel, it struck a familiar note in their hearts. These are the Savior's sheep, and these are they who will follow Him.

First, let's be certain that we understand that the Lord was using a metaphor when He described His Followers as "Sheep". Some people may take offense at this comparison. This analogy will not set well with those of us who are afflicted with pride. Of course, our intelligence is not like a sheep's. However, the contrast, or the difference between the intelligence and power of the shepherd, compared to that of sheep is accurate, when we think of ourselves in comparison to the Lord! Those who are truly wise will listen to, and follow, their loving and all wise Shepherd.

Questions That We Each Need to Ask Ourselves: Am I One of the Lord's "Sheep", or Not, and Will I Follow Him, or Not?

Here is how to tell if you are one of those who are trying to hear the Savior's voice, so you can follow Him: Is there anything you have read in *The Holy Bible*, *The Book of Mormon*, or perhaps these books that has caused you to feel strongly that you should believe in and follow Jesus Christ?

If the answer to this question is "yes", then there is a second question: Are you willing to act upon these impressions you are receiving from the Holy Spirit? If the answer to this is yes, and if you then *do* act by finding Him and following Him, *then* you are one of His sheep. For those of you who feel in your hearts that this applies to you, go immediately to the Afterward at the end of these books, and do what it instructs you to do—before reading even one more word.

For those of you who have not yet felt a need, and a desire to learn more of Jesus Christ, and to follow Him—read on, until you feel these strong impressions. Please don't ignore them. You are hearing or *feeling* the Shepherd's voice. *Listen to your thoughts and feelings and then go to the Afterward to find those who will lead you to the Shepherd.*

A Shepherd Who Was Willing to Die to Protect and Preserve His Sheep

Another important teaching of the Savior, in this chapter is that it was the Father's will that:

... I lay down my life for the sheep (*John* 10:15, emphasis added).

Jesus Christ had power to both lay down his life and to "take it up again" (see verse 18). These were predictions of His crucifixion, and of His resurrection.

"I Am the Son of God"

Also, later in this chapter, the Savior gave the single clearest announcement of who He is, and of His relationship to God the Father. In verse 36, Jesus stated:

I am the Son of God.

The Good Shepherd's "Other Sheep"

In verse 16 of *John* 10, the Savior referred to His other sheep. He stated:

and other sheep I have which are not of this fold: them also I must bring, and they shall hear my voice and there shall be one fold and one Shepherd.

Who are these other sheep? The Savior answered this question Himself when He appeared to the people of the New World, as recorded in *The Book of Mormon*, and announced:

...ye are they of whom I said: Other sheep I have which are not of this fold; them also I must bring and they shall hear my voice; and there shall be one fold and one Shepherd (see *The Book of Mormon*, 3 *Nephi* 15:21).

These two verses, one in *The Holy Bible* and the other in *The Book of Mormon* link these two books. Both are books of scripture, and they both contain the teachings of Jesus Christ. In both *The Holy Bible* and *The Book of Mormon*, God has given us the record of His spiritual **Power Formula** for His children, and in both of these books we can hear the voice of our good Shepherd.

JOHN CHAPTER 11

John 11 deals mostly with Jesus Christ's raising of Lazarus from the dead. Also, there are some important statements in this chapter relating to the relationship between the Father and the Son. Before the Savior went to the tomb, wherein the body of Lazarus had been laid, He had already prayed to the Father regarding Lazarus. At the tomb the Savior prayed again thanking the Father for hearing His earlier prayer:

Then they took away the stone from the place where the dead was laid and Jesus lifted up His eyes, and said, "Father I thank thee that thou hast heard me, and I knew that Thou hearest me always; but because of the people which stand by I said it, that they may believe that Thou hast sent Me. When He had thus spoken, He cried with a loud voice, Lazarus come forth. And he that was dead came forth bound hand and foot with grave clothes and his face was bound with a napkin. Jesus sayeth unto them, loose him, and let him go (*John* 11:40-44).

Why would Jesus Christ pray to Himself? These verses, like so many others, show that the Christ and His Father are not same Being.

This chapter also deals with the gathering plot to kill Jesus. It is amazingly sad that among those who saw Lazarus being restored to life, were those who would use it as motivation to try to kill Jesus. The leaders of the Jews later said:

> If we let him alone all men will believe on Him: and the Romans will come and take away both our places and nation...from that day forth they took council together for to put him to death. Jesus therefore walked no more openly among the Jews [Jewish leaders] (verses 48 and 54).

These events remind me of something from a consultant who has been trained in the data written by L. Ron Hubbard said. He stated that anti-social or psychopathic personalities are angered by, and will try to stop others from doing good. What greater example do we have of the suppression of good than these people plotting to kill a man who had just raised someone from the dead? In John Chapter 12, we shall read that the "...chief priests..." even conspired to kill Lazarus.

Perhaps it is also true that the greater the good a person does, the greater the efforts of their enemies to stop them. This event was the Savior's crowning miracle. Although Jesus had healed multitudes in His life, and had previously raised two people for the dead, Lazarus had been dead for *three days*. Also, this miracle was done publicly. This was the absolute testimony of His Power and His Godhood.

However, even though some used this miracle as a reason to try to kill Jesus, there is also good news in this chapter. After seeing that Lazarus had been raised from the dead:

> Then many of the Jews, which came to [comfort] Mary [who was Lazarus's sister], and had seen the things which Jesus did, believed of Him (verse 45).

JOHN CHAPTER 12

In *John* 12, we also see examples both of loving worship of the Savior and of **Treason** against Him. These events occurred in the final week of the Savior's life. This chapter starts out in this way:

> Then Jesus six days before the Passover came to Bethany where Lazarus was, which had been dead, whom he had raised from the dead. There they made him a supper; and Martha served, but Lazarus was one of them that sat at the table with him. Then Mary took a pound of ointment, of spikenard, very costly and anointed the feet of Jesus, and wiped his feet with her hair; and the house was filled with the odor of the ointment. Then sayeth one of his disciples, Judas Iscariot, Simon's son, which should betray him. Why was not this ointment sold for 300 pence and given to the poor? This he said and not that he cared for the poor; but because he was a thief, and had the bag and bear what was put therein. Then Jesus said, let her alone: against the day of my burying hath she kept this (*John* 12:1-7).

By saying that "...against the day of my burying hath she kept this," Christ was referring to the fact that this was the anointing that was to be used prior to His burial. Jesus did not tolerate

Judas's attempt to suppress Mary. He immediately corrected Judas by saying "...Let her alone." Also, we gain a glimpse from these verses as to how the Condition of Judas Iscariot had deteriorated to a **Condition of Enemy.**

Judas had been given a responsibility among the Savior's apostles. He was evidently the treasurer, because he "had the bag" and bear what was put therein." This meant that he held the money bag, or in Greek, "the purse." Judas must have been stealing the funds of the group and using them for his own purposes, because John referred to him as "a thief." Because of his crime against the group and probably for other reasons Judas' spiritual condition fell. He became a secret or covert **Enemy** of Christ. His condition further fell to **Treason**, when he betrayed the Master for thirty pieces of silver. It may be good at this point, for the reader to review the Conditions. For the list of the Conditions please see page 3.

Only slightly higher on the list of Conditions than **Treason** is the Condition of **Enemy,** which was the condition of the Jewish leaders. Here again, the Jewish leaders tried to suppress and murder not only Christ, but also tried to suppress the evidence of His good works. Many people who had come to the feast of the Passover in Jerusalem knew that Jesus was there.

> ... and they came not for Jesus sake only, but that they might see Lazarus, whom
> he had raised from the dead. But the chief priests consulted that they might put
> Lazarus also to death; because that by reason of him many of the Jews went away
> and believed on Jesus (verses 9-11).

It is so difficult to understand how these leaders were so intent in suppressing Jesus that they even wanted to kill Lazarus, who was living evidence of the Savior's goodness and power.

So here we see the beginnings of the conspiracy. Those who were open in their opposition, and who were thus **Enemies** of the Savior, would soon be in league with one from Jesus' inner circle, Judas Iscariot, who was in the condition of **Treason.** This would prove to be a lethal combination.

Jesus was not unaware of the events going on around Him. He knew His mortal life and ministry was coming to an end. He tried to prepare His followers for the coming sad day. He taught them, using a metaphor:

> ...the hour is come that the Son of Man should be glorified. Verily, verily, [truly] I
> say unto you, except a corn [kernel] of wheat fall into the ground, it abideth
> alone. But if it die, it bringeth forth much fruit. He that loveth his life shall lose it,
> but he that hateth his life in this world shall keep it unto eternal life... Now is my
> soul is troubled and what shall I say? Father save me from this hour: but for this
> cause came I unto this hour. *Father, glorify thy name. Then there came a voice
> from Heaven saying, I have both glorified it and will glorify it again* (*John* 12:23-
> 25, 27, & 28).

Again, The Father's Voice Was Heard From Heaven

Here we have an example, not only of Christ praying to the Father, but also of the voice of the Father audibly answering the Savior's prayer. His voice came out of Heaven. The Father must have been a separate Person and He must have been in a different location than the Son, or the Son must be a ventriloquist.

On at least two other instances, in *The New Testament*, the Father's voice was heard from heaven, while His Son, Jesus Christ, stood upon the earth. These were at the time of the Savior's baptism (*New Test. Matthew* 3:13-17), and at the time of Jesus' transfiguration (*Matthew* 17:1-5). In none of these instances was the Savior trying to trick those who stood by through throwing His voice heavenward. It was not Jesus' voice they heard, it was the voice of His Father in Heaven. *Jesus was not a deceiver nor a ventriloquist. He is not the Father. He is the Son. He prayed to the Father and was answered by the Father, and witnesses heard the audible voice of the Father speaking.*

Why is it so Important to Realize that The Father and The Son are Two Different Persons?

By now, the reader may be wondering why so much has been written in these books to demonstrate that the Father and the Son are separate Beings. *The reason is simple. If the Father is actually also the Son, as so many Christian churches believe, there would be no reason and no need for the Father to do a **Power Formula** for His Son, and there would be no need for the Son to do **Power Change** with the Father!*

Christ went on to say:

> And I, if I be lifted up from the earth, will draw all men unto me." (*John* 12:32-33). This He said signifying what death he should die [i.e. crucifixion when He would be lifted up upon the cross].

Because of the gathering storm, the Savior temporarily stopped contact with His enemies. He wanted time to finish the **Power Formula** for the Apostles. How He did his **Power Formula** for His Apostles will be considered in *The Power Formulas Part Three*.

The hour of his death was close at hand, but not yet (*John* 12:34-37). The Apostle John made this interesting observation:

> Nevertheless, among the chief rulers also many believed on him; but because of the Pharisees they did not confess him, lest they should be put out of the
>
> synagogue; for they loved the praise of men more than the praise of God (*John* 12:42-43).

How sad! However, there is a good lesson we can learn from this: if we are ever faced with the choice of pleasing people or pleasing God, *always* make the choices that please God!

The Honor That Cometh From God Only

A related concept was one the Savior had taught in *John* chapter 5:

I receive not honor from men...How can ye believe, which receive honour one of another, and seek not the honour that cometh from God only (see *John* 5:41 and 44).

What is the honour that cometh from God only? Please read *Matthew* 25:34-40 to find out!

The Express Image of the Father

In *John* chapter 12, Jesus Christ also taught the people that:

> He that believeth on me, believeth not [only] on me, but on him that sent me. He that seeith me seeith him that sent me (*John* 12:44-45).

Some people have mistaken this verse for an indication that Jesus really is the Father. However, this is not the case. What Christ meant is "like Father, like Son." In fact, they were so much alike in appearance that the apostle Paul, in his letter to the *Hebrews*, described the Son as being "the express image of the Father's person" (*Hebrews* 1:1-3). By the way, the old English verbs "believeth" and "seeith" in these verses actually mean believes and sees. The "eth" and "ith" endings are equivalent to an "s" in modern English. This is true for both *The Holy Bible* and *The Book of Mormon*.

John chapter 12 concludes with one of the finest evidences that the Father had done a **Power Formula** for Jesus, and that Christ was carrying out principles, like those of the **Power Change Formula**, with his Father:

> For I have not spoken of myself but the Father which hath sent me; *he gave me a commandment, what I should say, and what I should speak* and I know that his commandment is life everlasting; *whatsoever I speak therefore even as the Father said unto me so I speak* (*John* 12:49-50, emphasis added).

The phrase: "*Whatsoever I speak therefore **even as** the Father said unto me so I speak*" is equivalent to the '**don't change anything**' of the **Power Change Formula**.

Three Power Formulas

As Jesus approached the end of his mortal life, He knew that he would soon be leaving the scene,. He turned his attention to preparing and training His apostles for the important responsibility they would soon carry of leading His Church on the earth. As mentioned previously, the Savior while carrying out a **Power Change Formula** with his Father, and He was also doing a **Power Formula** for His apostles.

Many of the teachings of Jesus Christ in *The New Testament* were directed not to the membership of the Church in general and to those who had not yet believed on Him. Rather, many of His teachings were directed to His apostles.

One of the common mistakes of many Christians is to assume that when Christ gave directions to the 12, these directions applied to all of Jesus Christ's followers. A living apostle has written regarding this subject. His teachings, although they are about a separate topic, litigation, shed light on the importance of the principle of understanding *to whom* revelations are directed:

> ...*some of these directions were given to Church leaders rather than to the general multitude of members and believers.* Modern prophets have clarified this point, but some conscientious members have still considered themselves bound by *scriptural directions that were not addressed to them* (Elder Dallin H. Oaks, *The Lords Way,* 1991, Deseret Book, Salt Lake City, page159, emphasis added).

Approximately 50 Percent of Jesus Christ's Teaching in the New Testament Were Directed to His Apostles

It is an interesting exercise to compare the amount of verses in *The New Testament* where the Savior was giving general teaching to the amount of verses where His teachings were directed to His apostles. This can be done using a "red letter" edition of *The New Testament*, where all of the Savior's words are printed in red letters. It was surprising to me, when this was done, to find that approximately 50 percent of Jesus Christ's teachings were addressed to His apostles, and not to a general audience.

In John chapter 20, and in other verses, we'll also read of a third set of instructions, or **Power Formulas**, that Jesus Christ gave. This was a **Power Formula** specifically for Peter, who served as the earthly leader of the Savior's Church, after the Savior ascended into heaven.

One further note, it is interesting to read of Christ preparing the apostles prior to His death, and to compare these events to the latter part of the life of the prophet Joseph Smith. In *The Power Formulas Part 3*, we will consider how Joseph Smith was also aware that his life was coming to a close. Also, we shall review how the prophet spent the latter part of his life working diligently to train the modern apostles to lead the Church after he was gone. It is amazing that both the Savior, and His prophet, Joseph Smith, used principles like those described in the **Power Formula** to help prepare leaders of The Church of Jesus Christ.

JOHN CHAPTER 13

In *John* chapter 13, the Savior continued to prepare His apostles. He instituted the ordinance of washing of feet. When He washed the feet of each of His apostles, Jesus Christ also instructed them to "wash one another's feet" (*John* 13:14). This is an ordinance that He instituted for His apostles.

Regarding the washing of feet, a modern day apostle James E. Talmage, has written in his book, *Jesus the Christ* (page. 619).

The ordinance of the washing of feet was re-established through revelation December 27, 1832 [to the Prophet Joseph Smith]. It was made a feature of administration to the school of the prophets and detailed instructions relating to its administration was given (*Doctrine and Covenants* 88:140-141). Further direction as to the ordinances involving washing was revealed January 19, 1841 (*Doctrine and Covenants* 124:37-39).

Soon after the washing of the feet, Judas left to betray the Savior, as Satan entered into him. Then Jesus said unto him, "that thou doest do quickly"(verse 27). With the departure of Judas, the Savior's emotional tone level appears to have immediately improved. Jesus then gave His apostles a new commandment:

> That ye love one another; as I have loved you, that ye also love one another. By this shall all men know that ye are my disciples, if ye have love one to another (verse 35).

As Jesus continued to teach and train His apostles, He was, in effect doing a **Power Formula** for them. As part of this training, He was also teaching them the principle of the **Power Change Formula**, in that their actions and even their emotions were to emulate His. As He so beautifully put it: "…love ye one another *as I have loved you*".

Disciples and Apostles

A word of clarification: the terms disciple and apostle are not synonymous. Anyone who follows the teachings of Jesus Christ is His disciple. However, only those whom the Lord specifically calls, and who are ordained by Him or by His apostles can be called apostles. The essential meaning of the word apostle is one sent specifically and individually by the Savior to represent, and to testify of, Him.

JOHN CHAPTER 14

The Truth

In John chapter 14, the Savior continued His teachings, and His **Power Formula** preparation of, His apostles. He also made known this crucial truth:

> I am the way, the truth, and the life. No man cometh unto the Father, but by me (*John* 14:6).

The One and Only

There is much good in the various religions of the world, and in the philosophies of men. However, good teachings and even good plans for living life are not enough. The only way to achieve our highest possible growth, and joy, is through accepting Jesus Christ and following His gospel, or **Power Formula**. This is the real purpose of His **Power Formula**: for us to become like, and to be with our Father in Heaven.

Without Jesus Christ, "...no man cometh unto the Father...". His gospel, His plan of life, His **Power Formula** is senior to all other religions and philosophical systems. For more information on this, see: "What think ye of Christ" in *Super Power*.

"If Ye Love Me…"

Jesus, in *John* chapter 14, taught how we can show our love for Him:

"If ye love me keep my commandments" (verse 15).

We could also put it this way: If ye love Me, do **Power Change** with Me by following My gospel, which is My **Power Formula**.

The Role of the Third Member of the Godhead, The Holy Ghost

Regarding the Holy Ghost or the Holy Spirit, here are some things we know: 1) He is a Personage of Spirit who, at present, doesn't have a physical body; 2) He is a God and a member of Godhead, with the Father and the Son; 3) the Father has not yet revealed the identity of the Holy Spirit; 4) He can comfort, inspire, protect, and help us to remember important things we have learned.

The First, Second and Third Comforters

In this chapter, the Savior prophesied: "I go unto my Father..." (see verse 12). However, He promised His apostles that they would not be left alone. He stated:

I will pray the Father, and He shall give you another Comforter that He may abide with you forever (verse 16).

This "other Comforter" is the Holy Ghost. Jesus Christ further taught us about the duties of the Holy Ghost, in this way:

But the Comforter, which is the Holy Ghost, whom the Father will send in my name, He will teach you all things and bring all things to remembrance, whatsoever I have said unto you (verse 26).

The Holy Ghost would comfort, teach and remind the apostles of the words they had heard the Savior teach, and the things they had seen Him do. The Savior also taught that He, Himself, would return and visit them, if they were worthy, and that the Father would also visit them:

I will not leave you comfortless: I will come to you...If a man love Me, he will keep My words: and My Father will love him, and *We will come unto him and make our abode with him* (*John* 14:18, 23, emphasis added).

In these verses, Jesus Christ referred to He and the Father, using the plural term: "We." They are not one, but Two. The Holy Ghost is the first Comforter, the Savior is the Second Comforter, and the Father is the Third Comforter. We can eventually receive all three Comforters if we sufficiently love Them and keep or follow Them. The way we do this is by doing as Jesus Christ taught: "If you love me, keep my commandments", and "...if a man love me, he will keep my words...".

Jesus Christ Quoted the Father

In verse 24 of *John* 14, Jesus again said His teachings that were, in fact, quotations from His Father:

...and the word which ye hear is not Mine, but the Father's which sent Me.

Here is yet another evidence that Jesus Christ and His Father are not the same Person. Another important lesson from this verse, and from the many others which teach the same principle, is that the gospel **Power Formula** that the Savior taught His apostles, and all of us, did not originate with Him. He received it from His Father, and in turn, Jesus Christ taught the gospel **Power Formula** to Peter, His apostles and to His other followers, or disciples.

In *Part Three* of the *Power Formulas*, we shall see how the Lord's apostles teach us the **Power Formula**, thereby also giving us the opportunity of doing **Power Change** with God.

As noted earlier, it was also in chapter 14 that Jesus Christ taught that:

My Father is greater than I (verse 28).

As we consider this statement, it only makes sense that because the Father was greater than the Savior, the Father should do a **Power Formula** for His Son, in order to help the Son become as great as He was. Also, because Jesus Christ was, at that time, not as great as His Father, He could do **Power Change** with His Father. If the Father and the Son were equals, or if they were the same Person, there would be no need for them to interact on a **Power Formula** and **Power Change** basis!

"...I Love the Father..."

After Jesus concluded the last supper, and the meeting in the upper room, He and the Eleven left to begin the walk to the Garden of Gethsemane. As they did so, the Savior taught them of His love for the Father, and His willingness to keep the Father's commandments even though it would cost Him His life:

> That the world may know that I love the Father; and *as the Father gave me commandment* [a Power Formula] *even so I do* [Power Change]. Arise, let us go hence (verse 31).

In teaching that He did "even so" as his Father directed Him to do, Jesus again demonstrated actions identical to the "don't change anything" principle of the **Power Change Formula.**

JOHN CHAPTER 15

In *John* chapter 15, the Savior taught His apostles of their relationship to Him. He did so by comparing their relationship to Him to His relationship with the Father. He taught:

> I am the true vine and my Father is the husbandman. Every branch in me that beareth not fruit he taketh away. And every branch that beareth fruit He purgest it, that it may bring forth more fruit...I am the vine, ye are the branches. He that abideth in me and I in Him the same shall bring forth much fruit: for without me, ye can do nothing...As the Father hath loved me, so I have loved you: continue ye in my love. If ye *keep my commandments* ye shall abide in my love; *even as I have kept my Father's commandments*, and abide in his love (verses 1,2,5,9,10, emphasis added).

The Flow of God's Power

In this metaphor, the vine, which represents Jesus Christ, is started by the Husbandman, who is God the Father. He conceived of it, and planted it. The vine grows, moisture and nutrients flow from the vine to its branches, (the apostles and prophets) and then to the fruit (us). In like manner, God's Power flows from the Father to the Son, and then to the apostles, and finally to the members of His Church.

The way which God's Power flows to us is through a chain **Power Formula, Power Change Formulas.** The Father has done a **Power Formula** for His Son. The Son is doing **Power Change** with the Father, and has done a **Power Formula** for His apostles. The apostles do **Power Change** with Him, and a **Power Formula** for us. We do **Power Change** by following the Lord's apostles and prophets. We then do a **Power Formula** for our children, and our children do **Power Change** by following their parents. In **Part Three**, a diagram is included which illustrates that flow of God's power to His.

In verse ten quoted above, we can observe again the principle of the **Power Change Formula.** The Savior had kept the commandments of the Father. In doing so, He was fulfilling **Power Change** with His Father. In these verses, He was asking His apostles to keep His commandments:

> ...*even as* I have kept my Father's commandments (Verse 10, emphasis added).

He thus instructed the apostles to do **Power Change** with Him, as He was doing **Power Change** with the Father... (Verse 10).

The Savior also testified to the completeness of His **Power Formula** for them in this way:

> Henceforth I call you not servants; for the servant knoweth not what his Lord doeth. But I have called you friends; *for all things I have heard of my Father I have made known unto you* (*John* 15:15, emphasis added).

JOHN CHAPTER 16

In chapter 16, the Savior continued to teach and prepare His apostles, as He and they walked to the Garden of Gethsemane. This chapter includes more teachings about the mission of the Holy Ghost. Also, Jesus Christ again prophesied of His death and resurrection.

Concerning the work of the Holy Ghost, Jesus Christ taught that one of the things the Holy Ghost does is:

> Reprove the world of sin... (*John* 16:8).

The Holy Ghost can touch our hearts, meaning our emotions, and let us know of our need for repentance. He does so by helping us to realize that we have sinned. As we come to realize how our counter survival and counter progression actions or inactions (sins) have harmed us and others, we can begin to *feel* remorse.

How to Repent

Recognition of our sins and remorse for our sins are the first two steps of the repentance process. Other steps of repentance include: confessing our sins to those we have harmed, and to God, making restitution if possible, discontinuing these harmful behaviors, and replacing these behaviors with helpful and positive behaviors.

The Holy Spirit is Also Doing Power Change with God, and He Brings Us God's Power Formula

The Holy Spirit can also guide you into all truth:

> *for He shall not speak of Himself; but whatsoever He shall hear, that shall He speak:* and He will surely shew you things to come" (*John* 16:13, emphasis added).

The verse shows that the Holy Spirit is also carrying out **Power Change** with God because "...*whatsoever He shall hear, that shall He speak...*" equals "...don't change anything..." Also, as the Holy Spirit inspires us, He is revealing **God's gospel Power Formula** to us.

"I Come Forth From the Father…Again, I leave the World and Go to the Father"

As they continued walking to Gethsemane, or while within the Garden, Jesus Christ again taught His apostles that He would soon be leaving to go to the Father:

> A little while and ye shall not see Me: and again a little while, and ye shall see Me, because I go to the Father. Then said some of His disciples among themselves, What is this that He sayeth unto us, a little while and ye shall not see Me: and then a little while ye shall see Me: and because I go to the Father…we cannot tell what He sayeth. (Verses 16-18)

The Savior explained His meaning in this way:

> I came forth from the Father and am come into the world: Again, I leave the world and go to the Father." His disciples said unto him, "Lo, now speakest thou plainly, and speaketh no proverb" (*John* 16:6-18; 28-29).

Jesus Christ's Victory: "…Be of Good Cheer, I Have Overcome the World"

Even though the apostles said they understood that He would be leaving them, the Savior knew that they did not fully comprehend what was about to happen, and that when these traumatic events occurred, they would be greatly troubled and temporarily scattered. He would be left to face the suffering of Gethsemane and His death on the cross, alone. However, His Father would still be with Him.

> Behold the hour cometh, yea, is now come, these shall be scattered every man to his own, and shall leave me alone: and yet I am not alone, because the Father is with me. These things I have spoken unto you, that ye might have peace. But in the world ye shall have tribulation: but be of good cheer; I have overcome the world (*John* 16:32-33).

In saying that He had overcome the world, Jesus Christ was prophesying of His imminent victory over the forces of darkness, and of His eventual completion of **Power Change** with the Father (see also *New Test. Revelation* 3:20-21).

JOHN CHAPTER 17

Before He was arrested, betrayed and crucified, Jesus Christ gave His last teachings in mortality to His apostles. These last teachings were given in the form of a prayer. This can be a great lesson to us, for as others pray vocally, they are often inspired to say what God would have them pray. If we are truly listening, we can hear revelation from God, as others, and we ourselves, pray!

The Savior's prayer, in *John* Chapter 17, has been called the great intercessory prayer. In this chapter, Jesus Christ prayed to His Father "…for His apostles and all the saints [or members of His church]..." (see chapter heading *John* chapter 17 in the Latter-day Saint version of *The Holy Bible*).

In this, the greatest of all recorded prayers, Jesus Christ gave this wonderful definition of eternal life:

> And this is eternal life, that they might know thee the only true God, and Jesus Christ, whom thou has sent (*John* 17:3).

In *Super Power* we will discuss the meaning of Eternal Life. *Knowing* God is more than *knowing about* God.

In the next verse, the Savior declared that He had completed the work, which His Father had assigned him:

> I have glorified thee on the earth: I have finished the work which thou gavest me to do and now, Oh Father, glorify thou me with thine own self with the glory which I had with thee before the world was (verses 4,5).

At this time, Jesus Christ was reporting to His father that He was in the process of completing **Power Change** for His mission in mortality. Furthermore, the Savior was requesting that He be allowed to receive the promised glory, when He had completed His mission.

Next, Jesus Christ reported to His Father on the **Power Formula** He was doing with that faithful 11 apostles, who where in the process of doing **Power Change** with Him:

> I have manifested thy name unto the men which Thou gavest me out of the world: thine they were and Thou gavest them me; and they have kept thy word. Now they have known that *all things whatsoever thou given me are of Thee. For I have given unto them the words which thou gavest me*, and they have received them, and have known surely that I came out from thee, and have believed that thou didst send me (*John* 17:6-8, emphasis added).

In short, the Savior reported to the Father that He had both been carrying out **Power Change** with Him, and He was doing a **Power Formula** for His apostles. Also, He was reporting to the Father that the faithful apostles were doing **Power Change** with Him. He then summarized this **Power Formula, Power Change** cycle of action in this way:

> *As thou hast sent me into the world, even so have I also sent them into the world* (*John* 17:18, emphasis added).

Our Advocate: Jesus Christ

The Savior went on to pray not only for the apostles, but for those whom these apostles would be leading and teaching:

> Neither pray I or these alone, but for them also which shall believe on me through their word; that they may be one; as thou, Father, are in me, and I in thee. That they may also be one in us that the world may believe that thou has sent me (*John* 17:20-21).

The Savior interceded for us with God the Father. He asked the Father that we be allowed to be with Them in the next life. He prayed:

> *Father I will that they also, whom thou hast given me, be with me where I am,* that they may behold my glory, which thou hast given me: for thou lovest me before the foundation of the world (*John* 17: 24, emphasis added).

This is the goal of the **Power Formulas** and **Power Change Formulas** between the Father and the Son, and between the Son and us: that we will be able to be "...with Me where I am...". In a modern revelation, through the prophet Joseph Smith, the Savior further explained how He is our Advocate with the Father:

> *Listen to him who is the advocate with the Father, who is pleading your cause before him*—
> Saying: Father, behold the sufferings and death of him who did no sin, in whom thou wast well pleased; behold the blood of thy Son which was shed, the blood of him whom thou gavest that thyself might be glorified;
> *Wherefore, Father, spare these my brethren that believe on my name, that they may come unto me and have everlasting life.*
> Hearken, O ye people of my church, and ye elders listen together, and hear my voice while it is called today, and harden not your hearts;
> For verily I say unto you that I am Alpha and Omega, the beginning and the end, the light and the life of the world—a light that shineth in darkness and the darkness comprehendeth it not.
> I came unto mine own, and mine own received me not; but unto as many as received me gave I power to do many miracles, and to become the sons of God; and even unto them that believed on my name gave I power to obtain eternal life (*The Doctrine and Covenants* 45:3-8).

There was only one thing lacking before the Savior could conclude the mortal portion of **Power Change,** and before He could return to his Father. He needed to make the great atoning sacrifice.

JOHN CHAPTER 18

Our Savior's Love Was Made Manifest in His Concern for the Survival of His

Apostles, and in His Willingness to Suffer and Die for Us

John chapter 18 begins with a story of how Jesus was betrayed by Judas. When the "band of men and officials from the chief priests and Pharisees..." came to arrest Him:

> Jesus therefore, knowing all things that should come upon him, went forth, and said unto them, Whom seek ye?
>
> They answered him, Jesus of Nazareth. Jesus saith unto them, I am He. And Judas also, which betrayed him, stood with them.
>
> As soon then as He had said unto them, I am He, they went backward, and fell to the ground.
>
> Then asked He them again, Whom seek ye? And they said, Jesus of Nazareth.
>
> **Jesus answered, I have told you that I am He: if therefore ye seek me, let these go their way** (verses 4-8).

This chapter also tells the story of how Peter took up his sword, thinking that he would defend Jesus. In his zeal, he smote off the ear of one of the high priest's servants who came with the group to arrest Jesus (see verses 10-11). As is sometimes the case, the different gospel writers gave different accounts. In the book of *Luke*, we are told that the Savior, "touched...his ear and healed him" (*Luke* 22:51).

Jesus Christ's Suffering for Our Sins in the Garden of Gethsemane

Luke also recounted the Savior's suffering for our sins prior to His arrest. The Savior took Peter, James and John with Him into the Garden of Gethsemane, where Jesus knelt in prayer. He said to His Father:

> ...if thou be willing remove this cup from me, nevertheless *not my will be done but thine be done*. And there appeared an angel unto him from Heaven strengthening him and being in agony he prayed more earnestly *and his sweat as it were great drops of blood falling down to the ground* (*Luke* 22:42-44, emphasis added).

We shall consider more about the Savior's suffering, in our behalf, later.

Here is yet another example of Christ praying to the Father. He also drew a distinction between the will of His Father and His own will. Again, what further proof do we need that Jesus Christ and God the Father are not the same person?

"...Jehovah was Convicted of Blasphemy Against Jehovah"

After the betrayal by Judas, the Savior was taken from the Garden of Gethsemane by an armed guard. He was taken to be judged. Regarding the so-called trial which lead to the Savior's crucifixion, Apostle James E. Talmage wrote:

...the crucial question followed immediately: "Art thou then the Son of God? He said unto them, ye say that I am. And they said, what need we any further witnesses? For we ourselves have heard of his own mouth" (*Luke* 22:66-71). *Jehovah was convicted of blasphemy against Jehovah.* The only mortal being to whom the awful crime of blasphemy, in claiming divine attributes and Powers of God were impossible, stood before the judges of Israel condemned as a blasphemer (*Jesus the Christ*, page 629, emphasis added).

The conviction of Jehovah for blasphemy against Jehovah is the greatest example of tragic irony in all of history!

The leaders of the Jews had determined that Jesus should die. However, they did not have the authority to put someone to death. Only their Roman dictator could pronounce, and cause a sentence of death to be carried out. Therefore, they took the Savior before Pilate to be condemned.

After speaking with Jesus, Pilate did not find cause to order His death. Therefore, Pilate sought to release Him. It was a custom that a prisoner could be released at this feast of the Passover. Pilate told the people:

> Ye have a custom that I should release one unto you at the Passover; will ye therefore that I release unto you the King of the Jews? Then cried they all again saying, Not this man but Barabas. Now Barabas was a robber (*John* 18:39-40).

JOHN CHAPTER 19

In John chapter 19, the account of the Savior's crucifixion was told. Also, prior to the crucifixion, the Savior was scourged, meaning He was whipped. Pilate hoped that this punishment would be sufficient and that the people would reconsider their demand that Jesus be crucified. But they cried out:

> Away with him. Crucify Him." Pilate sayeth unto them. Shall I crucify your King? The chief priest answered, we have no king but Caesar. Then delivered He him therefore to be crucified. And they took Jesus, and led Him away (*John* 19:15-16).

Prayer on the Cross

John's gospel was not the only account of the crucifixion. Luke recorded two important prayers by the Savior to His Father, which occurred during the crucifixion:

> ...then said Jesus, "Father, forgive them for they know not what they do...," and later: And when Jesus had cried with a loud voice, he said, Father into thy hands I commend my spirit; and having thus said, he gave up the ghost (*Luke* 23:34, 46).

Regarding the manner of the Savior's death, James E. Talmage wrote:

...Death by crucifixion was at once [both] the most lingering and the most painful form of execution. The victim lived in ever increasing torture, generally for many hours, sometimes for days. The spikes so cruelly driven through hands and feet penetrated and crushed sensitive nerves and quivering tendons, yet inflicted no mortal wound. Death came through the exhaustion by intense and unrelenting pain through localized inflammation and congestion of the organs instant to the strain and unnatural posture of the body (*Jesus the Christ*, page 655).

Jesus Christ Suffered in Our Place, Before and During the Crucifixion

James E. Talmage also taught that as horrible as crucifixion was, the Savior had already passed through greater suffering in the garden of Gethsemane, when:

In some manner actual and terribly real though to man incomprehensible, the Savior took upon Himself the burden of the sins of mankind from Adam to the end of the world. Modern revelation assists us to a partial understanding of the awful experience. In March 1830, the glorified Lord, Jesus Christ, thus spoke, 'for behold I God have suffered these things for all, that they might not suffer if they would repent, but if they would not repent, they must suffer, even as I, which suffering caused myself, even God the greatest of all to tremble because of pain, and to bleed at every pore, and to suffer both body and spirit. And would that I might not drink the bitter cup and shrink [to pull back from a painful experience]. Nevertheless, glory be to the Father, I partook and *finished my preparations* unto the children of men' (*Doctrine and Covenants* 19:16-19). From the terrible conflict in Gethsemane, Christ emerged a victor. Though in the dark tribulation of that fearful hour, He had pleaded that the bitter cup be removed from His lips. The request however oft repeated, was always conditional; *the accomplishment of the Father's will was never lost sight of as the object of the Son's supreme desire.* The further tragedy of the night, and the cruel inflictions that awaited him on the morrow, to culminate in *the frightful tortures of the cross could not exceed the bitter anguish to which He had successfully passed* (*Jesus the Christ*, page 613-614, emphasis added).

This quotation, from a modern apostle gives us an amazing, though partial, understanding of what the Savior went through for us. Not only was the experience horrible, it was also long, and it was a battle. As He knelt in prayer to His Father in the Garden, the Savior bore our sorrows and the horrendous weight of the burden of all our sins. Here are three inspired insights that James E. Talmage taught about the Savior's suffering in the Garden.

[1. **It was a]** "...terrible conflict...[from which] Christ emerged as the victor." [To my mind, this means that Satan, the adversary was present, possibly also with his legions, and they used all of their powers to afflict and torment the Savior in an effort to cause Him to give up the battle. However, He would not submit. The victory He won was also ours, for He fought it as our champion].

[2. **The intensity of the Savior's pain was "...unfathomable by the finite mind..."**. He described it in this way:] "...which suffering caused myself, even God, the greatest of all, to tremble because of pain and to bleed at every pore, and to suffer both body and spirit".

[3. **His suffering for us in the Garden was not of short duration.** Apostle James E. Talmage described the duration of the Savior's suffering as] "...that hour of anguish...".

Modern revelation to the prophet Joseph Smith quoted above confirmed that the unimaginable pressure of pain and suffering which the Savior experienced in the Garden did cause Him to actually sweat blood (see *The Doctrine and Covenants* 19:16-19)

It is my opinion that at least one cell of His precious blood, along with some of the serum that transports the cells in the blood, was spilled for every person on the earth. Also, it is my feeling that the loss of blood in Gethsemane, during his scourging, from the crown of thorns, and on the cross at Calvary, eventually led to a rupture of His heart, and to His death. Our sins caused Him to not only suffer, but our sins also cost Him His life. This was the price He was willing to pay because of His love for you and for me, and for His Father.

Jesus Christ Won the Victory Over Sin and Death on His Own

From Matthews' gospel, we learn that the Savior also spoke to his Father again from on the cross:

> and about the 9th hour Jesus cried with a loud voice saying, "Eli, Eli lama sabacthani? That is to say, My God, my God, why hath thou forsaken me?" (*Matthew* 27:46).

Why did Christ say this? James E. Talmage, who was a modern apostle, answered that question in his book, *Jesus the Christ.* Regarding the final events on the cross, when Christ stated, "My God, my God why hast thou forsaken me?" Apostle Talmage wrote:

> What mind of man can fathom the significance of that awful cry? It seems that *in addition to the fearful suffering incident to [caused by] the crucifixion, the agony of Gethsemane had returned, intensified beyond human power to endure. In that bitterest hour, the dying Christ was alone in most terrible reality. That the supreme sacrifice of the Son might be consummated in all it's fullness, the Father seems to have withdrawn His support of His immediate presence, leaving to the Savior of men the glory of complete victory over the forces of sin and death.* The cry from the cross though heard by all, who were near was understood by few..." [*Later, after further suffering, Christ*]: *"...realizing He was no longer forsaken, but that His atoning sacrifice had been accepted by the Father, and that His mission in the flesh had been carried to glorious consummation, exclaimed in a loud voice of holy triumph: 'It is finished!'* In reverence, resignation, and relief He addressed the Father saying: 'Father, into thy hands I command my spirit.' He bowed his head and voluntarily gave up his life. Jesus the Christ was dead.

His life had not been taken from Him except as He willed to permit. Sweet and welcome would have been the relief of death in any of the earlier stages of his suffering from Gethsemane to the cross. He lived until all things were accomplished as had been appointed. In the latter days, the voice of the Lord Jesus hath been heard affirming the actuality of His suffering and death, and the eternal purposes thereby accomplished. *Here and heed His words: "For, behold, the Lord your Redeemer suffered death in the flesh; wherefore he suffered the pain of all men that all might repent and come unto Him"* (*Doctrine and Covenants* 18:11), *Jesus the Christ*, pages 660, 661,662, emphasis added).

The Price of Progress

We might ask ourselves what was happening to the Father during this time while His Son was on the cross? What was the Father experiencing? Although we don't know for sure what was happening, here is a story that may shed some light on the answer to this question.

This is a story of a young astronaut and his father. This astronaut, Roger Chaffe, was killed in the Apollo 1 disaster. He and the other two members in the Apollo 1 crew were killed during a drill when their spacecraft was destroyed by fire. This tragedy was caused by an electrical spark igniting the 100 percent oxygen in the capsule. In the investigation that followed this tragedy, many design flaws in the Apollo spacecraft were discovered and corrected, including changing the gas inside the capsule to a mixture which was not flammable. Without these corrections, and without the catastrophe that led to these improvements in the Apollo capsule, we would probably never have made it to the moon.

At the cemetery, after the funeral, a reporter asked Roger's father if he was upset about the death of his son, possibly in an effort to see if Roger's father would blame someone. Mr. Chaffe replied as he hung his head in sorrow: **"No...sometimes the price of progress comes high."**

It was touching to hear Mr. Chaffe say these words on a television program about the Apollo Moon expeditions. Also, this story brought to mind the Savior and His Father. The Father withdrew his immediate presence from His son during the last few moments of his crucifixion. According to Elder James E. Talmage, in the book *Jesus the Christ* quoted above, this was to allow the Son to have the final and personal victory over the forces of sin and death, without His Father's help. This was the conclusion of the Savior's mortal mission portion of His **Power Change** with the Father. In fact, when the Savior announced that 'it is finished', it was the same as saying the atoning sacrifice portion of My **Power Change** with the Father is finished!

The Father's Suffering

Believing Christians often think of the great sufferings of the Son during the crucifixion and also during Gethsemane when He suffered for all the sins. However, there was also another One suffering. Our Father in heaven could have easily rescued His Son personally, or by sending His angels. Rather, the Father allowed His Son to experience the agonizing torment of the crucifixion and suffering in the Garden of Gethsemane for us. In doing so, our Father in heaven was willing to personally suffer, because of His love for us. He was also willing to allow His Son, Jesus Christ, to suffer and die so we could progress, and return to Him.

As Roger Chaffe's father said, "Sometimes the price of progress comes high." This is especially true of the price of our progress. In order for us to be able to return to our Father in heaven, the price was the agonizing suffering and death of Jesus Christ *and* the agony that the Father must have re-experienced, while allowing His Son to be sacrificed for us.

The Love of the Father and the Son for Us

For God, [the Father], so loved the world that he gave His only begotten Son, that whosoever believeth in Him should not perish, but have everlasting life (*John* 3:16). [Also, speaking of His own love for us, Jesus said] Greater love hath no man than this, than he lay down his life for his friends (*John* 15:13).

A Price We Can Not Pay

Speaking of the price the Savior paid for our sins, a Christian rock song has these lyrics (paraphrased): 'No one wants to pay the asking price', and 'You stand by [me] the sinner, even though all the things I've done have left you bleeding' (*Undone* by the group F.F.H.).

Another way to say this is found in the lyrics of another Christian rock song, 'He loved me so much, that He would rather die than ever live without me!' (*To Ever Live Without Me*, Artist: Jody McBrayer).

JOHN CHAPTER 20

Oh Happy Day!

The 20th chapter of John's gospel tells a happy story of the Savior's resurrection, and of His appearance to many of His followers. The first person He appeared to was Mary Magdalene.

But Mary stood without the sepulcher weeping: and as she wept, she stooped down and looked into the sepulcher and seeith [saw] two angels in white, the one sitting at the head, and the other at the feet, where the body of Jesus had lain. And they say unto her, woman, why weepest thou? She [not realizing that these two were angels] sayeth unto them, because they have taken away my Lord and I know not where they have laid him. And when she had thus said, she turned herself back and saw Jesus standing, and knew not that it was Jesus. Jesus sayeth unto her, Woman, why weepest thou? Whom seekest thou? She, supposing him to be the gardener sayeth unto Him, Sir, if thou hast born him hence, tell me where thou hast laid Him and I will take Him away. Jesus sayeth unto her, Mary. She turned herself and sayeth unto him, Rabboni; which is to say, Master. Jesus sayeth unto her, Touch me not; *for I am not yet ascended to my Father*, but go to my brethren and say unto them, I ascend unto my Father, and your Father; and to my God and your God (*John* 20:11-17, emphasis added).

Mary did go to the apostles and told them that she had seen the Savior. Jesus appeared to ten of the apostles as well. He then made a statement that summarizes the entire **Power Formula** and **Power Change** sequences of events described in the *New Testament*.

> Then the same day at evening, being the first day of the week, when the doors were shut where the disciples were assembled for fear of the Jews, came Jesus and stood in the midst, and sayeth unto them, Peace be unto you. When he had so said, he shewed unto them his hands, and his side. Then were the disciples glad when they saw the Lord. **Then said Jesus unto them, peace be unto you; as my Father hath sent to me, even so I send you** (*John* 20:19-21, emphasis added).

Just as The Father had prepared His Son Jesus Christ, to complete the mission of being our Savior, by doing a **Power Formula** for Him, and as the Savior had completed the **Power Change** by following the direction and example of His Father, so also was Jesus Christ completing a **Power Formula** for His apostles. They, in turn, were to complete **Power Change** by following Him and doing the works that they had seen Jesus do. Also as Jesus Christ was sent by the Father, "even so" the apostles were sent by the Savior (see *John* 20:19-20).

Later in this chapter, the Savior again appeared to the apostles. This time, the eleventh apostle, Thomas, was also present. Thomas learned for himself that the Savior's body was a real physical body, when the Savior invited Thomas to feel the wounds in His hands and His side (see *John* 20:27-28).

The Purposes of John's Gospel

This chapter ends with these words:

> And many other signs truly did Jesus in the presence of His disciples, which are not written in this book. *But these are written that [1] ye might believe that Jesus is the Christ, the Son of God, and [2] that by believing, ye might have [eternal] life through His name [meaning by following Him and thus doing **Power Change** with Him]* (*John* 20:30-31).

In this short verse, the Apostle John summarized his purposes in writing His gospel.

Forty More Days of Power Formula Preparation for the Apostles

We learn from other sources that following His resurrection, the Savior continued to appear to and teach His apostles for a period of 40 days (*New Test, Acts*1:1-3). It was during this time that He completed his **Power Formula** for them. After this time of preparation, and after they had received the life-changing presence of the Holy Ghost to inspire and help them, they were prepared to lead His Church, and to direct the great missionary effort to follow.

JOHN CHAPTER 21

Chapter 21 tells of one of the times when the Savior appeared to and taught His apostles following His resurrection. This was at the Sea of Tiberius, or Galilee. Peter and others of the apostles had been fishing, without success. Jesus spoke to them from the shore. He instructed that they cast their nets on the right side of their ship.

> ...They cast, and therefore and now they were not able to draw in for the multitude of fishes. Therefore that disciple whom Jesus loved [John] sayeth unto Peter, it is the Lord... (*John* 21:6,7).

Jesus Christ's Third Power Formula Was for Peter, Who Would Lead His Church: "Feed My Sheep"

They returned to shore and dined on fishes with the Lord Jesus. Peter was given the opportunity to repent for His three denials of the Savior. Jesus Christ admonished Peter to "Feed my sheep". The Savior then gave a two-word explanation of the **Power Change Formula**:

> ...And when he had spoken this, he said unto Him, *Follow me* [He repeated this instruction in verse 22:] "... *Follow thou me*" (*John* 21:19, 22 emphasis added).

Perfect Beings Gave Us a Perfect Example of the Power and Power Change Formulas

The Father had performed a **Power Formula** for His Son. The Son had completed the mortality portion of **Power Change** by doing and teaching all those things, and only those things, which He had seen His Father do. This was the **Power Change Formula** in perfection. The Son had also taught Peter, and His apostles, and all who would follow Him by becoming members of His Church, the doctrine that He had received from His Father.

Following the Son is Following the Father

Because the Son did and taught only those things He had seen His Father do and teach, when the apostles or when we follow the Son, we are also following the Father!

Modern Apostles also Feed His Sheep

The Savior taught **a Power Formula** for the prophet/president of His Church and for the other apostles. He had been their leader, and their good Shepherd. He was now going to be with His Father. His apostles would now be the shepherds. It would be their duty to "Feed my sheep." Ancient apostles and prophets, as well as modern apostles and prophets, do this by teaching the members of His Church the gospel and teachings of Jesus Christ. Thus, they both do **Power Change** with the Savior, and pass on His Gospel **Power Formula** to us.

One Reason Why the Lord Chooses, Ordains and Trains His Apostles

The apostle Paul explained that one reason why the Lord selects, trains and places "…apostles and prophets…" at the foundation of His church is for the:

"… perfecting of the saints" (see *New Test. Ephesians* 2:19-21).

A saint is a member of Christ's Church. Therefore, perfecting the saints simply means helping members of the Church to follow the Savior, and which is carrying out **Power Change** with Him.

The Link Between Power Change and the Next Power Formula

The great **Power Formula** and **Power Change Formula Cycle of Action** was now complete. Here is how the cycles work: the final step of the **Power Formula** given by the Person in Power to their successors is for the successors to do a **Power Formula** for those in a lower condition, than themselves. This allows others to also follow into a **Condition of Power**. Thus, in order for the successor to do **Power Change**, he or she must also make a record, and do a **Power Formula** for those who desire to follow them.

In this way, these cycles are perpetuated eternally. Perhaps this is one reason why the Lord has described His work as:

"…one eternal round, the same today, as yesterday and forever" (*Doctrine and Covenants* 35:7).

The Father and the Son's Three Objectives of Their Power and Power Change Formulas for Us

1) **They desire us to become perfect, as they are.** One object of **Power Formula** and **Power Change Formulas** employed from the Father to the Son, from the Son to the apostles, and from the apostles to us, is to make it possible for us to become:

…perfect even as my Father which is in Heaven is perfect (see *Matthew* 5:48).

and

Therefore I would that ye should be perfect even as I, or your Father who is in heaven is perfect (see 3 Nephi 12:48).

2) **They want us to receive a fullness of joy.** A second objective is to make it possible for us to experience a fullness of joy (see *John* 15:11 and *The Book of Mormon, 2 Nephi* 2:25 and 9:18). The fullness of joy comes when we dwell forever with our families in the presence of Jesus Christ and our Heavenly Parents.

3) **They want us to receive their power to do good forever.** A third purpose, or objective of God's **Power** and

Power Change Formulas for us is to empower us. The verses below from the apostle John's book of *Revelation* describe how this happens.

Power Change from the Father to the Son and From the Son to Us

Behold. I stand at the door and knock. If any man hear my voice, and open the door, I will come in to him, and will sup with him and he with me.

To him that overcometh will I grant to sit with me in my throne, even as I also overcame, and am set down with my Father in his throne. (*New Test. Revelation* 3:20-21, emphasis added).

In reference to these verses, the clear indication here is that sitting on the Savior's throne is symbolic of receiving His power and authority from Him. "Overcame" in this verse is synonymous with having believed in and followed Him, thus completing **Power Change,** with Jesus Christ. We can complete **Power Change** with the Savior by following His gospel plan or **Power Formula.** Just as Jesus overcame, or did **Power Change** with the Father, we can also overcome by doing **Power Change** with the Son.

When we do so, we will "...sit down with me [Jesus Christ] in my throne" and thus receive His Power, "...even as..." Jesus Christ has received the Father's power. What is His Power? Jesus Christ described the Power He received from His Father in this way:

...**all power is given me in heaven and in earth** (*New Test. Matthew* 28:18, emphasis added).

This is what Our Father in Heaven and His Son, Jesus Christ, want us to receive. Whether we do receive Their power to do good and to love, is up to us.

A Preview of The Power Formulas, Part Three, and Why it is Hoped that You Won't Have to Read it

In *The Power Formulas Part 3, Jesus Christ, The Church of Jesus Christ, and the Power Formulas*, we will see how the Savior, through His apostles and prophets, does a **Power Formula** for us, and how we can do **Power Change** by learning, believing, and living the gospel of Jesus Christ. However, if something in the *New Testament* or in these books has touched your heart, you are encouraged to learn and to start living by God's **Power Formula** now. There is no need to read Part Three, if your heart has been touched.

Our Father in Heaven and Jesus Christ want us to start with the spiritual **Non Existence Formula,** by coming unto Jesus Christ and His Church, so we can eventually do **Power Change** with Them. They want us to start as soon as we feel the convincing power of the Holy Spirit testifying to us of Their existence, and of the truth of Their gospel. They also want us to continue to follow the Savior and progress so we can eventually receive Their **Super Power Formula** in Their House, the Holy Temple.

These books are some of my efforts to do just that. My hope and prayer is that you will choose to follow Jesus Christ so that you can eventually do **Power Change** and **Super Power**

Change with your Heavenly Father and with His son Jesus the Christ so you can experience the fullness of joy, the love and the power to do good that They have. This is what the Savior meant when He said: "To him [and her] that overcometh will I grant to sit with Me in My throne..."

If you feel that you are ready to do so, please go to the *Afterword*, at the end of these volumes, for instructions about what to do next.

May we one day meet with each other and with our Heavenly Parents, and with Their Son, our Savior. May we each receive the fulness of Their joy, Their love, and of Their Power to do good.

End of Part Two, of The Power Formulas

THE POWER FORMULAS

Part Three

Jesus Christ,
The Church of Jesus Christ
and the Power Formulas

The Father and Jesus Christ have Instructed Us to do Non Existence and Power Change with Them by Following the Example of Jesus Christ

And the Father said: Repent ye, repent ye, and be baptized in the name of my Beloved Son. And also, the voice of the Son came unto me, saying: He that is baptized in my name, to him will the Father give the Holy Ghost, like unto me, [**Spiritual Non-Existence Formula**]; wherefore, *follow me and do the things which ye have seen me do* [**Power Change** with God] *(The Book of Mormon,* 2nd Nephi 31:11-12, emphasis added*).*

Introduction to Part Three of the Power Formulas

In *Part 3,* we will also look at how the Savior has completed all the steps of the **Power Formula** for His *New Testament* apostles and prophets, and for the members of His ancient Church. We will also see how the Savior has caused that a modern **Power Formula** record should be made for us, just as mentioned in step 2 of the **Power Formula**. We will also see how He got these records into our hands, thereby fulfilling step 3 of the **Power Formula**.

In *Part 3,* we will also identify how Jesus Christ and The Father have done everything They can to make it possible for us to succeed in doing **Power Change** with Them. This is step 4 of Their **Power Formulas** for us.

"In the Mouths of Two or Three Witnesses Shall Every Word be Established" (New Test. 2nd Corinthians 13:1)

In *The Power Formulas, Part Two,* we reviewed how Our Father in Heaven has done a **Power Formula** for His Son, Jesus Christ, and how the Son has done **Power Change** with His Father. Near the end of *Part Two* were these words:

> Here is how the cycle works: the final step of the **Power Formula** given by the Person in Power to their successors is for the successors, who have moved into a **Condition of Power**, by doing **Power Change**, to then do a **Power Formula** for those in a lower condition, than themselves. This allows others to also follow into a **Condition of Power**. Thus, in order for the successor to do **Power Change**, he or she must also make a record, and do a **Power Formula** for those who desire to follow them.

Jesus Christ has organized His Church upon the earth at least three times. In each case, He has, through His inspired servants, made a record, or **Power Formula**, for us to follow. Each of these scriptural records provides a witness and a guide, which make it possible for us to do **Power Change** with God. These three records are: 1) *The Holy Bible,* 2) *The Book of Mormon,* and 3) *The Doctrine and Covenants of The Church of Jesus Christ of Latter-day Saints, and The Pearl*

Great Price.

The Savior's Nine Power Formulas

This truth also applied to Jesus Christ. While doing **Power Change** with His Father, He also was doing three **Power Formulas.** One was for the general membership and the leaders of His Church. A second **Power Formula** was for the apostles, and the third was for Peter as the leader among the apostles.

Among these special blessings and special powers given to Peter were the Savior's bestowal of the Keys of Priesthood leadership. The bestowal of these keys indicated that Peter was the presiding apostle in the Lord's Church (*Matthew* 16:13-19).

Jesus Christ has also repeated the same three **Power Formulas** patterns in Ancient America as recorded in *The Book of Mormon,* and in the latter days, with the restoration of His Church. Thus, we have nine **Power Formulas** from Jesus Christ recorded in the scriptures.

Power Change, and "...The Presiding Apostles of Old..." and Modern Times

Prior to His ascension into Heaven, Jesus Christ instructed Peter to do **Power Change** with Him as the Church's earthly leader, even though doing so would also eventually lead to Peter's execution. The Savior instructed Peter with these simple words: "...Follow me" (*John* 21:15-19). It should be noted that Peter did not function alone. He had two associates or counselors in the Presidency of the Lord's Church. These were James and John. A modern apostle, James E. Talmage, in his book *Jesus the Christ,* described Peter, James and John as "...the presiding apostles of old..." (*see page 768*).

It was these three: Peter, James and John, who were sent by the Lord to restore the higher priesthood, and to ordain the prophet Joseph Smith and his associate, Oliver Cowdery as apostles.

After reviewing the Savior's three *New Testament* **Power Formulas,** we can make some conclusions regarding the relative amount of His teachings, which were directed toward the apostles, as compared to those directed toward everyone. Here is a surprising fact, as mentioned in *Part Two:* approximately 50 percent of Jesus Christ's teachings and instructions in the *New Testament* were given to His apostles rather than to the people in general.

Old Testament Examples of the Power and Power Change Formulas

The reader may be wondering, "What about the *Old Testament?*" *Part 2* of *The Power Formulas* considered only the *New Testament* portion of *The Holy Bible* record. The reason that we did not dwell on the *Old Testament* is that, for the most part, it is a record of people who were operating in **Conditions** well below **Power** or even **Non Existence** in regard to their spiritual states.

A living apostle has taught about how the Old Testament record differs from the New Testament, in these ways:

While the Old Testament is a study of prophets and a people, the New Testament is focused on the life and influence of the only Man who came into mortality with dual citizenship in heaven and on earth—our Savior and Redeemer, Jesus Christ (Elder L. Tom Perry, "The Sabbath and the Sacrament", *Ensign*, May 2011, page 6).

While it is true that the Lord often had individual prophets who were operating in a **Condition** of spiritual **Power**, as a group, the people of the Old Testament were living far below their privileges. An example of this is seen at the time Moses brought the children, or descendants, of Israel out of Egypt. The Lord wanted these people to prepare themselves so that they could be like Moses.

God wanted them to become: "a treasure...a kingdom of priests, and a holy nation" [i.e., in a **Condition of Spiritual Power**] (*Exodus* 10:3-6). However, they demonstrated by their worship of the golden calf, and in many other ways, that they were not ready for these blessings.

Because they forgot their Lord so soon, and because of their worship of idols, God withdrew His Gospel **Power Formula** and the higher, or Melchizedek, Priesthood from them and gave them instead a lesser law. This was the Law of Moses (see *Exodus* 34:1-2 of the Joseph Smith translation of *The Holy Bible*). The *lesser law* corresponds to *lesser spiritual* **Conditions**. Perhaps, because the Law of Moses was given to a people in relatively low spiritual **Conditions**, its directives were very tight in their control, and its punishments were very severe.

Power and Power Change Formulas in the Old Testament

Our purpose in these books is to concentrate on the highest spiritual **Condition**: the **Condition of Spiritual Power**. However, please don't misunderstand, there is much of great worth, truth, and beauty in the Old Testament. Two examples of a **Power Formula** and **Power Change** relationships in the *Old Testament* are seen between the Lord and the Prophet Moses and later between Moses, and his successor, Joshua.

Although we won't take the time to fully consider how the Lord, Moses and Joshua interacted at this time, we will consider, in outline form, the elements of **Power Formula** and **Power Change** between them.

The Power Formula and Power Change Between the Lord and Moses

Power Formula Step One between the Lord and Moses ("...don't disconnect") (see *Old Test. Exodus* chapter 2, and 33:7-11).

Power Formula Steps Two and Three between the Lord and Moses ("...make a record..." and "get it into the hands of the guy who is going to take care of it..."). (see *Exodus* 31:18, and *Exodus* 9:10).

Power Formula Step Four between the Lord and Moses ("Do all you can to make the post occupiable"). The five books of Moses are full of examples of the miracles that God performed through Moses. A well-known example of these miracles was when the Lord, through Moses, parted the Red Sea so the children of Israel could cross on dry ground, thus escaping the army that was pursing them. Also, when a rebellion was starting "...against Moses..." the Lord personally corrected those who doubted Moses and spoke to them in support of Moses (see *Old*

Test. Numbers 12:1-8).

Power Change between the Lord and Moses ("Don't change anything...") (see *Exodus* 7:1-6).

Power Formula and Power Change Between Moses and Joshua

Power Formula Step One between Moses and Joshua ("...don't disconnect."), (see *Deuteronomy* 32:44), (Hoshea is another way of spelling Joshua's name), (also see *Deuteronomy* 34:9).

Power Formula Step Two and Three between Moses and Joshua ("...make a record... [and] ...get it into the hands of the guy who is going to take care of it.") (In *Deuteronomy* 31 Moses gave Joshua verbal counsel on how to lead the people of Israel; also the written records of the law were placed in the ark of the covenant. Joshua, as the leader of the people, would be in charge of, and have access to these scriptural records).

Power Formula Step Four between Moses and Joshua ("Do all you can to make the post occupiable") (*Old Test. Numbers* 27:15-23, and *Deuteronomy* 34:9).

Power Change between Joshua and Moses ("...don't change anything") (see *Joshua* 1: 7-8 and 3:7. Also see *Joshua* 24:26).

Power Formulas from God in The Book of Mormon

Up until the time of the Savior's appearance to the people in *The Book of Mormon*, these people were also operating under the lesser, or Mosaic Law. However, like the people of the Old Testament, they did have prophets among them, whose spiritual condition was **Power**. These prophets, like Moses, Joshua and others in the *Old Testament* tried to elevate the spiritual condition of their people. *The Power Formulas Part One* discusses examples of the Lord's **Power Formulas** and **Power Change** among *The Book of Mormon* Record Keepers and others.

The Condition of the Lord's Church Today

In *Part 3*, we will consider how statistical measurements, when applied to the Church of Jesus Christ of Latter-day Saints, demonstrate that it is operating in a **Condition of Power**. Finally, *Part 3* will review how both the Savior, and His prophet, Joseph Smith, spent their last days on earth completing **Power Formula** training for the apostles who would be leading the Church after their departures.

After *Part 3*, we will consider *Super Power*, meaning God's Power, and how we can do **Super Power Change** with God through temple instruction and ordinances. In addition, our attention will turn to the spirits of those who have lived on the earth without an adequate opportunity to receive God's **Power** and **Super Power Formulas**. We will discover that God's plan of happiness is totally fair and just—no one is left without the opportunity of receiving all of God's blessings and powers.

The final volume of this series, *Super Power*, will consider how we can the do a **Power Formula** for our families by teaching and demonstrating how to live a Christ-like life of love and service, and by helping them to prepare to enter the Holy Temple.

Chapter One

Jesus Christ's New Testament Record Contains Power Formulas for Peter, His Apostles, for the Members of His Ancient Church, and for Us

It is not be the purpose of this book to thoroughly review the life of Jesus Christ. That work has been done by others. Please see *Jesus the Christ* by James E. Talmage. The author was an apostle of the Church of Jesus Christ of Latter-day Saints. He has written a wonderful account of the Savior's life and teachings, some of which has been reviewed, in *Part Two*. Our purposes in considering elements of the life of Christ, includes those listed below.

1. While upon the earth, the Savior was engaged in two great cycles of action. First, regarding His relationship to His Father in Heaven, Jesus Christ was performing **Power Change**. Please see *Part Two* for this information;
2. Regarding His relationship to the apostle Peter, to His other apostles and to His other followers, Jesus Christ was doing **Non Existence** through **Power Formulas**.

The Savior has different expectations for His apostles than for the general members of His Church. He expected the apostles to do **Power Change** with Him as the earthly leaders who would supervise the Church's great missionary efforts, and who would govern His Church and kingdom. These were responsibilities that were *not* placed on the general membership of His church.

How Jesus Christ did Not Disconnect from His Followers in The New Testament (Power Formula Step 1)

We will now look at the evidence found in the *The New Testament* of the **Power Formula** like actions demonstrated by the Savior during His life upon the earth. We will start by showing examples of how the Savior's life embodied: "The first law of the condition of power...don't disconnect..."

A good example from the *New Testament* would be the instance where the Savior's disciples sought to limit people's access to Jesus Christ. Specifically, when some little children were brought to Jesus, probably by their parents, and some of His disciples "rebuked them." However, the Savior said:

> ...Suffer [allow] the little children, and forbid them not to come unto me; for of such is the kingdom of Heaven. And he laid His hands on them [probably giving each of them a blessing],... (*John* 19:13-15).

Another example of how the Savior connected with others is seen when Jesus Christ went looking for a man who had been cast out of the synagogue after Jesus had healed him of his blindness. Jesus found this man, comforted him and taught him the gospel (*John* 9:1-38). The Savior also associated with publicans, or tax collectors, who were detested by many (*Matthew* 9:9-10). He also touched a leper to heal him (*Matthew* 8:1-3). He maintained connection with all who wanted to associate with Him.

It is possible, that some may think that the Savior disconnected from His followers when He died. While it is true they were deprived of His physical presence for a short time, He did return to visit and teach them after His resurrection, on more than one occasion. In addition, they could always pray to the Father and receive help and comfort, because the Savior specifically promised them that the Father would send them the Holy Ghost. It is through the Holy Ghost, that the Savior maintains long-term connections to His apostles and to each of us who want to be connected to Him.

The Savior also promised His faithful apostles:

> I will not leave you comfortless: I will come to you," and "...I am with you alway[s], even unto the end of the world. Amen" (*John* 14:18 and *Matthew* 28:20).

God's Ultimate Purpose

In fact, the ultimate purpose of our Father in Heaven preparing the Savior for us, and of Jesus Christ fulfilling His mission of being the Messiah and our Savior, was to allow us to be connected to Them eternally, by being like Them, and living with Them in Their Celestial Kingdom.

How Jesus Christ Made the New Testament Record for Us (Power Formula Step 2)

The second step in the **Power Formula** is to "...make a record...write up your whole post...". As far as we know, the Savior did not actually write any of the scriptures that are found in the *New Testament*. However, as noted in *Part Two*, there is an instance where He did write a very important scripture in the *Old Testament*. This is found in the book of *Exodus*, Chapter 31:18 where we learn that the Ten Commandments were actually written on two stone tablets by the finger of the Lord, Jesus Christ, who is also Jehovah (see *Exodus* 31:18 and *Deuteronomy* 9:10). The words from these tablets were then recorded by Moses in the book of *Exodus* (see *Exodus* Chapter 20).

The books of the *New Testament* were written, for the most part, by apostles of Jesus Christ. The only three writers that may not have been apostles are Luke, Mark and Jude. It is possible that these men may have been members of the seventy, who Jesus Christ also called, ordained, and sent as missionaries. It should be noted that Luke and Mark did participate in missionary service. Also, Mark, Luke and/or Jude may have been ordained as apostles at a later date following the death of other apostles.

The Savior's specific instructions for His followers to make a record of His teachings are not contained in the four New Testament gospels. However, there is an instance where the Savior apparently repeated some of His teachings so that a record could be made. The gospel of John details the visit of Nicodemus, a man of high standing among the Jewish people, to the Savior by night.

This was a very important teaching moment for the Savior. In fact, it appears that it was during this interview with Nicodemus that the Savior gave His first teachings following His baptism, and the temptations in the wilderness. It is important to note that these teachings were in regard to the doctrine of spiritual rebirth, which are equivalent to a **Spiritual Non Existence Formula**. His teachings to Nicodemus were meant to instruct him, and each of us, on how we can return to be with our Father in Heaven.

In writing about this incident, Elder James E. Talmage, in the book, *Jesus the Christ* has taught:

> If Jesus and Nicodemus were the only persons present at the interview, John, the writer must have been informed thereof by one of the two. As John was one of the earliest disciples and afterward one of the apostles, and as he was distinguished in the apostolic community by His close personal companionship with the Lord, *it is highly probable that he heard the account from the lips of Jesus. It was evidently John's purpose to record the great lesson of the occasion,* rather than to tell the circumstantial story. The record begins and ends with equal abruptness; unimportant incidents are omitted; every line is of significance; the writer fully realized the deep import of His subject and treated it accordingly (*Jesus the Christ*, pages 149 and 153, emphasis added).

The Savior knew that John would be recording His teachings. It is likely that the Savior had asked John to do so.

We know other instances where the Lord's apostles and prophets have been specifically instructed to write down God's teachings so we would have a record of them. One such incident occurred in *The Book of Mormon* in 3rd Nephi. This incident will be reviewed in Chapter 2. Another example follows.

The Apostle John was Commanded by Jesus Christ to Write The New Testament Book of Revelation

In *Revelation* 1:11, we learn that the Lord Jesus Christ commanded the apostle John to make a record of his vision. Also, in the 21st chapter of *Revelation*, the Savior gave what is perhaps the greatest promise of comfort and hope for those who endure in following the Savior. In these verses, the Savior again instructed John to write His words:

> And God shall wipe away all tears from their eyes, and there shall be no death, neither sorrow, nor crying, neither shall there be any more pain; for the former things are passed away. And he sat upon the throne said, Behold, I make all things new. *And he said unto me Write: for these words are true and faithful* (*Revelation* 21:4-5, emphasis added).

"All Scripture is Given by Inspiration...", Therefore the Scriptures are God's Records for Us

In His second epistle or letter to Timothy in *The New Testament*, the apostle Paul wrote:

All scripture is given by inspiration of God and is profitable for doctrine, for reproof, for correction, or instruction in righteousness (2 *Timothy* 3:16).

Since all scriptures are given by inspiration, it is obvious that the Savior wanted the scriptural records to be made and kept. Whether He personally instructed His disciples to make these records, or if He inspired them to do so through the Holy Ghost, it makes no difference. These are *His* records, and He has caused that these records were made for our benefit.

How the Lord has Gotten the Records into Our Hands (Power Formula Step 3)

The Lord has used various means to get His scriptural records to us. *The Holy Bible* has been translated into Greek and into other languages including English. This translation process wasn't perfect. Some errors were introduced. One of The Church of Jesus Christ of Latter-day Saint's revealed Articles of Faith states:

We believe *The Bible* to be the word of God as far as it is translated correctly" (*The Pearl of Great Price, The Articles of Faith*, number 8, page 60).

One reason that the Lord has caused other scriptures to come forth, including *The Book of Mormon*, is because of these errors in the translation of *The Holy Bible*, and because of the confusion that has occurred as a result of these errors.

As noted in *Part One* of the series, *The Book of Mormon* came forth through a prophet by inspired translation. The Lord has also given us *The Doctrine and Covenants* and *The Pearl of Great Price* through modern prophets. Furthermore, the Church of Jesus Christ of Latter-day Saints believes that the Lord's records for us are not finished. Rather, the Church's position is that:

...we believe that God will yet reveal many great and important things pertaining to the kingdom of Heaven (see *The Pearl of Great Price, Articles of Faith*, number 9, page 60, emphasis added).

How the Savior Does All That He Can Do to Make the Post Occupiable (Power Formula Step 4) for the Members of His Church in The New Testament Times and Now

After getting the record into our hands, which is the 3rd step in the **Power Formula**, the Savior has done, and continues to do, all that He can do, "to make the post occupiable" for us. The first question we need to ask ourselves is: what exactly is this "post"? The post or position that our Father in Heaven and Jesus Christ want us to occupy is for us to be sons and daughters of God. This means They want us to be Their heirs, and to receive "all that my Father hath" (see *Doctrine and Covenants* 84:38).

The Father and the Son have done much to make this possible for us. Included in the list of things that They have done to help us become Their heirs, are those below.

1. They have planned for, prepared for, and accomplished the Savior's atonement, so that our sins can be forgiven.
2. They have made it possible for us to have the companionship and guidance of the Holy Ghost, the third member of the Godhead. This gift is given to those who follow Them by having faith in the Father and the Son, repenting, being baptized for the remission of their sins and receiving the gift of the Holy Ghost, by the laying on of hands of Their representatives who have been given the priesthood authority and power to do so.
3. They have called apostles and prophets to receive and make a record of Their teachings which contain Their **Power Formula** for us.
4. Because of Their loving kindness for us, They have granted unto us Their grace, which is Their "...divine means of help or strength, given through the bounteous mercy and love of Jesus Christ...this *grace is the enabling Power that allows men and women to lay hold on eternal life and exaltation, after they have expended their own best efforts. Divine grace is needed by every soul*...However, grace cannot suffice without the total effort on the part of the recipient. Hence the explanation: 'It is by grace that we are saved after all that we can do' (*2nd Nephi* 25:23). *It is truly the grace of Jesus Christ that makes salvation possible*. This principle is expressed in Jesus' parable of the vine and the branches" [see] *John* 15:1-11. (Bible Dictionary, The Church of Jesus Christ of Latter-day Saints, see the heading of Grace, emphasis added*).
5. They have accomplished the resurrection, thus providing perfect and immortal bodies for all God's children.

The Principles of Power Formula and Power Change as Taught by the Apostles of Jesus Christ to the Members of The Church of Jesus Christ in The New Testament Books, After the Four Gospels

In *Part Two*, we reviewed information from the gospels of *The New Testament*, and especially from John's gospel, which demonstrated that principles like those of the **Power** and **Power Change Formulas** were present in *The Holy Bible*. We have also reviewed a few examples from *The Old Testament*. Other examples can be found in *The New Testament* books, after the four gospels.

Not only did the apostles follow Jesus Christ, thereby doing **Power Change** with Him, they also taught the gospel **Non Existence Formula** to those who were not yet members of the Church, through missionaries. These apostles also taught God's **Power Formula** to the members of the Savior's Church. In addition, these apostles instructed the Church members to follow them, thereby allowing the members of the Lord's Church to also do **Power Change** with the Savior.

We will now consider some examples of these truths from *The New Testament* Books that followed the gospels. In the first letter to the members of the Church, or saints, at Corinth, the apostle Paul wrote:

> *Be ye followers of me, even as I also am of Christ.* Now I praise you, brethren that ye **remember me in all things and keep the ordinances, as I delivered them to you.** But I would have you know that **the head of every man is Christ; and the head of the woman is the man; and the head of Christ is God** (*1st Corinthians* 11:1-3, emphasis added).

In these verses, the Apostle Paul outlined a series of **Power Formula** and **Power Change** cycles which have been accomplished by our Father in Heaven, Jesus Christ His apostles, and which are to be accomplished by us.

How God's Power Gets to Us—Four Cycles

Each of these **Power Formulas** and **Power Change cycles** include a **Power Formula** from the One in power and **Power Change Formula** by those who would receive power. This information is similar to that already addressed in *Part Two* under *John* Chapter 15. Below, in outline form, are the four cycles.

1. The first of four cycles in the transmission of God's Power through a **Power Formula** and **Power Change** was between the Father and the Son, or as Paul, the apostle, put it, "...And the head of Christ is God". The Father also has done a **Power Formula** for the Holy Ghost, and He is doing **Power Change** with God (see *John* 16:13).
2. Cycle two is from Christ and the Holy Spirit to the apostles which Paul taught in this way: "Be ye followers of me **even as I also am [a follower] of Christ**".
3. The 3rd cycle is between "every man" (meaning between priesthood holders of the Lord's Church and the apostles and prophets that Christ has appointed to represent Him upon the earth. Again, as Paul taught, **"Be ye followers of me [an apostle]**, even as I am also of Christ".
4. The 4th cycle is one in where these priesthood holders teach the gospel and set the example for their families, starting with their wives. Paul taught this principle in this way. "And the head of the woman [and their children] is the man".

This does not mean that a man is the "boss" of his wife. The husband and His wife are equals. Because of the priesthood he holds, the Lord expects him to instruct his wife and children in the principles of the gospel, and to set the example for them. In this way, fathers can lead their families in love to the Savior, and the Savior can lead them to their Father in Heaven.

In each case, the one giving the **Power Formula** teaches true principles to those receiving the **Power Formula**. These persons are to then carry out these principles, exactly, with the Savior's help or grace, which He usually extends to us by the Power of the Holy Spirit. As we follow the Father, the Son, and the Holy Spirit, and with Their help, we can eventually accomplish **Power**

Change with God *(see diagram).*

FIRST MISSION: Proclaiming the Gospel to the Living	SECOND MISSION: Perfecting the Saints	THIRD MISSION: Redeeming the Dead

The Meaning of "...Perfecting the Saints"

The diagram above lists one of the Church's missions as "Perfecting the saints." Where does this phrase come from and what does it mean? The Apostle Paul gave a metaphor to describe the organization of the Lord's Church. Speaking to new members of the Church Paul taught:

> Now therefore ye are no more strangers and foreigners, but fellow citizens with the saints [members of the Church], and of the household of God;
>
> **And are built upon the foundation of the apostles and prophets, Jesus Christ himself being the chief corner stone;**
>
> **In whom all the building fitly framed together groweth unto an holy temple in the Lord** (*N. Test. Ephesians* 2:19-21, emphasis added).

Paul also gave us this job description of the Lord's Church and its earthly leaders, the prophets, apostles and other priesthood holders:

> **And he gave some, apostles; and some, prophets; and some, evangelists; and some, pastors and teachers;**
> **For the *perfecting of the saints*, for the work of the ministry, for the edifying of the body of Christ:**
> **Till we all come in the unity of the faith, and of the knowledge of the Son of God, unto a perfect man, unto the measure of the stature of the fullness of Christ:** (*N. Test., Ephesians* 4:11-13, emphasis added).

What did Paul mean when in verse 12 of Ephesians 4 where he wrote that Jesus Christ gave us His Church organization and leaders for "the perfecting of the Saints"? Paul answered that question in the next verse:

Till we all come …unto [become] a perfect man [or woman and] unto the measure of the stature [height] of the fullness of Christ [become like Christ].

Jesus Christ commanded us to become perfect (see Matthew 5:48). In the verses above, one of His apostles explained that it is through His Church that this can occur. By becoming a member of His Church, and by keeping His commandments and receiving the Savior's grace and His **Super Power Formula** in the temple, we can eventually become:

…even as I [Jesus Christ] am and I am even as the Father… (*BofM 3 Nephi* 28:10)

Thus, the mission assigned to His Church by God of "perfecting the saints" means just what it says: *perfecting* the saints!

As we considered the diagram, which outlines the series of **Power** and **Power Change Formulas** from Our Father in Heaven, to us, we saw that the Lord has given three missions to His Church.

These were:

1. Proclaiming the Gospel (missionary work);

2. Perfecting the Saints (helping the members of the Church become like their Savior, and their Heavenly Parents);

3. Redeeming the dead through genealogical research and temple ordinances in their behalf.

The first and third of these missions have something in common. They both are designed to take the Lord's Gospel **Power** and **Super Power Formulas** to others. The first mission is to take these **Formulas** to the living. The third mission is to take these **Formulas** to the dead. The goal of both of these missions is to make it possible for individuals and families to develop faith in God the Father, His Son Jesus Christ, and the Holy Ghost, and then to become members of The Church of Jesus Christ. This fact is illustrated in the next diagram:

The Condition of Those Who are Perfected by Jesus Christ

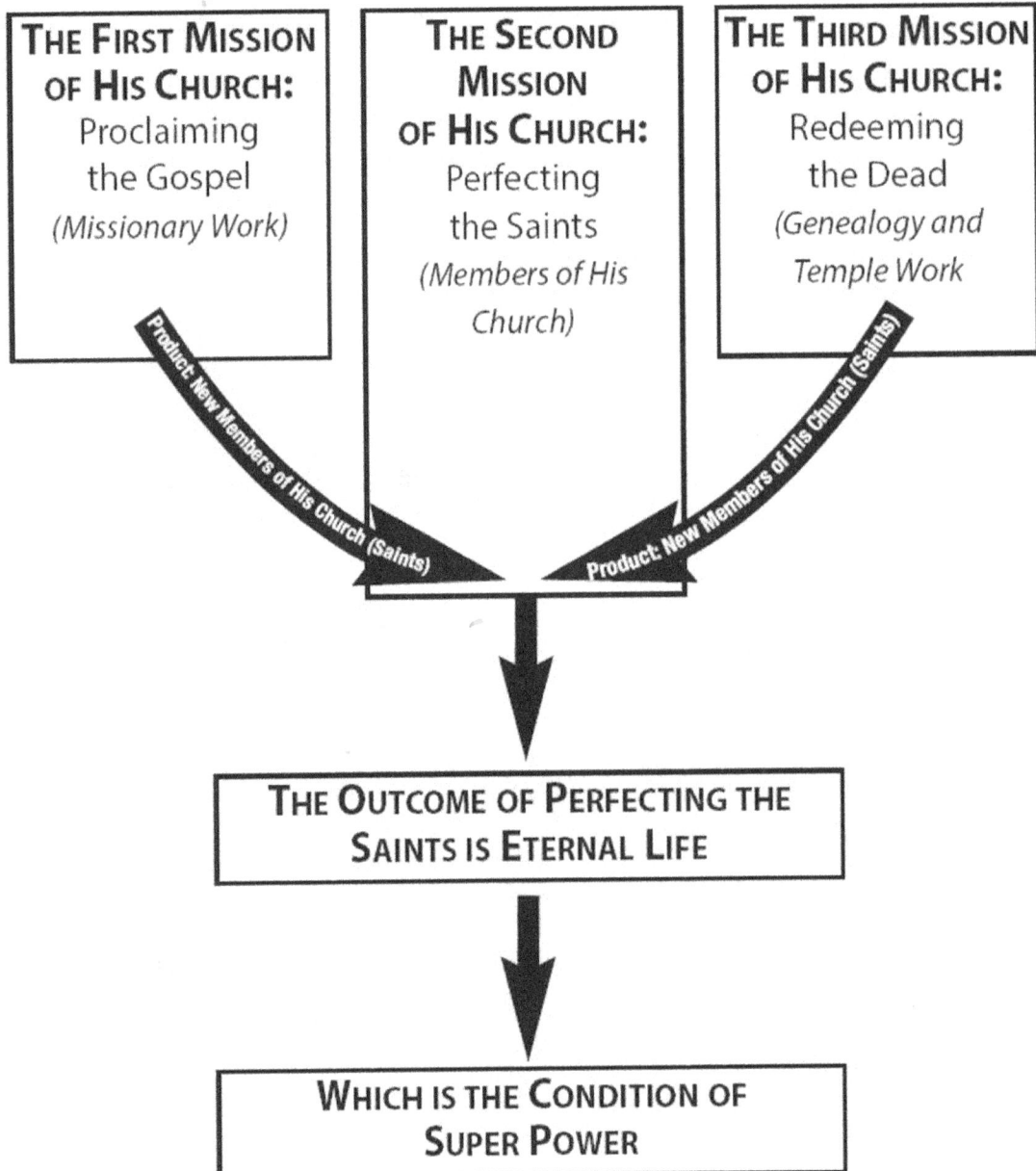

THE FIRST MISSION OF HIS CHURCH:
Proclaiming the Gospel
(Missionary Work)

THE SECOND MISSION OF HIS CHURCH:
Perfecting the Saints
(Members of His Church)

THE THIRD MISSION OF HIS CHURCH:
Redeeming the Dead
(Genealogy and Temple Work

Product: New Members of His Church (Saints)

Product: New Members of His Church (Saints)

THE OUTCOME OF PERFECTING THE SAINTS IS ETERNAL LIFE

WHICH IS THE CONDITION OF SUPER POWER

The three missions become one: perfecting the saints.

Our Father in Heaven has also assigned Himself a mission. He described the mission in this way:

> For behold, this is my work and my glory—to bring to pass the immortality and eternal life of man (*Pearl of Great Price, Moses* 1:39).

Once we understand that Eternal Life means life with our Eternal Parents, it only takes an instant to see that the missions of God and of His Church are the same. That mission is to allow us to become like our Savior and our Heavenly Parents, and to dwell with Them.

If we then apply this outcome to the **Conditions Formulas**, we get this diagram:

THE CYCLES OF POWER AND POWER CHANGE FORMULAS, FROM GOD TO US THROUGH HIS SON JESUS CHRIST AND THROUGH THE CHURCH OF JESUS CHRIST OF LATTER-DAY SAINTS

These three columns each represent one of the three parts of the Mission of the Church of Jesus Christ of Latter-day Saints

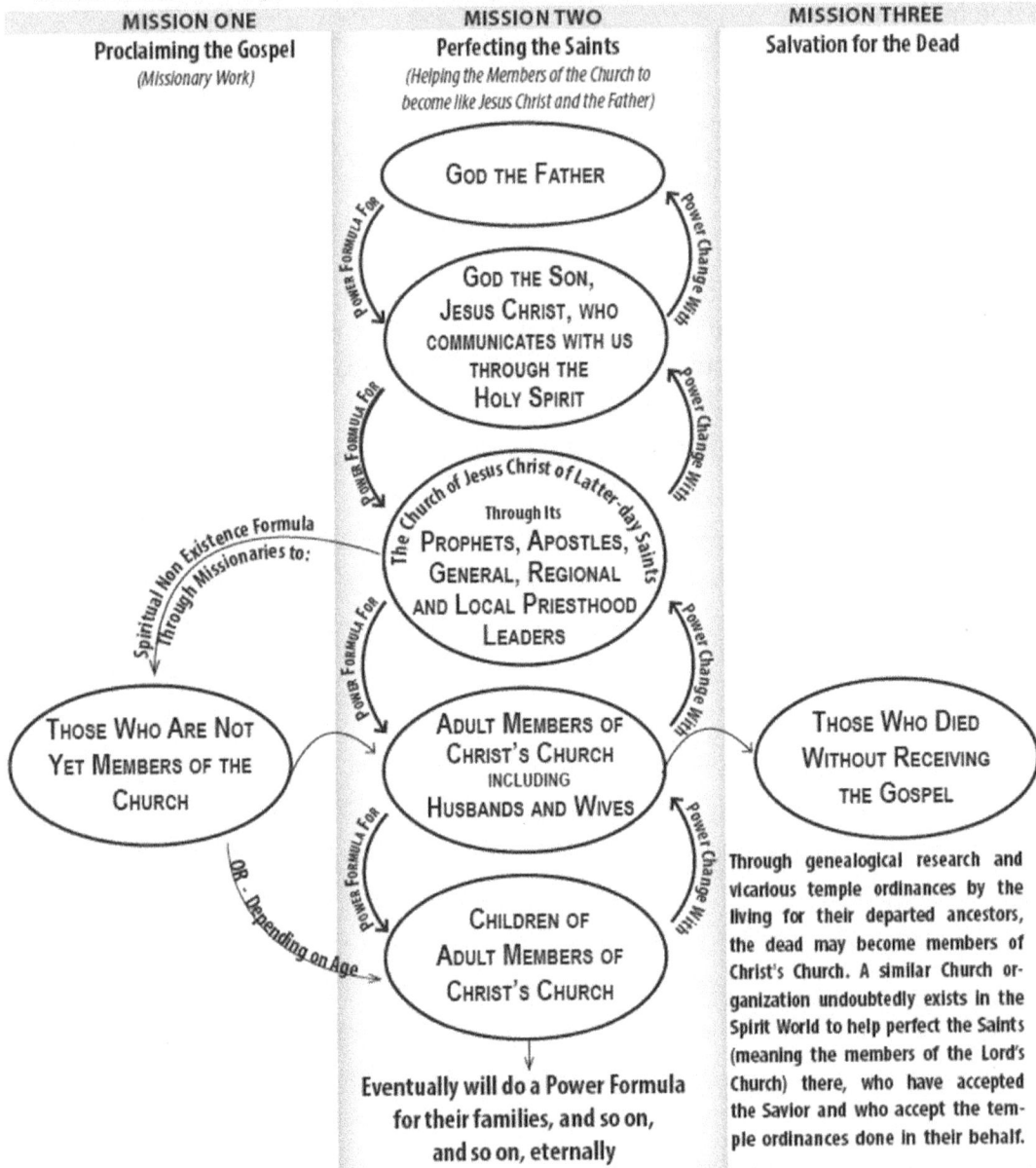

MISSION ONE
Proclaiming the Gospel
(Missionary Work)

MISSION TWO
Perfecting the Saints
(Helping the Members of the Church to become like Jesus Christ and the Father)

MISSION THREE
Salvation for the Dead

GOD THE FATHER

Power Formula For

Power Change With

GOD THE SON, JESUS CHRIST, WHO COMMUNICATES WITH US THROUGH THE HOLY SPIRIT

Power Formula For

Power Change With

The Church of Jesus Christ of Latter-day Saints

Through Its
PROPHETS, APOSTLES, GENERAL, REGIONAL AND LOCAL PRIESTHOOD LEADERS

Spiritual Non Existence Formula Through Missionaries to:

Power Formula For

Power Change With

THOSE WHO ARE NOT YET MEMBERS OF THE CHURCH

ADULT MEMBERS OF CHRIST'S CHURCH INCLUDING HUSBANDS AND WIVES

THOSE WHO DIED WITHOUT RECEIVING THE GOSPEL

OR - Depending on Age

Power Formula For

Power Change With

CHILDREN OF ADULT MEMBERS OF CHRIST'S CHURCH

Eventually will do a Power Formula for their families, and so on, and so on, eternally

Through genealogical research and vicarious temple ordinances by the living for their departed ancestors, the dead may become members of Christ's Church. A similar Church organization undoubtedly exists in the Spirit World to help perfect the Saints (meaning the members of the Lord's Church) there, who have accepted the Savior and who accept the temple ordinances done in their behalf.

THROUGH THEIR PERFECT PLAN, THE FATHER, SON AND THE HOLY SPIRIT HAVE IT ALL COVERED.
NO ONE IS LEFT OUT OF THE OPPORTUNITY TO DO **POWER** AND **SUPER POWER CHANGE** WITH GOD!

The Apostle Paul and the Power Change Formula

It is interesting to note that Paul taught those that he was training, that they were to be followers of himself "even as" he was following Jesus Christ. They were also to keep the ordinances "as I delivered them unto you," meaning they were not to change them. These teachings contain the same principles as the **Power Change Formula**, which states:

> The Formula for the Power Change condition is: when taking over a new post, *Change nothing* until you are thoroughly familiar with your new zone of Power..." you just *don't Change anything...go through the exact same routine every day as your predecessor went through.* Sign nothing that he wouldn't sign. *Don't change a single order...* (L. Ron Hubbard, *Modern Management Technology Defined,* Los Angeles, Bridge Publications, 1976 see Power Change, page. 400).

Similar principles were also taught by the Savior's prophets on the western hemisphere, and these principles are recorded in *The Book of Mormon.* We will review this second witness and **Power Formula** in the next chapter.

Chapter Two

Jesus Christ's Book of Mormon Record Contains Power Formulas for Nephi, His Twelve Disciples, for the Members of His Ancient American Church, His Restored, Latter-day Church and for Everyone Else

Just as He had done in the Holy Land, Jesus Christ also did more than one Power Formula in the New World

Immediately after His appearance, and after having the people come to meet and to touch Him, Jesus Christ called for Nephi, the current Prophet Record Keeper, to come forward. Then, in view of all the people, the Savior ordained Nephi, giving him priesthood power and authority, and making Nephi the leader of His Church in ancient America (see *The Book of Mormon, 3 Nephi* 11:18-21). Nephi's position was similar to Peter's, in that he was the presiding earthly authority over this portion of the Lord's Church.

Next the Lord chose eleven other disciples and gave them power also (Verse 22).

As He had done in *The New Testament*, Jesus Christ gave some of His *Book of Mormon* teachings to: 1) all church members; 2) some of His teachings were directed to His Twelve chosen leaders; and 3) some of His teachings or **Power Formula** was intended for the leader of the Twelve, who was Nephi. In this way, Jesus Christ did **Power Formulas** on three levels.

For specific information on how Jesus' actions fulfilled the steps of the **Power Formula** among His ancient American Church members, please see the *Power Formulas, Part One*, Chapter 13.

Jesus Christ and the Power Formula Step One: Not Disconnecting, in The Book of Mormon

In *Part One*, we reviewed the event in *The Book of Mormon* when the resurrected Savior appeared to the people on the American continent. At that time, He actually had each one of them come forward and meet Him, and touch the wounds in His body, that they might bear record of Him to their children, and to others. This is another example of how the Savior maintained connection to His followers.

In this way, Jesus Christ fulfilled step 1 of the **Power Formula** with these people. He also maintained a revelatory connection to His prophet record keepers, and through them to the members of His ancient American church. Also, the gift of the Holy Ghost was given to these people. This is another way that the Savior stayed connected to them.

Another Name for God's Authority, Power and Super Power is the Priesthood

The power and authority, which God grants to man to perform sacred ordinances, is called the Priesthood. This power has two divisions. The first is known as the Priesthood of Aaron or the Aaronic Priesthood. Aaron was the brother of Moses, and he was ordained by Moses to function as a Priest among the people of ancient Israel. This lesser Priesthood or "Aaronic" includes the authority to baptize, and it is equivalent to God's Power.

However, the authority to confer the Gift of the Holy Ghost is not included in the Aaronic Priesthood. The higher Priesthood has been given the name: Melchizedek Priesthood. This Priesthood, which is mentioned in *The Holy Bible* (see *Hebrews* 5:6; 7:17 and 21), includes the authority to confer the Gift of the Holy Ghost and to perform many other sacred ordinances including the ordinances of the Holy Temple.

Jesus Christ also gave His Twelve leaders on the ancient American Continent this higher Power and Authority (see *The Book of Mormon, Moroni* 2:1-3).

Why God's Higher Priesthood or Super Power is Called The Melchizedek Priesthood

In a modern revelation, the Lord has explained why His higher Priesthood was given the name: Melchizedek Priesthood:

> There are, in the church, two priesthoods, namely, the Melchizedek and Aaronic, including the Levitical Priesthood.
>
> Why the first is called the Melchizedek Priesthood is because Melchizedek was such a great high priest.
>
> Before his day it was called the Holy Priesthood, after the Order of the Son of God.
>
> But out of respect or reverence to the name of the Supreme Being, to avoid the too frequent repetition of his name, they, the Church, in ancient days, called that priesthood after Melchizedek, or the Melchizedek Priesthood.
>
> All other authorities or offices in the Church are appendages to this priesthood (*Doctrine and Covenants* 107:1-5).

Jesus Christ and the Power Formula Step Two, Making a Record, in The Book of Mormon

As He had done prior to coming to visit the people of ancient America, Jesus Christ had His prophet Record Keepers engrave His teachings on metal plates. His instructions to Nephi were to "...write the things which I have told you..." (see *3 Nephi* 23:4).

While visiting among these ancient Americans, Jesus Christ placed a great emphasis on the importance of His sacred record. In fact, Jesus Christ even performed a quality control check on the contents of His Record in this way:

> ...Behold, other scriptures I would that ye should write, that ye have not. And it came to pass that He said unto Nephi: bring forth the Record which ye have kept... (*3 Nephi* 23:6-7, emphasis added).

The Savior then reviewed the records, and then He reminded Nephi of the fulfillment of a prophecy that he had not included in his writings. The Lord then

> ...commanded that it should be written; therefore it was written according as He commanded (*3 Nephi* 23:13).

The Author, The Editor and The Executive of The Book of Mormon

By reviewing and correcting the Record, the Savior demonstrated that it was indeed His Record. The Savior was both the author and the editor of *The Book of Mormon*. He really didn't need to look at the Record. He already knew what it contained, and what had been left out. *The act of reviewing the Record served as a witness, and a symbol, that it was His Book.* What greater testimony could we have of the importance of *The Book of Mormon*?

L. Ron Hubbard taught an Executive is one who:

> ...is able to get others to get the work done, and able to get policy known and used (*Modern Management Defined*, Bridge Publication, Los Angeles, 1976, page 185, see Executive Ability).

The Savior has done just that when it comes to getting us the **Power Formula** Records contained in both *The Holy Bible* and *The Book of Mormon*. He has done so by inspiring His prophets, either directly, or through His angels, or through the Holy Ghost with His teachings. The Savior then directed His prophets to write down these teachings for our benefit so that God's policies are "...known and used".

By having His servant Nephi: "...write the things which I have told you...," and by having Nephi add additional engravings, the Executive of our salvation, Jesus Christ, fulfilled the action we now call Step 2 of the **Power Formula**: "...make a record..."

Jesus Christ and the Third Step of the Power Formula, "...Get it [the Record] into the Hands of the Guy Who is Going Take Care of it," in The Book of Mormon

This step of the **Power Formula** was literally fulfilled when the Savior returned the metal plate Record to Nephi.

Jesus Christ and the Fourth Step of the Power Formula: "Do All You Can to Make the Post Occupiable," in The Book of Mormon, and What is the Post We are to Eventually Occupy?

The final step in the **Power Formula** is to: "Do all you can to make the post occupiable." Before we consider what the Savior has done to help us achieve a state of spiritual power, we first need to better understand what is meant by "...the post..." In the previous chapter, which looked at Jesus Christ's New Testament Church, we reviewed the meaning of "...the post..." that the

Father and the Son want us to occupy. In that section, it was written that this post was for us to become Their heirs. We will now consider further what it means to become an heir of God.

While Jesus Christ was visiting His followers and organizing His Church among *The Book of Mormon* people, He taught them that they were to "...be perfect even as I, or your Father who is in heaven is perfect" (3 *Nephi* 12:48).

Also, while training His Twelve disciples to be the leaders of His Church in ancient America, the Savior taught them that they should be "...even as I am" (*3 Nephi* 28:10). Our potential is to become perfect beings. We will then be like our Savior in knowledge love, and power. This is the "post", meaning the type of Beings that the Gospel **Power Formula** is designed to prepare us to become! This is also what it means to become an heir of God, meaning that we are to become perfect, even as They are!

The Savior also taught that we can receive "...all that My Father hath..."(*Doctrine and Covenants* 84:38). This is also what it means to become an heir of God.

It would be very difficult, and perhaps even impossible to make an all-inclusive list of the things that our Heavenly Parents and Jesus Christ have done to help us accomplish this supernal goal. However, here is another short list of some of the things that our Heavenly Father and Jesus Christ have done, or will do, to help us become like Them.

1. Our spirits are the offspring of our Father and our Mother in Heaven.
2. The Father, through His Son, created this earth, the sun, the moon and the stars, all of which were necessary for us to obtain our physical bodies.
3. They have given us our freedom to choose.
4. They have blessed us with the Atonement of Jesus Christ, which makes forgiveness of our sins possible.
5. They have provided the resurrection for all of us.
6. They have prepared the scriptures, which are Their **Power Formula** Records for us.
7. They have organized The Church of Jesus Christ and sent missionaries to teach Their Gospel **Power Formula** to us.
8. They have instructed Their servants the apostles, prophets, the seventy, regional and local Church priesthood leaders in how to help us.
9. They have sent us the Holy Ghost, to be our Witness, Guide and Comforter.
10. They have made it possible for us to have eternal marriages and families (more on this later).
11. They will make personal visitations to us when we are prepared.
12. They will make this earth a Celestial World for us to dwell on eternally, with Them, and with our families.

What more could we ask for? They have literally done, and continue to "...do all [They] can to make the post occupiable", as described in Step 4 of the **Power Formula**. They have done Their part. The rest is up to us!

Jesus Christ Also Taught the Principle of Power Change in The Book of Mormon: Do

the Works, "...Which Ye Have Seen Me Do Even That Shall Ye Do"

As noted in *Part One*: "The Savior also taught a principle we can equate with the **Power Change Formula**. This principle was for each person to follow His example. In other words, we are to:

...do the works which ye have seen me do...(*3 Nephi* 27:21).

If we had been asked to try to put in words how the Savior might have taught the principle of **Power Change**, we could not have done so any better than this!"

Later, the Savior also taught this principle, not just in the terms of what we should *do*, but also in terms of what we should *be*. At this time, He was speaking to the twelve disciples. However, this principle applies to all who follow the Savior:

...Therefore what manner of men ought ye to be? Verily I say unto you, even as I am" (3 *Nephi* 27:27).

Those Who Do Power Change With God Will Eventually Be "Even As" Jesus Christ and His Father

What will be the ultimate Condition of those who do **Power Change** by following the Savior? What would such individuals be like? The Savior taught three of His disciples, and again by inference, all of us, that it is possible for us to become even as He and our Heavenly Parents are:

...ye shall be even as I am, and I am even as the Father... (3 *Nephi* 28:10).

Chapter Three

Jesus Christ, The Church of Jesus Christ of Latter-day Saints and The Power Formulas

In Chapter Three, we will consider how God's **Power** and **Power Change Formulas** given us in *The Holy Bible* and *The Book of Mormon* are linked to the restoration of The Church of Jesus Christ, and to the availability of God's **Power Formulas** for us, today. Also, we will consider what happened to the Church of Jesus Christ that the Savior had established both in the Holy Land and on the ancient American continent, and why it was necessary for Him to restore His Church in modern times.

Because of persecution from without, and because of contentions and defections from within, the Church of Jesus Christ, both in the Old World and in the New World anciently, ceased to exist. This occurred soon after the Savior ascended into Heaven.

Another way of saying this, is that those who's spiritual **Conditions** were in the **Enemy** and the **Treason** categories succeeded in their efforts to persecute and suppress the Church below **Non Existence**, and ultimately into the lowest condition: **Confusion**. The historical name for this **Condition of Spiritual Confusion** is the *Dark Ages.*

With the falling away of the Church, God's **Power Formula** was no longer available. However, portions of the truth still remained, and eventually well-intentioned people tried to "reform" the Church during the Protestant Reformation.

Lost Foundation Restored

On the American continent, and in the Holy Land, the leaders of the Church were eventually killed, or taken from among the people. The apostle Paul described the organization of the Lord's Church as being like a Temple. In this description, Paul explained that the Church was "...built upon the foundation of apostles and prophets, Jesus Christ Himself being the chief cornerstone" (*New T. Ephesians* 2:20).

The analogy is clear. A building cannot continue to stand without its foundation. This is why, with the loss of its inspired leadership, the Church of Jesus Christ was lost from the earth anciently, in both the Old and the New Worlds. Also, it is very significant that with the loss of foundation of the Church organization, there was also an actual loss of temples and temple ordinances. In addition with the restoration of The Church of Jesus Christ to the earth in 1830, came the restoration of God's temples to the earth.

Because the Church had been *formed* by Jesus Christ, and not by men, it was not possible for men to *re-form* the Church, after it was gone. In order for The Church of Jesus Christ to exist once again, there would need to be a *restoration,* by Jesus Christ Himself. The *Reformation* was not adequate. A *Restoration* was required.

This is exactly what happened. The Age of Enlightenment eventually brought democracy and freedom of religion. Once a nation had been established with enough freedom to make such a restoration possible, Jesus Christ called and empowered new apostles and prophets, thus re-laying the foundation of His Church.

As part of the restoration of His Church, Jesus Christ has revealed anew His **Gospel Power Formula** through the prophet Joseph Smith, and to His other modern apostles and prophets. This has again made it possible for us to do **Power Change** with God.

How Jesus Christ Restored His Church and His Gospel Power Formula to the Earth

In order for the Lord to reveal His **Power Formula**, it was first necessary for Him to call and prepare a prophet, through whom He could give revelations. To call a prophet, it was necessary for the Savior to Personally connect, by revealing Himself to His prophet. Also, this prophet would need to be given God's Power, or priesthood, so other apostles and prophets could be called, empowered and trained. Through His apostles and prophets the Lord would start the cycle again, and "make a record" of His revelations. Next, through His prophets and apostles, the Lord would get that record into our hands.

Through His living apostles and prophets and through the help of the Holy Ghost, the Lord Jesus Christ has done everything possible to help us succeed. It was through His living apostles and prophets that the Savior has completed all the steps of His **Power Formula** for us today.

It is plain to see that the calling of new apostles and prophets was the necessary first action by God in restoring His **Power Formula** to the Earth. We will now look more closely at how the Savior has completed these steps of the **Power Formula** for His Church in these latter days.

Power Formula Step One: How the Father and the Son Connected with Joseph Smith, Prior to Giving Him Their Power Formula Records for Our Time

In 1820, Joseph Smith was a 14-year-old boy living with his family in the upper part of the state of New York. Although he believed in Heavenly Father and in Jesus Christ, Joseph did not belong to a church. He was diligently trying to decide which church to join. During this time, Joseph was reading in *The Holy Bible*, and he came across this passage in the book of *James*:

> If any of you lack wisdom, let him ask of God, that giveth to all men liberally, and upbraideth [punishes] not; and it shall be given [to] him (*James* 1:5)

This scripture provided the way for Joseph Smith to find out which church was right. Young Joseph, believing in the promise of this ancient apostle, James, decided that he would pray to God and ask Him which church he should join. Joseph went to a grove of trees near his home, and, early on a beautiful spring day, he knelt in prayer.

In answer to his prayer, a pillar of light appeared above his head, and in this light he saw two Persons. One of Them said, pointing to the other: "This is my beloved Son, hear Him." Joseph Smith was visited by God, the Father, and His Son, Jesus Christ! He asked Jesus which church he should join. He was told that he should join none of them, because none of them were the Savior's Church.

The Lord's Church was not, at that time, upon the earth. The prophet, Joseph Smith would become the instrument through which the true Church, and the Power of Jesus Christ, were restored to the earth (see *The Pearl of Great Price*, Joseph Smith History verses 1-12).

Part of that restoration came in the form of *The Book of Mormon*. An angel, named Moroni, appeared to Joseph and showed him the place where *The Book of Mormon* record was located. This same Moroni was the final record keeper, who had placed the metal plate record in a hillside approximately 1,200 years previously.

For the next four years, as Joseph matured, he also received training in the form of visits and instructions from the angel Moroni, to prepare him to receive and translate the record. In the fourth year, Joseph was allowed to go the hill where the record was stored. Joseph was directed to lift a stone that was covering a stone box located near the top of the hill. Inside the box were the golden plates that contained *The Book of Mormon* record.

Also, in the box was a device that God had prepared to help Joseph translate the Book. This device was called a Urim and Thummim. *The Holy Bible* also mentions a Urim and Thummim (see *Exodus* 28:30).

Joseph removed these articles from the box, and he took them to his home. With the Lord's help he was able to translate the engravings from a portion of the plates into English. This translation was published as *The Book of Mormon* in 1830 (see *The Pearl of Great Price*, Joseph Smith History, verses 21-75).

Power Formula Step 2: Jesus Christ Caused Three Records: The Holy Bible, The Book of Mormon, and a Record of the Revelations given to Joseph Smith to be Made Available to Help His Church

The Law of Witnesses

In addition to providing *The Book of Mormon* **Power Formula** to the members of His Church, or "saints", in these final or "latter-days", before the Savior returns to the earth, He has also provided *The Holy Bible*. As we have shown in Part 2 and in Chapter One of this *Part Three*, *The Holy Bible* is also a record of God's **Power Formula** for His children. The Church of Jesus Christ of Latter-day Saints believes:

> *The Bible* to be the word of God, as far as it is translated correctly. We also believe *The Book of Mormon* to be the word of God (*The Pearl of Great Price, Article of Faith* #8, page 60).

The book referenced above, *The Pearl of Great Price*, along with *The Doctrine and Covenants of The Church of Jesus Christ of Latter-day Saints*, contain the scriptural record of the revelations that God has given to the Prophet Joseph Smith, and to other modern apostles and prophets. These modern revelations are the third **Power Formula Record** that we have received from the Lord. The Lord has obeyed His own law that:

...in the mouth of two or three witnesses, shall every word be established (see *New Test. Matthew* 18:16; also see *The Book of Mormon Ether* 5:4; and *The Doctrine and Covenants* 128:3).

"...The Record Is True", and Re-laying the Foundation

In the first revelation, or "section," of *The Doctrine and Covenants*, the Lord explained why He called Joseph Smith to be His prophet:

> Wherefore, I the Lord, knowing the calamity which should come upon the inhabitants of the earth, called upon my servant Joseph Smith, Jun., and spake unto him from heaven and gave him commandments...And after having received the record of the Nephites, yea, even my servant Joseph Smith Jun., might have power to translate through the mercy of God, by the power of God, *The Book of Mormon. And also those, to whom these commandments were given, might have power to lay the foundation of this church*, and bring it forth out of obscurity and out of darkness, *the only true and living church upon the face of the whole earth*... What I the Lord have spoken, I have spoken, and I excuse not myself; and though the heavens and the earth pass away, my word shall not pass away, but shall all be fulfilled, *whether by mine own voice or by the voice of my servants, it is the same. For behold, and lo, the Lord is God, and the Spirit beareth record, and the record is true,* and the truth abideth forever and ever, Amen (Doctrine and Covenants 1:18, 29, 30, 38, and 39, emphasis added).

As He did in *The Holy Bible* and *The Book of Mormon* **Power Formulas**, Jesus Christ delegated and assigned the responsibility of actually making the record to His prophets and apostles. An example of the Lord's servants being instructed to **make a record** occurred in the life of a modern apostle, Joseph Smith.

The prophet and an associate were instructed to "write while we were yet in the spirit." This was during a vision in which Joseph Smith and Sidney Rigdon saw the degrees of glory, or the Heavens, that are available for our Father's children (see *Doctrine and Covenants* 76:80, see also *New Testament, see also 2nd Corinthians* 12:2).

Power Formula Step 3, How Jesus Christ Got His Record Into The Hands Of The Members of The Church Of Jesus Christ Of Latter-Day Saints

One of the beautiful things about having a prophet **make a record**, is that the record will already be in the hands of that prophet, and he can then follow the **Power Formula** record himself. The prophet can also teach others from it. In this way people can learn how to do **Power Change** with God. This is exactly what happened to the prophet Joseph Smith, and to The Church of Jesus Christ of Latter-day Saints.

Step 4 of the Savior's Power Formula for the Prophet Joseph Smith. How Jesus Christ Has Done Everything Possible To Help Him Function as the Prophet and the Earthly President of the Savior's Church

As reviewed above, the Lord Jesus Christ testified of the prophet's calling in these words:

> Wherefore, I the Lord, knowing the calamity which should come upon the inhabitants of the earth, called upon my servant Joseph Smith, Jun., and spake unto him from heaven, and gave him commandments;
>
> And also gave commandments to others, that they should proclaim these things unto the world; and all this that it might be fulfilled, which was written by the prophets...
>
> That the fullness of my gospel might be proclaimed by the weak and the simple unto the ends of the world, and before kings and rulers.
>
> [Also]
>
> And also with Peter, and James, and John, whom I have sent unto you, by whom I have ordained you and confirmed you to be apostles, and especial witnesses of my name, and bear the keys of your ministry and of the same things which I revealed unto them;
>
> Unto whom I have committed the keys of my kingdom, and a dispensation of the gospel for the last times; and for the fullness of times, in the which I will gather together in one all things, both which are in heaven, and which are on earth;
>
> And also with all those whom my Father hath given me out of the world.
>
> [Also]
>
> But, behold, verily, verily, I say unto thee, [that while Joseph Smith is living] no one shall be appointed to receive commandments and revelations in this church excepting my servant Joseph Smith, Jun., for he receiveth them even as Moses...
>
> For I have given him the keys of the mysteries, and the revelations which are sealed, until I shall appoint unto them another in his stead (*Doctrine and Covenants* 1:17, 18, 23; 27:12-14; 28:2, 7).

Step 4 of the Savior's Power Formula for all Members of His Church

Chapters one and two of *The Power Formulas, Part Three* both included lists of some of the things that the Lord has done and is doing to help the members of His Church. With the restoration of His Church and His **Gospel Power Formula** in these latter days, all of these blessings, are now available to us. Below is another list of some of the things that God the Father, His Son, Jesus Christ, and the Holy Ghost have done to "make the post [of being Their Heirs] occupiable" for us.

1. They have created this earth, the sun, the moon and the stars, all of which were necessary for there to be life on this planet, so we could obtain our physical bodies.
2. They have revealed truth through Their prophets, through the scriptures, and through inspiration from the Holy Ghost.
3. They have given us our freedom to choose.
4. They have made it possible for us to be forgiven of our sins through the atoning sacrifice

of Jesus Christ.

5. They have provided the resurrection, which will give each of us a perfect and immortal body.
6. They have given us families.
7. They have given us Their Church.
8. They have given us Their Priesthood power and authority.
9. They have given us Their temple ordinances and training.
10. They have made it possible for us to be blessed by missionary service, both for those who receive their **Gospel Power Formula**, and those who share it with others.
11. They have made it possible for the dead to also advance and progress through missionary work in the Spirit World, and through vicarious temple ordinances done by the living in behalf of the dead.
12. They answer our prayers. This includes our sincere prayers to learn the truth about Jesus Christ, His Church and His Gospel **Power Formula.**

Chapter Four

'BY THEIR FRUITS [STATS] YE SHALL KNOW THEM':
Evidences That The Church of Jesus Christ of Latter-day Saints Is God's Restored and True Church

Identifying Evidence #1 of Christ's True Church: Temples, Ancient and Modern

While the Savior was upon the earth, He frequently went to the temple in Jerusalem to teach the people. He also cleared the temple grounds twice of money changers, calling it "My Father's house," and later, "My house" (*New Test. John* 2:16; *Matthew* 21:12). He also prophesied that one of the consequences of the people of Israel rejecting Him as their Messiah and King was that His once Holy Temple, would become "...your house" (New Test. Matthew 23:37-38). Also, because of their general rejection of Him as their Messiah, the temple would eventually be destroyed (see *New Test. Matthew* 24:1-2).

Temples and Temple Worship are Evidences of Jesus Christ's True Church Upon the Earth

As part of the restoration of Jesus Christ's Church and His **Gospel Power Formula**, the restoration of temple worship has occurred. In His temples we can receive additional help and Power from God (*Doctrine and Covenants* 124:39). These blessings of the Temple, and how they extend the opportunity to do **Power Change** with God to those died without receiving it while they lived on the earth, will be discussed in the final book of this series, **Super Power**.

Identifying Evidence #2 of Christ's True Church:
Living Apostles and Prophets

In Chapter One of this book, we considered Paul's description of the Church organization as being like a building, and specifically, like "...*a temple...*" (see *New Test. Ephesians* 2:19-20). You will recall that he compared the apostles and prophets to the foundation, with Jesus Christ being the chief corner stone. We have also pointed out how the Lord's Church fell anciently when it lost this foundation of apostles and prophets.

"...Until New Apostles Are Sent..."

For The Church of Jesus Christ to again exist on the earth, it was necessary for the Savior to call new apostles. This truth was recognized by Roger Williams who lived before the time of Joseph Smith. He was a founding father of the state of Rhode Island, and of the first Baptist Church in America. He taught that there was:

...no regularly constituted Church of Christ on earth, nor any person authorized to administer any church ordinance, nor can there be until new apostles are sent by the great head of the Church, for whose coming I am seeking (*Picturesque America*, p. 503).

You will also recall in the verses cited above from The *Doctrine and Covenants* section one, that:

Those to whom these commandments were given, might have power to lay the foundation of this Church... (*Doctrine and Covenants* 1:30, emphasis added).

The foundation of Christ's Church was laid when the Savior sent His ancient apostles, Peter, James and John, to ordain Joseph Smith, and his associate Oliver Cowdery with His higher priesthood power and to the office of apostles of Jesus Christ.

Identifying Evidence #3 of Christ's True Church: Missionary Work,

The Church of Jesus Christ was soon organized as it had been anciently with Apostles and Prophets, the Seventy, High Priests, Elders and all of the other offices of the Priesthood. Also, just as during the time of Christ's mortal ministry, His Church began to send out missionaries throughout the world in these latter days. The Church of Jesus Christ of Latter-day Saints is one of the fastest growing Christian churches on earth. Today there are more than 52,000 full-time missionaries, most serving at their own expense, throughout the world. Recently, the Lord, through His living prophet Thomas S. Monson has announced a lowering of the age at which the young men and young women of the Church can serve missions. This has resulted in a 200% to 400% increase in the number of missionary applications! There are also many more part-time missionaries serving. It is my privilege to be one of these.

We know from reading the rest of the New Testament, that missionary work did not cease after Jesus Christ left the earth. His apostles, and other missionaries carried the **Gospel Spiritual Non Existence and Power Formula** messages to many nations (see *Acts* 5:42, and 10:42).

One of the great evidences of the falling away of Christ's Church with the death of His apostles is that the Lord's organized program of missionary work ceased. Likewise, one of the great evidences of the restoration of Christ's Church to the earth in these latter days was that after the Lord had called modern apostles and prophets, there was a reinstatement of missionary work. Also, this missionary work was carried out just as it had been organized by the Savior and His apostles anciently.

In February of 1831, less than one year after the Church of Jesus Christ had been restored to the earth, The Savior gave this revelation to Joseph Smith:

HEARKEN [hear and obey], O ye elders of my Church...And ye shall go forth in the power of my Spirit, preaching my gospel, two by two in my name... (*Doctrine and Covenants* 42:1 and 6, emphasis added).

As noted earlier, this was how the Savior sent out the Seventy to do missionary work during His mortal ministry: "...two and two..." (*New Testament, Luke* 10:1).

Many other revelations on the subject of missionary work were given to the prophet Joseph Smith. Among these revelations were instructions that missionaries be sent to Great Britain. These revelations came during a period when the Church was receiving much persecution. If the Church was being directed by men rather than the Lord, they would have probably "circled the wagons", to protect themselves, and would have avoided sending out some of their finest members and leaders as missionaries. However, this was not the Church of men. The Lord had other plans for His Kingdom.

The first missionaries sent to Great Britain went in the year 1837. *By 1850, 60 percent of the Latter-day Saints on earth lived not in the United States, but in Great Britain!* Most of those who joined the Church in England eventually came to America to be with their Latter-day Saint brothers and sisters here.

Among these who came to America were William Heaton and James Bowers. Both of these men, after joining the Church, became local missionaries, in England, prior to coming to the United States. Both men sailed to America with their families in 1856 aboard the ship *The Enoch Train.* Both were in the first group of handcart pioneers who walked across the Midwest of the American continent, pulling and pushing their meager belongings with them.

William and his family made it to Utah, so did the family of James Bowers. However, James Bowers did not live to see the valley of the Great Salt Lake. James was among those who died while crossing the central plains. He was buried somewhere along the "Mormon" trail in Iowa.

After settling in Utah, both of their families were called by Brigham Young, the second prophet and president of the Church, to move to Nevada to start a new community along the Muddy River. A son of James Bowers, named Isaiah, later married a daughter of William Heaton. Her name was Maria. Isaiah and Maria were two of my great, great grandparents on our mother's side of our family.

On my father's side of our family, he was the first person to become a Latter-day Saint. My father was taught the gospel by missionaries and joined the Church in his early twenties. Since that time, a number of dad's relatives have also joined the Church, including his mother, his aunt and some of his cousins. Perhaps you now understand how the restoration of The Church of Jesus Christ and the revelations, which restored the Lord's great missionary program have, quite literally, shaped the lives of our family. Also, the lives of millions of other people have been changed as a result of the missionary program of the Lord's Church.

In a recent General Conference of the Church, one of the Savior's living apostles spoke of the great missionary program of the Church and summarized the message that the Lord's missionaries are declaring to the world, in this way:

> From the early days of the Restoration, the Brethren [meaning the apostles, prophets and the seventy] have been very serious about their charge to declare the gospel. In 1837, only seven years after the organization of the Church, at a time of poverty and persecution, missionaries were sent to teach the gospel in England. Within the next few years, missionaries were preaching in such diverse places as Austria, French Polynesia, India, Barbados, Chile, and China.
>
> The Lord has blessed this work, and the Church is being established across the world. This meeting is being translated into 90 languages. We are grateful for the

52,225 full-time missionaries serving in more than 150 countries. *The sun never sets on righteous missionaries testifying of the Savior.* Think of the spiritual power of 52,000 missionaries, endowed with the Spirit of the Lord, boldly declaring that there is *"no other name given nor any other way nor means whereby salvation can come...only in and through the name of Christ"* (*The Book of Mormon, Mosiah* 3:17) (*Preparing the World for the Second Coming,* Elder Neil L. Andersen, *The Ensign of The Church of Jesus Christ of Latter-day Saints,* May 2011, page 51, emphasis added).

"...By Their Fruits [Stats] Ye Shall Know Them...." (True Prophets and False Prophets, and How You Can Tell Them Apart)

Prior to His crucifixion, the Savior was teaching the people His famous Sermon on the Mount. As part of this discourse, Jesus warned the people to beware of false prophets. He then went on to explain how we can tell the difference between a true and a false prophet.

It is interesting to note that by giving the people a way to make the distinction between a true and a false prophet, Jesus was, in effect, also teaching that there would indeed be true prophets. Otherwise there would have been no need to give us a way to decide who is a true and who is a false prophet. If there were to be no further prophets after the ascension of Jesus and the death of His apostles, He could have just said beware of all who come claiming to be prophets.

Matthew, who was an apostle of Jesus Christ, recorded these teachings in what is now the seventh chapter of his gospel, as follows:

> Beware of false prophets, which come to you in sheep's clothing, but inwardly are ravening wolves. *Ye shall know them by their fruits.* Do men gather grapes of thorns, or figs of thistles? *Even so every good tree bringeth forth good fruit; but a corrupt tree bringeth forth evil fruit. A good tree cannot bring forth evil fruit, neither can a corrupt tree bring forth good fruit...Wherefore by their fruits ye shall know them"* (*New Test. Matthew* 7:15-20, emphasis added).

We will now look at some of the fruits, or statistics, of The Church of Jesus Christ of Latter-day Saints. Specifically we will consider these five areas 1) Church growth; 2) successful marriages and family life; 3) promotion of life (birth rate); 4) Service and volunteerism statistics for the State of Utah; and 5) the life expectancy, or survival statistics of active adult members of The Church of Jesus Christ of Latter-day Saints.

Positive Statistical Trend or 'Fruit' Number One: Church Growth

While Jesus was yet living upon the earth, He started the great missionary program of His Church. First,

> ...He called His twelve disciples together and gave them power and authority over all devils, and to cure diseases. And He sent them to preach the Kingdom of God,

and to heal the sick (*New Test. Luke* 9:1-2).

The next chapter of Luke re-counts the story of the Seventy who were also called and sent by the Lord, as additional missionaries:

> ...two and two before His face into every city and place wither [where] He Himself would come (Luke 10:1).

This is also how missionaries are sent by the Lord and His Church today: "...two and two...".

After His work of preparing His apostles was done, and just before He ascended into heaven, the Savior gave *His apostles* what some people have called the 'great commission':

> Go ye therefore, and teach all nations, baptizing them in the name of Father, and of the Son, and of the Holy Ghost: Teaching them to observe all things whatsoever I have commanded you... (*New Test. Matthew* 28:19-20).

Just as the Savior gave His great commission to the ancient apostles to do missionary work He has repeated it to His Restored Church through His modern apostles.

> Go ye into all the world, preach the gospel to every creature, acting in the authority which I have given you, baptizing in the name of the Father, and of the Son, and of the Holy Ghost.
> And he that believeth and is baptized shall be saved, and he that believeth not shall be damned (Doctrine and Covenants 68:8-9).
>
> [Also]
>
> Which Twelve hold the keys to open up the authority of my kingdom upon the four corners of the earth, and after that to send my word to every creature (Doctrine and Covenants 124:128).

Also, just a few months ago, President Thomas S. Monson, who is an apostle and a prophet has taught of our duty to take the gospel to the world, with these words:

> Tonight there are many thousands of our number who are serving the Lord full-time as His missionaries. In response to a call, they have left behind home, family, friends, and school and have gone forward to serve. Those who don't understand ask the question, "Why do they respond so readily and willingly give so much?"
> Our missionaries could well answer in the words of Paul, that peerless missionary of an earlier day: "For though I preach the gospel, I have nothing to glory of: for necessity is laid upon me; yea, woe is unto me, if I preach not the gospel!"

The holy scriptures contain no proclamation more relevant, no responsibility more binding, no instruction more direct than the injunction given by the resurrected Lord as He appeared in Galilee to the eleven disciples. Said He:

"All power is given unto me in heaven and in earth.
"Go ye therefore, and teach all nations, baptizing them in the name of the Father, and of the Son, and of the Holy Ghost:
"Teaching them to observe all things whatsoever I have commanded you: and, lo, I am with you always[a], even unto the end of the world."

This divine command, coupled with its glorious promise, is our watchword today, as it was in the meridian of time. Missionary work is an identifying feature of The Church of Jesus Christ of Latter-day Saints. Always has it been; ever shall it be. As the Prophet Joseph Smith declared, "After all that has been said, the greatest and most important duty is to preach the Gospel."

Within two short years, all of the full-time missionaries currently serving in this royal army of God will have concluded their full-time labors and will have returned to their homes and loved ones. Their replacements are found tonight in the ranks of the Aaronic Priesthood of the Church. Young men, are you ready to respond? Are you willing to work? Are you prepared to serve?

President John Taylor summed up the requirements: "The kind of men we want as bearers of this gospel message are men who have faith in God; men who have faith in their religion; men who honor their priesthood; … men full of the Holy Ghost and the power of God[;] … men of honor, integrity, virtue and purity."

Brethren, to each of us comes the mandate to share the gospel of Christ. When our lives comply with God's own standard, those within our sphere of influence will never speak the lament, "The harvest is past, the summer is ended, and we are not saved."

The perfect *Shepherd of souls, the Missionary who redeemed mankind, gave us His divine assurance:*

"If it so be that you should labor all your days in crying repentance unto this people, and bring, save it be one soul unto me, how great shall be your joy with him in the kingdom of my Father!

"And now, if your joy will be great with one soul that you have brought unto me into the kingdom of my Father, how great will be your joy if you should bring many souls unto me!" (Doctrine and Covenants 18:15)

Of Him who spoke these words, I declare my personal witness. He is the Son of God, our Redeemer, and our Savior.

I pray that we will have the courage to extend the hand of fellowship, the tenacity to try and try again, and the humility needed to seek guidance from our Father as we fulfill our mandate to share the gospel. The responsibility is upon us, brethren. In the name of Jesus Christ, amen (October 2012 LDS General Conference talk by President Thomas S. Monson, "See Others as They May Become").

A Major World Faith

Since the restoration of the Church of Jesus Christ, the Lord has continued to call missionaries through His apostles and prophets. As mentioned previously, today there are more than 52,000 missionaries serving full time. Most serve for a period of two years at their own expense.

Rodney Stark, a sociologist, who is not a member of the Church, has studied and written about the growth of the Church. In an article he wrote about this subject, he quoted other researchers in this way:

> ...The Mormons have nearly as many missionaries in the field as do all of the Protestant bodies of North America combined (*Stark and Bainbridge* 1984).

In this same article, Rodney Stark has written that:

> ...If growth during the next century is like that of the past, the Mormons will become a major world faith. If, for example, we assume they will grow by 30 percent per decade, then in 2080 there will be more than sixty million Mormons. But since World War II, the Mormon growth rate has been far higher than 30 percent per decade. If we set the rate at 50 percent, then in 2080 there will be 265 million Mormons.

Concerning the reasons for the strong growth statistics of the Church, Rodney Stark wrote:

> One reason for Mormon growth is that their fertility is sufficiently high to offset both mortality and defection. But a more important reason is a rapid rate of conversion. Indeed, the majority of Mormons today were not born in the faith, but converted to it (Stark, Rodney, *The Rise of a New World Faith*, originally published in *REVIEW OF RELIGIOUS RESEARCH* 26:18-27, emphasis added).

The Limitations of Statistics

Does the rapid growth of The Church of Jesus Christ of Latter-day Saints prove that it is God's true Church on the earth? No. They're other churches that are also growing rapidly. Among these is the Church of Scientology, International. Also, statistics regarding the growth of the churches are not complete. For instance, some statistics are mostly just for the United States and Canada. Also, much of the data is not recent.

"Extremely Reliable" Statistics

However, regarding statistics generated by The Church of Jesus Christ of Latter-day Saints, Rodney Stark has commented that:

> It is worth noting that Mormon statistics are extremely reliable (is there another denomination that actually sends out auditors to check local figures?). [Rodney Stark also wrote of the]: ...extraordinary efforts of Mormon social scientists to

study their faith. Through the years, I have consulted with many denominational research departments and have read countless reports of their results. I have often been favorably impressed. Yet the research efforts of other denominations shrink to insignificance when compared with the quality, scope, and sophistication of the work of the Mormon social research department. One might as well be comparing missionary efforts *(see above reference,* emphasis added).

Recently, it was announced that The Church of Jesus Christ of Latter-day Saints has grown from its original six members in 1830, to become the 4th or 5th largest Church in the United States.

Positive Statistical Trend or "Fruit" Number Two: Successful Marriages and Family Life

Among the revelations given by the Lord Jesus Christ through the prophet Joseph Smith are many about marriage and the family. One of these revelations contains this remarkable promise:

> If a man marry a wife by my word, which is my law, and by the new and everlasting covenant, and it is sealed unto them by the Holy Spirit of promise [the Holy Ghost], by him who is anointed, unto whom I have appointed this power and the keys of this priesthood; and it shall be said unto them: Ye shall come forth in the first resurrection; and...it shall done unto them in all things whatsoever my servant hath put upon them, *in time and through all eternity; and shall be of full force when they are out of this world...*" *(Doctrine and Covenants* 132:19, emphasis added).

In other words, marriages performed in Latter-day Saint Temples can last through "...time and through all eternity".

Eternal Marriage and Eternal Families

As mentioned above, these temple marriages, or sealings, are different than all other types of marriages. Marriages that are not performed in the temples are for this life only, or, as stated in many ceremonies, these marriages only last: "until death do you part" [or until death do you divorce]. These couples are often told that they are married "for the period of your mortal lives".

In contrast, marriages, which are performed in the temple, are for this life *and for all eternity.* Not only are the parents married forever, their children are also sealed to them, *forming an eternal family unit.*

How is it possible for a wedding to unite couples and families forever? The answer to this question is found in the *New Testament.* The priesthood power and keys of authority to use this power were given by the Savior to Peter, and to the other apostles. Jesus Christ taught these apostles that:

> ...whatsoever ye shall bind on earth shall be bound in heaven... (*Matthew* 16:19, and 18:18).

As part of the restoration of His Church to the earth in these latter days, Jesus Christ sent the ancient apostles Peter, James and John to confer this same priesthood power and authority and the keys upon Joseph Smith. The authority to bind a marriage not only for this life, but also in heaven has been passed on to others so that they are authorized to seal marriages forever.

Lessons from the Movie Casper: "Can I Keep You?" and "Until We are Together Again"

Recently, while re-watching the movie *Casper*, my heart was touched. For those of you have not seen this movie, it is about a father and his teenage daughter who are struggling after the untimely death of his wife and her mother. A theme of the story is the father's continuing love for his wife, and his desire to be with her again.

The father and his daughter meet four ghosts who are occupying a scary old mansion. Three of these ghosts are cranky and pesky. However, one, the younger nephew of the three, is Casper, "the friendly ghost". Some of you may remember watching old cartoons about Casper.

During the course of their adventures, Casper falls in love with the daughter. In one scene, while he is saying good night to her as she is falling asleep, Casper whispers in her ear: "Can I keep you?"

The beauty and the truth of this question, and of the love that prompted it, are almost overwhelming. For isn't this the deepest desire of our hearts? We want desperately to keep our relationships with our loved ones, for losing them is the greatest "sting" of death.

Later in the movie, the father is able to see and speak to the spirit of his wife. When the time comes for her to leave, he asked her: "Where are you going?" She tells him: "To where I can watch over both of you until we are together again." Such ideas are more than just nice sentiments, and more than things we wish were true.

For nearly 170 years now, the Lord's servants who hold His priesthood power authority and keys, have been sealing marriages for time and for all eternity in the Lord's temples. Some may believe that these concepts of eternal love, eternal marriages and eternal families are too good to be true, and that the reality of what the Lord has in store for us in the next life is really something less wonderful than these eternal relationships with those we love. However, just the opposite is true! The future that the Lord has prepared for us is even greater than we can imagine, rather than less than we now hope for!

The apostle and prophet, Paul, taught this truth in this way:

> But as it is written, eye hath not seen, nor ear heard, neither have entered into the heart of man, the things which God hath prepared for them that love him (*New Testament, 1 Corinthians* 2:9).

Alone in a Mansion?

The Savior taught:

> Let not your heart be troubled: ye believe in God, believe also in me. In my

Father's house are many mansions: if it were not so, I would have told you. I go to prepare a place for you" (*John* 14:1-2).

What good would it be to live in a beautiful mansion in the celestial world by ourselves? Our mansions will never be home or heaven without having our loved ones with us there! We will not be alone if we follow the Savior's **gospel Power Formula**, we will be together forever with our families. This is one of the most wonderful of the "...things which God has prepared for those who love Him" (*New Testament, 1 Corinthians* 2:9).

Thanks to the Father and the Son, there is a way for us to *not* lose them. By following Their plan, yes—we 'can keep' them, *and* we can also be together again with our Heavenly Parents, and our Savior forever! It doesn't, and it can't get any better than this! Thank you Father, thank you, Savior, and thank you Holy Spirit for taking away the 'sting of death', and replacing it with 'a fullness of joy'!

The Pearl of Greatest Price

Matthew's gospel records the parable of the Pearl of Great Price with these words:

> Again, the kingdom of heaven is like unto a merchant man,
> seeking goodly pearls:
>
> Who, when he had found one pearl of great price, went and
> sold all that he had, and bought it (*Matthew* 13:45-46).

This parable has a number of important elements. First, it uses the metaphor of a merchant seeking "goodly pearls". A merchant is one who buys and sells merchandise. Second, he was *actively seeking* these pearls. Third, when he found the greatest pearl, he was all in and fully invested in obtaining it.

This is a description of how one investigates truth should react when he or she finally receives the Gospel of Jesus Christ, which is God's **Power** and **Super Power Formulas**.

We should not hesitate or equivocate in our commitment to follow what God has revealed to us that we should do. We are to follow Jesus Christ with all our hearts and not look back. If we do so, we will loose the Pearl of Great Price, which is being with God in "...the Kingdom of Heaven...".

This is a great goal and a high reward. However, there is a higher goal, which leads to the greatest reward. That is to not only be with God in the Kingdom of Heaven, but to be there with our families, and with our Savior, and our Heavenly Parents eternally. **This is The Pearl of Greatest Price**!

Ultimate Success

Here is my recollection of a story told on the radio about a young lady named Anne Duke. She was a Christian, but not a Latter-day Saint. She and her husband were very much in love. He had just finished medical school. While traveling home, their car was struck by a runaway semi-truck; and they were both killed.

While her parents were going through Anne's belongings, they ran across something she had written in her diary. This was her definition of success: 'Ultimate success equals being with God face to face, in Heaven, forever.' What a great definition of success!

However, there is a more complete definition of ultimate success. With the added perspective of the Restored Gospel of Jesus Christ, we can complete the definition of ultimate success in this way: Ultimate success is being with our families and with our Savior, and with our Heavenly Parents, face to face in Heaven, forever! This is my greatest hope for all of us, that we may have this "ultimate success".

The Stabilizing Effects of Eternal Marriage and Family Relationships

Returning now to a review of the research statistics regarding Latter-day Saint family life, another social scientist, Daniel K. Judd did a literature review of research concerning the mental health of members of The Church of Jesus Christ of Latter-day Saints. He wrote:

> Analysis of the data indicates that Latter-day Saints who live their lives consistent with their religious beliefs experience *greater general well-being* and *marital and family stability*, and *less delinquency, depression, anxiety* and *substance abuse* than those who do not...a comparison between religious groups [Catholics, Liberal Protestants, Conservative Protestants, Latter-day Saints and those with no religion] revealed that '*Mormons tend to have the highest rate of marriage and fertility, but the lowest rates of divorce*' (Daniel K. Judd, *Latter-day Saint Social Life*, chapter 17, published by the Religious Studies Center, Brigham Young University, Provo, Utah, 1998, emphasis added).

In his review of the literature regarding Latter-day Saints whose marriages were sealed in the temple, Daniel K. Judd has written:

> ...Latter-day Saints who marry in a temple ceremony are less likely to divorce than those married outside the temple (Thomas 1983). Heaton (1988) reports that among men and women who were married in the temple, six percent of the men and seven percent of the women had later been divorced... (Daniel K. Judd, *Latter-day Saint Social Life*, chapter 17, published by the Religious Studies Center, Brigham Young University, Provo, Utah, 1998).

What a remarkable statistic! This means that, when this was reported, between 93 and 94 percent of those who were married in the temple don't get divorced! This is especially remarkable when compared to the overall divorce statistics for marriages in the United States. It has been widely reported that in the U.S. approximately 50 percent of all marriages end in divorce. This means that five of every ten marriages in the United States do not survive. In the U.S.A., it is 'until divorce do you part', as often as it is 'until death do you part'!

Divorce Proofing Your Marriage

For Latter-day Saint temple marriages, the above statistics indicate that less than one in ten marriages are dissolved by divorce. Thus, those who choose to have their marriages sealed in the temple are about *seven times* less likely to divorce than the general U.S. population! This is as close to making a marriage divorce proof as you are ever likely to see.

Also, to further divorce proof you marriage, here is a suggestion: In addition to having your marriage sealed in the temple, if you as a couple will pray together every night, you will not get a divorce. This counsel was given by a living apostle, Russell M. Ballard (from an address given at the Conference of the West Valley Utah Stake of The Church of Jesus Christ of Latter-day Saints).

With divorce, many social problems increase. These include delinquency, teenage pregnancy, and drug abuse. It is probable that the reason that, as quoted above:

> ...Latter-day Saints who live their lives consistent with their religious beliefs experience greater general well being and marital and family stability, and less delinquency, depression, anxiety, and substance abuse than those who do not... [is, at least in part, because of the higher marriage survival rate among such people] (Daniel K. Judd, *Latter-day Saint Social Life*, chapter 17, published by the Religious Studies Center, Brigham Young University, Provo, Utah, 1998).

In the next section we shall look at another beneficial result of the strength of Latter-day Saint temple marriages: the blessing of additional children.

Positive Statistical Trend, or "Fruit"
Number Three: Promotion of Lives (Increased Birth Rate)

It is not surprising that when marriages survive better, there is an increase in the number of children born to these couples. Another social scientist, Tim B. Heaton, has written the following regarding Latter-day Saint family size:

> Fertility refers to actual childbearing rather to the biological capacity to give birth. LDS [Latter-day Saint] theology supports attitudes and behaviors that directly influence fertility' (Bean, Mineau, and Anderton 1990). Consistent with a pronatalist [pro birth] doctrine, LDS fertility in the United States has been higher than the U.S. average, probably since the inception of the Church...Latter-day Saints who regularly attend church average one child more per family than Catholics, and the difference is even greater in comparison with both liberal and conservative Protestants (Tim B. Heaton, *Latter-day Saint Social Life*, chapter 4, published by the Religious Studies Center, Brigham Young University, Provo, Utah, 1998, emphasis added).

"Be Fruitful and Multiply and Replenish the Earth..."

From June 1830 through February 1831, the Lord revealed to Joseph Smith selections from *The Book of Moses*. These revelations, which clarified many of the teachings that God had given to this ancient prophet, were included in the forth volume of Latter-day Saint scripture: *The Pearl of Great Price*.

As part of *The Book of Moses*, the Lord re-revealed His commandment given to Adam and Eve, and to their descendants:

> And I God blessed them, and said unto them: Be fruitful, and multiply, and replenish the earth... (*The Pearl of Great Price, The Book of Moses* 2: 28, emphasis added). [This same commandment is also found in the book of *Genesis* of *The Holy Bible (Old Test. Genesis.* 1:22]

Most committed Latter-day Saints tend to give high regard to the instructions from God, given through His prophets, both ancient and modern. It is understandable, therefore, that they would choose to have large families.

"Children Are An Heritage of the Lord..." and "His Reward" to Parents

The Old Testament prophet and king, David, in his *Psalms*, wrote about children in this way:

> ...*children are an heritage of the Lord: and the fruit of the womb [a child] is his reward.* As arrows are in the hand of a mighty man; so are children of the youth. *Happy is the man that hath his quiver full of them...*" (*Psalms* 127:3-5, emphasis added).

"My Jewels"

Through another Old Testament prophet, Malachi, and to the modern prophet, Joseph Smith, the Lord has revealed how He feels about His faithful and loving children:

> And they shall be mine, saith the Lord of hosts [or multitude] in that day when I make up my jewels; and I will spare them, as a man spareth his own son that serveth him (Malachi 3:17, emphasis added, see also *The Doctrine and Covenants* 101:3).

Loving parents the world over, whether they be Latter-day Saints, or not, feel the same way about their children. Our children are our "jewels", or, as this word could also be translated, our "Royal Treasure." Each child is so special and precious! Our relationships to our children, our spouse, and to the Father and the Son, are the sources of our greatest joys in life.

There is no way to overstate how much each child means to their loving parents. Therefore, having additional children is the greatest blessing the Lord has given to members of The Church of Jesus Christ. Also, if we have additional children and raise them to receive the blessings of the

Gospel Power Formula, including temple marriage, this will help their marriages to survive, and we will probably also have more grandchildren, great grandchildren and so on!

The blessing of additional children even exceeds another blessing of being a member of the Lord's Church: that of a substantially increased life-span, which we will review in Positive Statistical Trend or "Fruit" Number Five.

The way we feel about our children and grandchildren is attached as a sign on one of the mirrors in our house:

We Will Love You Forever !

Our Mark Upon the World

Earlier, we reviewed some sweet truths taught by the family-friendly movie *Casper*. This was in the section titled: "Can I Keep You?" To finish this section we will look at what may be the best line in any movie. This comes from another family movie, *Jack Frost*. In one scene, a father, who has died tragically, returns as a snowman to visit his son.

This father had worked hard at his job. He had also been part of a rock band. Because of his busy schedule, he had often been absent from home. He had spent much time playing with the band, and trying to become rich and famous by getting a recording contract. As a result of all his outside activities, he had not spent as much time with his son as the boy wanted. The father regularly missed his son's hockey games, which had disappointed the son. When he returned to visit his son, he looked back over his life. This father told his boy:

> Son, I was so busy trying to make my mark upon the world, that I didn't realize that *you* are my mark upon the world (paraphrased).

Positive Statistical Trend or "Fruit" Number Four: Service and Voluntarism

Service is very important to the Latter-day Saints. *The Book of Mormon* teaches that:

> ...when ye are in the service of your fellow beings, ye are only in the service of your God (*Mosiah* 2:17).

Regarding service, a recent newspaper article reported that, for the fifth straight year, the State of Utah has ranked first in the *Volunteering in America Report*. Admittedly, this statistic is for a State, and not for a specific religion. However, the State of Utah has the highest percentage of Latter-day Saints of any state in the nation. Sociologists and statisticians would probably acknowledge that the main reason for Utah having such a high rate of voluntarism, is its large population of Latter-day saints.

According to this news story:

> Utah earned eight No. 1 rankings, including for volunteer hours per resident (No. 2 Iowa's 40.1 hour average is less than half Utah's 86.9 hours). [Also], "Provo

[Utah, the home of the Church's Brigham Young University] is the top ranked midsize city for voluntarism, with a [participation] rate of 63.6 percent and a per-resident average of 149.7 hours of service each year... (Deseret Morning News, June 16, 2010, pages B1 and B5).

In another story, to my recollection, it was reported that a government leader in a southern U.S. community thanked the volunteers who came to help the people of his area after a natural disaster. This leader thanked the members of the 'two Churches' who came to help them. These two churches were 'The Church of Jesus Christ of Latter-day Saints, and the Mormons'.

The Fifth Valid Therapy

Wayne Dyer is a famous psychologist, author and speaker. In a recorded seminar he had given for P.B.S., he described the benefits of service. A paraphrased version of what he said was that researchers have studied the effects of service on the serotonin level in the brain. Serotonin is a neurotransmitter, or brain chemical. Among its effects, serotonin helps to increase our feeling of well being or happiness. According to the information presented in this seminar, the serotonin levels increased in the brains of people who did acts of service for others. This is an amazing, and a very important finding.

L. Ron Hubbard wrote about our emotional tone level and how it can be elevated. He described: "...four valid therapies..." [which can raise a person's emotional tone. In brief these were:]

> 1) ...dianetic processing...; 2) ...education...; 3) ...changing his environment...; and 4) ...regulating the amount of MEST [Matter, Energy, Space and Time] which the individual should control... (L. Ron Hubbard, *Science of Survival*, Bridge Publications, Los Angeles, 1951, page 18).

If the study referred to above by Wayne Dyer is true, then we can now identify a fifth way to raise our emotional tone levels. That way or, "...valid therapy..." is by doing Service for others.

Also, this same study resulted in two other amazing discoveries. In addition to raising the serotonin level, and thus the emotional tone levels in the brains of those who give service, the serotonin level is also increased in the brains of those who *received* the service. Even more amazing was that the serotonin levels also increased in those who simply *observed* an act of service being performed for others!

Love and Service

Do we serve those we love, or is it that we love those we serve? An answer to this question is found in one of the Church's lesson manuals. Here is a great pearl:

> Some of us serve only those we enjoy being around and avoid all others. However, Jesus commanded us to love and serve everyone...(see *The Book of Mormon*,

Mosiah 4:15-19)... [Also], "...when we serve others, we gain important blessings. Through service, we increase our ability to love" (*Gospel Principles*, The Church of Jesus Christ of Latter-day Saints, Salt Lake City, 1978, 2009, page 164).

To me, this means that if we are finding it hard to love someone, perhaps because they have offended or hurt us, we should serve them *more*, instead of less. This will increase our ability to love that person! Many people think we serve the people we love, when in fact, the truth is that we also have more love for those we serve.

"Well Done..."

One more thing about service, it is an absolute requirement for those who want to be with their Heavenly Father and their Savior in the next life. It is only those who give loving service that the Lord will say: "Well done thou good and faithful servant. Enter into the joy of your Lord" (see *New Testament, Matthew* 25:34-40).

Science Has Identified Other Ways to Improve Mood Without Taking Medication

As listed above, one of the way L. Ron Hubbard listed of improving a person's emotional tone level was: "...3 Changing his environment...". Here are some ways to improve tone level by changing our environment without having to resort to the use of antidepressant medications: 1) Light therapy, and 2) exercise. Also, science has indicated that we can improve our mood by changing our internal environment with supplementation with: 3) Vitamin D3 (5,000 IU daily), and 4) Purified Fish oil 3,000 – 4,000 mg daily.

The data on light therapy recommends sitting with your eyes open, but not staring into the light at a distance of 12-17 inches. The light should be from a 10,000 Lux daylight bulb source for 20-30 minutes. The best time to do so is first thing in the morning. One such light that has the advantage of allowing you to read, or eat your breakfast, or even do computer work while sitting in front of it is the "Boxelight", available through Northern Light Technologies.

The Sixth Valid Therapy

In *The Power Formulas Part One*, we identified another way to raise emotional tone. This is the process of conversion by coming unto Jesus Christ, and thus being "born of God". This was seen in the example of Alma, whose tone level was raised from the lowest levels to the highest possible level (see *The Power Formulas Part One*, chapter 8, and *The Book of Mormon, Alma* 36, and *Mosiah* 27).

This sixth way to raise emotional tone level is essentially different than all the others. The difference is in the completeness and the duration of the change. Spiritual rebirth, which comes through having faith in Jesus Christ and His Father, repenting of our sins, being baptized for the forgiveness of those sins, and receiving the Gift of the Holy Ghost, has the potential of being the permanent cure for chronic tone level problems, and for the other problems of life. This is the Lord's way to overcome all our challenges and weaknesses.

One more thing. It is those who have come unto Christ and received this change of heart, and the "Sixth Valid Therapy", who are more likely to then give loving service, and thus receive the benefit of the Fifth Valid Therapy: Service.

More on Service:
How God Usually Meets Our Needs

President Spencer W. Kimball, one of the prophets of the Church, said:

> God does notice us, and He watches over us, but *it is usually through another mortal that He meets our needs. Therefore, it is vital that we serve each other...* (quoted from an address given by Elder Steven E. Snow, at the October General Conference of the Church, see the Church's magazine, *The Ensign*, November 2007, page 103).

The Only Measure of True Greatness

One of my favorite quotations is about service. It is that:

> ...service was [and is] the only measure of true greatness (James E. Talmage, *Jesus the Christ*, see pages 503 and 504).

This thought is so important, that our children have been encouraged to memorize it. It is also printed and attached to a mirror in our home.

Positive Statistical Trend or" Fruit" Number Five: Survival

To survive:

> ...is the goal of life itself...[according to L. Ron Hubbard.] This, the dynamic principle of man's existence, was discovered by L. Ron Hubbard and from this many hitherto unanswered questions were resolved. The goal of life can be considered to be infinite survival. That man seeks to survive has long been known, but that it is his primary motivation is new. Man as a life form can be demonstrated to obey in all his actions and purposes the one command: 'SURVIVE!' Also, L. Ron Hubbard's ...second major work on Dianetics was titled: *Science of Survival...* (*What is Scientology?*, based on the works of L. Ron Hubbard, Bridge Publications, Los Angeles, 1993, 1998, pages 144, and 587).

In *Part One of the Power Formulas*, we considered the fact that our **Conditions** are reflections of the likelihood of our survival. Chapter One of that book included these words: "The condition of any group or individual, determines their present potential for survival. Activities, which produce a condition of high survival ability, for oneself and others, are considered ethical. Those actions which endanger survival are considered to be unethical."

Because the **Power Formula** is one of the **Conditions Formulas**, it is also related to survival. Those in a **Condition of Power** have the highest potential to survive in their position or "post." Since this is the case, it should not be surprising that those who have received and followed God's spiritual **Power Formula** here on earth have superior survival statistics in their individual lives.

As part of His **Gospel Power Formula**, which the Lord has revealed, through Joseph Smith, and through the succeeding prophets of The Church of Jesus Christ of Latter-day Saints, we have received inspired directions regarding health. In 1833, the Savior revealed "A Word of Wisdom" instructing that we abstain from tobacco, alcohol, hot drinks, meaning coffee and tea, and that meat be eaten only "sparingly" (see *The Doctrine and Covenants* Sect. 89).

This revelation also contained this promise to those who would follow the Lord's Word of Wisdom:

> ...all saints who remember to keep and do these sayings, walking in obedience to the commandments, *shall receive health* in their navel and marrow in their bones; and shall find wisdom and great treasures of knowledge, even hidden treasures; and shall run and not be weary, and shall walk and not faint. And I, the Lord, give unto them a promise, that *the destroying angel shall pass by them*, as the children of Israel, and not slay them. Amen (*Doctrine and Covenants* 89:18-21, emphasis added).

Plus 8 and Plus 11

In an article titled: Health Practices and Mortality among Active California Mormons, 1980-1993, James E. Enstrom made the following observations:

> High priests who never smoked cigarettes, and engage in regular physical activity have SMRs [Standardized Mortality Ratios] relative to U.S. whites for cardiovascular diseases, and all causes that are among the lowest ever reported. The reductions in cancer, cardiovascular, and total death rates are especially large in the middle age ranges. Indeed, these active Mormons are currently achieving the 50 percent reduction mortality rate that has been set as a goal for the year 2000 by the National Cancer Institute (Breslow and Cumberland 1988)...

Russell M. Nelson, who was a world renowned heart surgeon, prior to being called by the Lord to serve as one of His living apostles, has spoken about Latter-day Saint longevity, from a more recent study:

> Some of you may wonder about the name Mormon. It is a nickname for us. It is not our real name, though we are widely known as Mormons. The term is derived from a book of sacred scripture known as the Book of Mormon.
> The true name of the Church is The Church of Jesus Christ of Latter-day Saints. It is the reestablished original Church of Jesus Christ. When He walked upon the earth, He organized His Church. He called Apostles, Seventies, and other leaders to whom He gave priesthood authority to act in His name.[3] After Christ and His Apostles passed away, men changed the ordinances and doctrine.

The original Church and the priesthood were lost. After the Dark Ages, and under the direction of Heavenly Father, Jesus Christ brought back His Church. Now it lives again, restored and functioning under His divine direction.

We follow the Lord Jesus Christ and teach of Him. We know that after His glorious triumph over death, the resurrected Lord appeared to His disciples on numerous occasions. He ate with them. He walked with them. Before His final Ascension, He commissioned them to "go … and teach all nations, baptizing them in the name of the Father, and of the Son, and of the Holy Ghost." The Apostles heeded that instruction. They also called upon others to help them fulfill the Lord's command.

Today, under the direction of modern apostles and prophets, that same charge has been extended to missionaries of The Church of Jesus Christ of Latter-day Saints. These missionaries serve in more than 150 nations. As representatives of the Lord Jesus Christ, they strive to fulfill that divine command—renewed in our day by the Lord Himself—to take the fullness of the gospel abroad and bless the lives of people everywhere.

Missionaries in their late teens or early 20s are young in ways of the world. But they are blessed with gifts—such as the power of the Holy Spirit, the love of God, and testimonies of the truth—that make them powerful ambassadors of the Lord. They share the good news of the gospel that will bring true joy and everlasting happiness to all who heed their message. And in many instances they do so in a country and a language foreign to them.

Missionaries strive to follow Jesus Christ in both word and deed. They preach of Jesus Christ and of His Atonement. They teach of the literal Restoration of Christ's ancient Church through the Lord's first latter-day prophet, Joseph Smith.

You may have previously encountered, or even ignored, our missionaries. My hope is that you will not fear them but learn from them. They can be a heaven-sent resource to you.

That happened to Jerry, a Protestant gentleman in his mid-60s who lives in Mesa, Arizona. Jerry's father was a Baptist minister; his mother, a Methodist minister. One day Jerry's close friend Pricilla shared with him the pain she felt from the death of her child during childbirth and a bitter divorce that occurred shortly thereafter. Struggling as a single mother, Pricilla has four children—three daughters and a son. As she opened her heart to Jerry, she confessed that she was thinking of taking her own life. With all the strength and love Jerry could muster, he tried to help her understand that her life had value. He invited her to attend his church, but Pricilla explained that she had given up on God.

Jerry did not know what to do. Later, while watering trees in his yard, this man of faith prayed to God for guidance. As he prayed, he heard a voice in his mind saying, "Stop the boys on the bikes." Jerry, a little bewildered, wondered what this meant. As he reflected on this impression, he gazed up the street and saw two young men in white shirts and ties riding bicycles toward his home. Stunned by this "coincidence," he watched them ride by. Then, realizing that the situation required him to act, he shouted out, "Hey, you, please stop! I need to talk to you!"

With a puzzled but excited look, the young men stopped. As they approached, Jerry noticed that they wore name tags identifying them as missionaries in The Church of Jesus Christ of Latter-day Saints. Jerry looked at them and said, "This may sound a little weird, but I was praying and was told to 'stop the boys on the bikes.' I looked up the street, and here you are. Can you help me?"

The missionaries smiled, and one said, "Yes, I am sure we can."

Jerry explained the worrisome plight of Pricilla. Soon the missionaries were meeting with Pricilla, her children, and Jerry. They discussed the purpose of life and God's eternal plan for them. Jerry, Pricilla, and her children grew in faith through sincere prayer, their study of *The Book of Mormon*, and the loving fellowship with members of the Church. Jerry's already strong faith in Jesus Christ grew even stronger. Pricilla's doubts and thoughts of suicide turned to hope and happiness. They were baptized and became members of Christ's restored Church.

Yes, missionaries can help in many ways. For example, some of you might want to know more about your ancestors. You may know the names of your parents and your four grandparents, but what about your eight great-grandparents? Do you know their names? Would you like to know more about them? Ask the missionaries! They can help you! They have ready access to the vast family history records of The Church of Jesus Christ of Latter-day Saints.

Some of you are members but not presently participating. You love the Lord and often think of returning to His fold. But you don't know how to start. I suggest that you ask the missionaries! They can help you! They can also help by teaching your loved ones. We and the missionaries love you and desire to bring joy and the light of the gospel back into your lives.

Some of you may want to know how to conquer an addiction or live longer and enjoy better health. Ask the missionaries! They can help you! Independent studies have shown that, as a group, members of The Church of Jesus Christ of Latter-day Saints are a healthy lot. Their death rates are among the lowest and their longevity greater than any yet reported in any well-defined group studied over a lengthy period of time in the United States. (See James E. Enstrom and Lester Breslow, "Lifestyle and Reduced Mortality Among Active California Mormons, 1980-2004," Preventative Medicine, Vol 46 (2008), 135.) (Elder Russell M. Nelson, "Ask the Missionaries! They Can Help You" Ensign of the Church of Jesus Christ of Latter-day Saints, November 1012, pages 18-20).

The most important statistics regarding survival among Latter-day Saints reported in this study were these:

> ...Compared to U.S. whites, *life expectancy from age 25 among those in the high priest cohort adhering to three health practices (never smoked cigarettes, regular physical activity and proper sleep) is 11 years greater for males and 8 years greater for females* (*Latter-day Saint Social Life*, Religious Studies Center, Brigham Young University, Provo, Utah, 1998, page 470 [previous paragraph] and page 464, emphasis added).

From these statistics, we can see how, for so many people, the destroying angel... has passed them by.

The Gift of Extended Life, and What Can Be Done with It

What does it mean to have 8-11 more years of life? What can be done with this increased time? For many Latter-day Saints, these years mean added time to serve others. Many older couples and senior single individuals choose to serve missions. These are often humanitarian missions, such as teaching languages, or training people in third world countries about sanitation and basic health care practices. Some senior missionaries also join with the younger missionaries in teaching people about the gospel of Jesus Christ. Some seniors actually serve multiple missions after their retirement.

Some senior Latter-day Saints also take advantage of their extra years of life to improve their minds through study, and travel. Many also serve in the Church's temples, where they help both the living, and those who have completed their mortal experience, to progress. We will consider more about the importance of temple service in *Super Power.*

One of the Greatest Pleasures in Life

These extra years of life also allow them to enjoy one of the greatest pleasures in life: the joy of being with, and getting to know their grandchildren! Not only is this one of the most joyful things in life, it also allows the grandparents more time to give love, positive teachings and examples to their grandchildren.

As Latter-day Saint grandparents live longer, and thus have more interaction with their grandchildren, is it not likely that this will increase the probability that their grandchildren will also receive the blessings of longer life, more successful marriages and greater posterity themselves?

This increase in life span also allows many members of The Church of Jesus Christ of Latter-day Saints to get to know and love their great grandchildren, as well, (thanks to my wife, Karla, for sharing this insight).

10 Percent In, 10 or 15 Percent Out

How do these increases in life expectancy translate into percentages of improvement in life span? For men, 11 years is over a 15 percent increase in their time to live. For women, an 8-year increase is a 10 percent addition to their life. What would you do with a 10 or 15 percent increase in your lifetime?!

The Lord has also commanded the Latter-day Saints to live by the law of tithing. This means that the members of the Church are expected to donate ten percent of their income to the Church. These sacred funds are then used to help accomplish the Lord's purposes on the earth, such as the building of temples and education. Giving ten percent of your income to the Church may seem like a great sacrifice to some people, but blessings come from keeping commandments.

Although the correlation is not a direct one, who wouldn't be willing to part with ten percent of their income and follow the health practices referenced in this study, to get 10 or 15 percent more life?!

Also, in a revelation given to the Old Testament prophet, Malachi, the Lord promised great blessings to those who pay tithing.

Will a man rob God? Yet ye have robbed me. But ye say, wherein have we robbed thee? In tithes and offerings. Ye are cursed with a curse: for ye have robbed me, even this whole nation. Bring ye all the tithes into the storehouse, that there may be meat in mine house, and prove me now herewith, saith the LORD of hosts, if I will not *open you the windows of heaven, and pour you out a blessing, that there shall not be room enough to receive it* (*Old Test. Malachi* 3:8-10, emphasis added).

Perhaps four of these blessings coming down to us from "the windows of heaven" are better health, longer life, more successful marriages, and more descendants!

Survival Rates Compared For Latter-day Saint Women and Men, and Their Average life Expectancies

Although LDS men had more improvement in their life expectancy than did LDS women in this study, the women still had an overall longer life expectancy than did the men. To my understanding, this is also true for society in general. Active Latter-day Saint women, in this study were found to have an amazing *average life expectancy of 88 years*, while their male counterparts could expect to live an of *average 85 years*. These are remarkable statistics!

Of course, if the average life expectancy for adult Latter-day Saint females, who follow the practices shown above, is 88 years, this means that many live well beyond this age.

My practice as a podiatrist, includes sometimes doing house calls. We recently treated a 101 1/2-year-old woman who lives by herself in her own home. When we arrived, she was teaching a piano lesson to a young student! She explained: "I have three students", and she doesn't charge them. Also, she makes yarn caps for little babies, which she donates to the Church's Humanitarian Center. These caps, along with many other goods, are sent to those in need in many nations.

About four decades ago, it was my privilege to serve as a missionary in Maryland and Pennsylvania. Our mission president was a fine man named George Baker. He was married to a remarkable woman, named Della Baker.

Our family kept in touch with "Sister Baker" over the years. Recently, we attended Sister Baker's funeral. She lived to be 103 years old! We earlier had the opportunity to hear her teach a Sunday school class while she was in her 90's.

Latter-day Saint Views Regarding Life and Death

It is well known that Latter-day Saints are Pro Life and Pro Family. What may not be a well known are their attitudes towards death. Perhaps this is best seen by attending L.D.S. funerals. These are amazing meetings, especially when compared to funerals for those who don't have a belief in life after death, or in the eternal nature of the family.

The funerals for believing and practicing Latter-day Saints are not usually sad occasions. Often, there is more laughter than tears at these funerals. There is also much inspiration, and the comforting influence of the Holy Ghost is always present at these meetings.

By way of an example, at a funeral for a friend's 94-year-old father, his three children were the speakers. One of his sons told of how his father faced life with courage and a sense of humor. This son said his father would joke, 'I know more people on the other side than on this side,' and 'I live on guts and pills!' Also, 'If you live long enough, you will get everything!' He also joked, 'I am so old, I no longer buy green bananas!'

This son also wore a tuxedo to the funeral out of respect for his father. He also said that he knew that his father was now with his mother, who had died earlier. His parents were married for eternity in a Latter-day Saint temple.

This father had been a great athlete. He was an all conference college football player. His sons had followed him as athletes. He loved sports, and never missed attending his son's games as they were growing up. His other son went on to play professional football. This son spoke lovingly of his father. He concluded his talk by saying, 'He is my father forever!' This is also my belief and feeling about my father.

How the Blessings or the "Fruits" of the Restored Church Have Helped Our Family

We recently lost dad. It was my privilege to be one of the speakers at his funeral. Here is a story, about Dad which was part of that talk. Dad had been a policeman and a detective in Salt Lake City. He had spent some time as a motorcycle officer. He knew the dangers of motorcycles.

In my late teens, it was my desire to own and ride a motorcycle. Most of my friends had one. The money had been saved, and the motorcycle had been picked out. The time came to tell my parents about this decision. My dad responded with humor and love. *Tough love*. He said, "Son, that sounds like it would be fun for you, but where are you going to live afterwards?!"

No motorcycle was purchased, and perhaps my life was preserved. There is no resentment about what he said. Instead, my feelings for Dad are feelings of love and gratitude. His spirit still lives. He still loves us and prays for us. We will eventually be reunited as a family.

Just a few more things about my dad, and about his and Mom's family. He was a convert to The Church of Jesus Christ of Latter-day Saints. He and Mom had their marriage sealed in the temple while I was on my mission. This means that couples who were married outside the temple can go together to the temple and have their marriage relationship made eternal. They had four children and eighteen grandchildren. Six of these descendants have received the blessing of serving a full time mission for the Church.

Mom and Dad were married for 63 years. He served his community, not only as a policeman, but as a boys' baseball coach in, and later as the director of the Salt Lake City Cops League. When he passed away, he was in his 85th year. Our mother is in her eighties. She enjoys good health, and we expect her to be with us for many years.

Does this sound familiar? My parent's lives are a perfect reflection of the "fruits" of the Gospel of Jesus Christ, which have been reviewed in this chapter! Dad was a "poster boy" for the benefits and blessings of God's Power Formula, and The Church of Jesus Christ, which the Savior has restored to the earth through his latter-day prophet, Joseph Smith.

Not the Only, and Not Every

The Church of Jesus Christ of Latter-day Saints is not the only religion whose followers live significantly longer than the average. Also, not all Latter-day Saints will live to an advanced age or avoid cancer and heart disease. Not all Latter-day Saint temple marriages will survive, and not all of the couples in such marriages will be blessed with more than the average number of children and other descendants. In addition, not all Latter-day Saints receive the benefits of doing voluntary service for others.

However, if you are an active member of the Church, meaning one who follows the revealed teachings of **God's Gospel Power Formula,** which is found in the scriptures and in the words of the Church's prophets and apostles, your chances of receiving the above noted blessings are significantly increased.

The Purpose of Reviewing These Statistics

What is the point of looking at these statistics? Is it an effort to boast about our Church, and what it can do for individuals, and for families? No — (well, maybe a little — sorry!). However, the real, and the important reason for pointing out the blessings of being a Latter-day Saint is that each of these positive statistical trends or "fruits", can be traced to revelations that Jesus Christ has given to the prophet Joseph Smith. If the accomplishments of the Church are positive or "...good fruits," how can the tree of revelation, and the prophet through whom these revelations were given, be other than good also? (see again, *New Test. Matthew* 7:15-20).

If the prophet Joseph Smith's revelations are positive and produce good results in the lives of those who follow his teachings, then, Joseph Smith is a true prophet, and the Church that was established through him, is the restored, and the true Church of Jesus Christ upon the earth!

Chapter FIVE

Jesus Christ and Joseph Smith Both Spent Their Final Days on Earth Completing Power Formulas for Their Successors

How The Savior Trained His Apostles

Months before His death, the Savior found ways to give further "...training and instruction..." to the Twelve:

> The supreme importance of our Lord's ministry, and the shortness of the time remaining to Him in the flesh, demanded more missionary laborers. The Twelve were to remain with Him to the end; every hour of possible instruction and training had to be utilized in their further preparation for the great responsibilities that would rest upon them after the Master's departure (*Jesus the Christ*, James E. Talmage, 1956, page 425).

Jesus Christ gave His last teachings and warnings to the general people probably three days before His crucifixion. The setting for this address, like so many of His sermons, was at the temple grounds in Jerusalem. In *Jesus the Christ*, modern apostle James E. Talmage described how the Savior devoted the rest of His mortal life to training and preparing the Twelve for their important future roles of leadership in His Kingdom:

> With the Lord's final departure from the temple, which probably occurred in the afternoon of the Tuesday of that last week, His public ministry was brought to its solemn ending. Whatever discourse, parable, or ordinance was to follow would be directed only to the further instruction and investiture of the apostles (*Jesus the Christ*, page 563).

The Savior continued to train His apostles personally for 40 days after His resurrection. After this time, Jesus Christ continued to give "...commandments unto the apostles...", "...through the Holy Ghost".

> The former treatise have I made, O Theophilus, of all that Jesus began both to do and teach,
>
> Until the day in which he was taken up, after that he through the Holy Ghost had given commandments unto the apostles whom he had chosen:
>
> To whom also he shewed himself alive after his passion by many infallible proofs, being seen of them forty days, and speaking of the things pertaining to the kingdom of

God (*New Test., Acts* 1:1-3)

In His training of the apostles, the Lord was actually completing His **Power Formula** for them.

How the Prophet Joseph Smith Trained the Modern Apostles of Jesus Christ

In like manner, as Joseph Smith approached his last days of mortality, he used this precious time preparing the apostles to step up and function as the leaders of the Lord's Church, after his death. Both the Savior, and later His modern prophet, Joseph Smith, knew that their time was short. Both of them prophesied of this fact.

Jesus prophesied:

> I came forth from the Father, and am come into the world: and again, I leave the world, and go to the Father (*John* 16:28).

Regarding the prophet Joseph Smith's prophecies of his own death, author Truman Madsen has written that Joseph Smith prophesied:

> ...I must seal my testimony with my blood. The testament is no force, Paul said, 'until the death of the testator'. Also, the brethren [probably referring to the modern apostles who served with the prophet] became anxious about his [Joseph's] life, so often did he express the sentiment that they must carry on in his absence. Brigham Young, for one recalled:
>
> I heard Joseph say many a time, 'I shall not live until I am forty years of age' (Truman G. Madsen, *Joseph Smith the Prophet*, Bookcraft, Salt Lake City, 1989, page 109).

Truman Madsen continued:

> As the end neared, *the prophet was concerned about the completion of the temple, about the records of the Church and about teaching in summary all that had theretofore been made known and to make sure that the brethren understood it. To that end he spent much of every day for three months with the Twelve and with others of the Church leaders, and often in counsel with husbands and wives, sharing, summarizing, reiterating restored truth and ordinances.* 'You give us no rest,' [Apostle] Orson Pratt said. 'The Spirit urges me,' the Prophet replied. Wilford Woodruff [who was also an apostle, and who later became the prophet and president of the Church] said: 'It was not merely a few hours...but he spent day after day, week after week, and month after month teaching [the Twelve] and a few others the things of the kingdom of God.' As the record shows, even though the temple was not complete, he administered the higher ordinances of the temple to certain of the more faithful and true. Thus, we

know of sixty to seventy couples who received temple blessings in the upper room over his store, before the Nauvoo Temple was completed... (*Joseph Smith the Prophet*, page 111, emphasis added).

Regarding this remarkable period of training and preparation of the Twelve, Truman G. Madsen also wrote:

> [Apostle] *Erastus Snow said of that period that he learned more in a few months in council with the Prophet than he had learned all his life before that.* Others, Parley P. Pratt among them, tried to keep notes. In that period, Joseph reviewed every restored principle, authority, and ordinance, completing it with a summary of the summary in a meeting in late May 1844, in which he said, in effect: '*Brethren, I have conferred upon you now, every key and principle and **power** that has been bestowed upon me. Now you must round up your shoulders and bear off the kingdom...*' In that same meeting the Prophet reconfirmed to the Twelve that Brigham Young, the presiding head of the Twelve (whom he had ordained thus at Quincy, Illinois, late in 1839), held the keys of the sealing power (Truman Madsen, *Joseph Smith the Prophet*, page 101, emphasis added).

The Cycle Repeated

Although it's amazing how both the Savior, and later His prophet spent the last days of their lives preparing their successors, it should not be surprising. Both Jesus Christ and Joseph Smith were teaching the same gospel, and both were doing a **Power Formula** for apostles and prophets.

The **Power Formula, Power Change Cycle of action** that Jesus Christ had completed with His ancient apostles in the Holy Land, and with His twelve disciples in His ancient American Church, was repeated with the modern apostles whom He had called to lead His Church in the latter days.

The prophet Joseph Smith's position or "post" in the restored Church of Jesus Christ was the same as Peter's in the early Church. Both were called to be the Senior Apostles of their day. Both were given separate instructions from the Savior, pertaining to their callings.

These revealed instructions can be seen in both the *New Testament*, for Peter, and in *The Doctrine and Covenants*, for Joseph Smith. That Joseph Smith, like Peter was to "feed my sheep", and did so, is shown in the above quotations. Joseph Smith, like Peter, was given the "Keys of My Kingdom" by the Savior. Also, when Joseph Smith was ordained to be the first modern apostle of Jesus Christ, it was Peter, with the assistance of his counselors, James and John, who ordained him.

These revealed and recorded instructions demonstrate that the Lord followed the same three **Power Formula** patterns in modern times as He had done anciently, on both hemispheres.

In review, the three **Power Formulas** that the Savior used each time He established His Church were: 1) for the general Church membership; 2) for His leaders, the apostles and disciples; and 3) for the Prophet and President of His Church.

The Savior's Church, The Church of Jesus Christ of Latter-day Saints, is still led by the Lord's apostles and prophets. These inspired leaders continue to teach us the Gospel of Jesus Christ, which is **God's Power Formula**. This gives us the opportunity to do **Power Change** with God.

In the next book, we will consider how we can do just that. We shall also consider one other "fruit" of **God's Gospel Power Formula**, and five great secrets that the Father and the Son have revealed about Themselves.

SUPER POWER

What is Super Power, and How and Where Can We Receive It?

In this final book of this series, about God's **Power Formulas**, we will complete a journey and a cycle that started 17 years ago. As we do so, we will begin by reviewing a concept contained on page one of *Part One.* Those of you who have read *The Power Formulas Part One* may recall that we were defining the word *power* as used in these books.

> "**Power** (pou'er), n.   1) Ability to do or act; capability of doing or accomplishing something...12) often powers of deity; divinity...23) to give power to; make powerful" (*Random House Dictionary of the English Language*, Stuart Berg Flexner, Editor, New York: Random House, 1987, p. 1516).
>
> What do we think of when we hear or read the word power? Many images come to mind. Some of these images are positive and some are not. Of the thirty-two definitions of power in the dictionary, these three define power as used in this book.
>
> Definition 23 speaks of transferring or giving power to someone else. The **Power Formula** is a formula for transferring power to others. Here is where the first definition comes in, because the **Power Formula** is actually a formula for transferring "the ability to do or act," and "the capability of doing or accomplishing something" to others.
>
> **The Power Formula** can be applied to any type of activity. One example would be a transfer of leadership within a business organization. However, the powers we are most interested in understanding are the powers of deity..., mentioned in definition 12 above...
>
> The Lord's powers encompass and **supercede** all other powers. We are narrowing down the meaning of power as used in this book. We will focus upon the "powers of deity," and upon how His abilities or powers can be transferred to us.

Another way of saying that the Lord's powers **super**sede all other powers is to describe His power as **Super Power**. Thus, **Super Power** is **God's power!**

In all other activities, the highest two Conditions are **Power Change** and **Power**. However, when we consider our Spiritual Condition, and our quest to follow the Savior's commandment that we are to become "...even as..." He and our Father in Heaven, then the two highest Conditions are **Super Power Change**, and **Super Power!**

Super Power and Priesthood

In the previous books of this series (see especially Chapter 2 of *Part Three*), we have defined God's power and authority as His **Priesthood**. The fullness of **God's Power**, or **Super Power**, is the fullness of His **Priesthood**. The Higher Priesthood is called the Melchizedek Priesthood, and in His fullness, it is God's **Super Power.**

Super Power is Also Eternal Life

Super Power is a **Condition**. Those who are in this **Condition** have many attributes. One of these attributes is having the actual **Power** or ability of God to do and accomplish good in the universe. However, having God's Power is not the only attribute possessed by those in the Condition of **Super Power**.

In *Part One*, we reviewed the definition of Eternal Life given by one of God's modern apostles. We also mentioned that the Condition of having **Eternal Life** *is* the Condition of **Super Power**. Here again is that quotation:

> God's life is eternal life, eternal life is God's life—the expressions are synonymous.
>
> Accordingly, eternal life is not a name that has reference only to the unending duration of a future life; immortality is to live forever in the resurrected state, and by the grace of God all men will gain this unending continuance of life. But only those who obey the fullness of the gospel law will inherit eternal life (D&C 29:43-44). It is "the greatest of all gifts of God" (D&C 14:7), for it is the kind, status, type and quality of life that God Himself enjoys. Thus, those who gain eternal life receive exaltation; they are sons [and daughters] of God, joint heirs with Christ,...they overcome all things, have all power and receive the fullness of the Father (Bruce R. McConkie, *Mormon Doctrine* (Salt Lake City: Bookcraft, 1966), p. 237.).

When we consider the overall state of those who ascend to the **Condition** of **Super Power**, we can see why the Conditions of **Super Power**, and having Eternal Life are synonymous.

Super Power and God's Temples

In this book, we will look at how our Father in Heaven, and His Son Jesus Christ have made it possible for us to receive Their **Super Power**. We will also consider how the restoration of God's temples to the earth plays an indispensable part in how we can receive Their power. There any many places and ways where we can learn of God. Churches and our homes are great places to learn about God and what He expects of us. However, God's **Super Power Formula** is only taught and received within the walls of His Holy Temples!

The Church of Jesus Christ of Latter-day Saints teaches that we can actually become like Our Father in Heaven and His Son Jesus Christ, and that we can actually receive Their power. The Church uses sacred temples for special ordinances pertaining to our eternal progression. In this book, we will discuss how these unique features: becoming like God, including receiving God's power, and temple instruction and ordinances, are related.

Preparing to Receive Super Power
(From the Condition of Spiritual Non Existence to Spiritual Power)

Preparation for the ordinances [of the temple] includes preliminary steps: of faith, repentance, baptism, confirmation, worthiness, a maturity and dignity worthy of one who comes invited as a guest into the house of the Lord (*Preparing to Enter the Holy Temple, a booklet published by the Church of Jesus Christ of Latter-day Saints*, page 2).

Just as it is necessary to ascend through the **Condition Formulas** from **Non Existence** through **Affluence**, before we can do **Power Change** in our earthly endeavors, it is also necessary to complete and possess the above-noted elements of growth, prior to receiving temple ordinances.

Service is an Essential Element to Receiving God's Super Power

We can learn and grow much through service, and without doing service we cannot become like our Savior. This is because we must "Follow Him". This includes doing service and loving our Father in Heaven and His children. We are to love others as the Savior does. We must be loving, and do service, in order to do **Super Power Change** with Jesus Christ, (see *The Book of Mormon, 3 Nephi* 27:21, *New Test., Luke* 25:40, and *Acts* 10:30). For more information about the benefits of service, please see the last chapter of *The Power Formulas, Part Three*.

We can be of service to our living brothers and sisters, and because of the Lord's temples, we can also be of service to those who have died.

Lessons Are Also Learned "…Down in the Valley"

Another way that we learn about God, and progress in becoming more like Him, is through experiencing challenges and difficulties in our lives. One of the Lord's modern prophets taught:

> It is not on the pinnacle of success and ease where men and women grow most. *It is often down in the valley of heartache and disappointment and reverses where men and women grow into strong character* (President Ezra Taft Benson, Conference Report of The Church of Jesus Christ of Latter-day Saints, Stockholm Sweden Area Conference, 1974, page 70, emphasis added).

Again, there are many places and ways that we can learn about God, there is only one place where the Lord reveals the fullness of His Gospel **Super Power Formula** to us. That place is in His Holy temples.

The Lord explained that one purpose of the building of the House of the Lord, or temple is to make a place where He could reveal His ordinances: 'And verily I say unto you, let this house be built unto my name, that I may reveal mine ordinances therein unto my people (see *Doctrine and Covenants* 124:38-41, which is also quoted in the Church's booklet: *Preparing to Enter the Holy Temple*, page 28).

Without the Temple, We Can Progress Only to a Condition of Spiritual Power

These preparatory steps are essential, before we can receive God's **Super Power Formula** in His temple. When we have been taught the record of His **Super Power Formula** in the temple, then, and only then, can we do **Super Power Change** with God. This is why the Lord has made it such a high priority for His Church to build Holy Temples. This is why the Lord has commanded the Church to build temples:

...*always*...to His Holy name...(*Doctrine and Covenants* 124:39, emphasis added).

Priesthood Ordinances Defined

Among the [priesthood] ordinances we perform in the Church are these: baptism, sacrament [receiving communion], naming and blessing of infants, administering to the sick [by giving blessings of healing and comfort], setting apart to callings in the Church, ordaining to offices [in the priesthood]. In addition there are *higher ordinances performed in the temples. These include washings, anointings, the endowment, and the sealing ordinance, spoken of generally as temple marriage* (*Preparing to go to the Holy Temple*, pages 28 and 29, emphasis added).

The Temples are Places Where We Can Be "Endowed with Power from On High"

We spoke earlier of the higher ordinances performed in the temple. These include the endowment. To endow is to enrich, to give to another something long lasting and of much worth. The temple endowment enriches in three ways: (a) *the one receiving the ordinance is given power from God.* 'Recipients are endowed with power from on high.' (b) A recipient is also endowed with information and knowledge,' (Bruce R. McConkie, *Mormon Doctrine*, 2nd ed. [Salt Lake City: Bookcraft, 1966], page 227); c) When sealed at the altar [to their spouse] a person is the recipient of **glorious blessings, *powers*, and *honors*** as part of his or her endowment (*Preparing to Enter the Holy Temple*, pages 29 and 31, emphasis added).

Investiture with "Glorious Blessings, Powers, and Honors..."

While re-reading *Jesus the Christ* recently regarding how the Savior concentrated on preparing the apostles during the last days of His mortal life, one word from that section stood out. That word is "investiture." Here again is that quotation:

With the Lord's final departure from the temple, which probably occurred in the afternoon of the Tuesday of that last week, His public ministry was brought to its solemn ending. Whatever of discourse, parable, or ordinance was to follow, would be directed only to the further instruction and *investiture* of the apostles" (*Jesus the Christ*, page 563, emphasis added).

Let's take a minute, and clear, or define this word, *investiture*.

> 1a: the ceremonial *conferral of symbols of office or honor*...b: an act of ratifying or establishing an office...2: *an act of infusing or enriching*...3: an act of clothing or decorating ('to dress a sovereign [a king or queen]...' R. C. Singleton..." (*Webster's Third New International Dictionary*, Merriam Webster Inc. Springfield Massachusetts, 1986, page 1190, emphasis added).

In the Temple, We Receive Both God's Teachings and an Investiture with His Power

The crowning blessings of the temple cannot be received by individuals. These blessings are reserved for couples who are worthily married in the ordinance of temple sealing which makes their marriage relationship eternal. Those who receive this ordinance, and then keep their covenants with the Lord and with each other, are promised that they shall inherit:

> ...thrones, kingdoms, principalities, and **powers**, dominions, all heights and depths... (*Doctrine and Covenants* 132:19, emphasis added).

Also, Latter-day Saints believe that the opportunity to receive these blessings is denied to no one. The ordinances of temple, including sealing, has been, is, or will be available to all. This occurs in one of the Lord's temples as living persons act as proxies in behalf of the individuals and couples who did not receive an adequate opportunity to receive these blessing in mortality.

Also, those who choose to live as single individuals may, of course, do so, both here and in the eternities.

Later in this book, we will further consider this concept of how the living can help those who have left mortality to progress. This is done as the living perform the temple ordinances for those who have finished mortality, and who are now in the Spirit World.

How Much Power Can We Receive, and How High Can We Ascend in Our Progression?

These questions are answered in this same revelation, quoted above, from the Lord to the prophet Joseph Smith. Prepare to be amazed by the Lord's answer. Speaking again of couples who faithfully keep the promises that they have made when they were sealed together in the temple, the Lord has taught that:

> ...they shall pass by the angels, and the gods, which are set there, to their exaltation and glory in all things, as has been sealed upon their heads, which glory shall be a

fullness and a continuation of the seeds forever and ever. **Then shall they be gods, because they have no end;** therefore shall they be from everlasting to everlasting, because they continue; then shall they be above all, because all things are subject unto them. **Then shall they be gods, because they have all power,** and the angels are subject unto them. Verily, verily, I say unto you, *except ye abide my law ye cannot attain to this glory* (*Doctrine and Covenants* 132:19-21, emphasis added).

Here, then, are the answers to the question listed at the beginning of this section:
1)   How much power can we receive? Answer: "...**all power**..."
2)   How high can we ascend in our progression? Answer: we can become "...**gods**..."

Is it Not Blasphemy to Say That We Can Become Gods?

The answer to this question is that this depends upon *who* is making this claim. It would be blasphemy if this claim was being made by a mortal person, for blasphemy is defined as:

> ...the act of claiming the attributes or prerogatives of deity... (*Webster's Third New International Dictionary*, Merriam Webster Inc., Springfield, Massachusetts, 1986, page 230).

However, this statement, that: "...they shall be gods..." was made by God and not by a mortal person. It is impossible for God to blaspheme Himself! Therefore, there is no blasphemy in this statement.

A God in Embryo

Apostle and author, James E. Talmage also commented on this question of our potential to progress:

> 'Mormonism' claims *an actual and literal relationship of parent and child between the Creator and man*—not in the figurative sense in which the engine may be called the child of the builder... but the connection between Father and offspring... [and:] ...the child may achieve the former status of the parent, and that in his mortal condition **man is a God in embryo**... 'Mormonism' claims that all nature, both on earth and in heaven, *operates on a plan of advancement; that the very eternal Father is a progressive Being,* that His perfection, while so complete as to be incomprehensible to man, *possesses this essential quality of true perfection—the capacity of eternal increase...in the far future, man may attain the status of a God.* Yet this does not mean that he shall be then the equal of the Deity we worship, nor does it mean that he shall ever overtake those intelligences that are already beyond him in advancement; for to assert such would be to argue that there is no progression beyond a certain stage of attainment. (James E.

Talmage, *The Articles of Faith*, The Church of Jesus Christ of Latter-day Saints, Salt Lake City, 1970, page 530, emphasis added).

In other words, God is a progressive Being not in His personal *qualities*, such as knowledge, love, or Power. Rather, His progression is in terms of the *quantity* of His creations, and the *quantity* of His children, and in our progression. Also, He has placed no limits on our potential to progress.

"The Great Secret"

In one of his last discourses before he was martyred, Joseph Smith, the prophet, spoke about the kind of being that God the Father is. This address was both a funeral sermon, and a talk to all the members of the Church at the Church's annual conference. One of the first topics he addressed was the character of God. Regarding this crucial subject the prophet taught:

> *If men do not comprehend the character of God, they do not comprehend themselves... It is necessary for us to have an understanding of God Himself in the beginning. If we start right, it is easy to go right all the time; but if we start wrong, we may go wrong, and it be a hard matter to get right.*

The prophet then proceeded to give this amazing explanation about:

> *...what kind of being God is...I will go back to the beginning before the world was, to show what kind of being God is...**God Himself was once as we are now, and is an exalted man, and sits enthroned in yonder heavens. That is the great secret.** If the veil were rent today, and the great God who holds this world in its orbit, and who upholds all worlds and all things by His power, was to make Himself visible, — **I say, if you were to see him today, you would see him like a man in form—like yourselves in all person, image, and very form as a man; for Adam was created in the very fashion image and likeness of God...**These are incomprehensible ideas to some, but they are simple. **It is the first principle of the gospel to know for a certainty the Character of God, and to know that we may converse with him as one man converses with another, and that he was once a man like us; yea, that God himself, the Father of us all, dwelt on an earth, the same as Jesus Christ Himself did...**(The Teachings of the Prophet Joseph Smith*, compiled by Joseph Fielding Smith, Deseret Book Company, Salt Lake City, 1969, pages 342-362, emphasis added, hereafter referred to as *Teachings*).

One of the things that is revealed by this, "...the great secret", is that God has progressed to His present Condition. He wasn't always God. This implies that even God the Father has received a **Super Power Formula**, and has done **Super Power Change** to become what He now is!

Power Change Between the Gods

Later in this same discourse, the prophet taught about the progressive relationship between the Father and His Son, Jesus Christ, in this way:

> What did Jesus do? Why *I do the things I saw My Father do...and I must do the same*, and when I get my kingdom, I shall present it to My Father, so that He may obtain kingdom upon kingdom, and it will exalt Him in glory. *He [the Father] will then take a higher exaltation and I will take His place, and thereby become exalted myself. So that **Jesus treads in the tracks of His Father**, and inherits what God [the Father] did before; and God [the Father] is thus glorified and exalted in the salvation and exaltation of all His Children* (see reference above, emphasis added).

What a marvelous description of the **Super Power Formula—Super Power Change** relationship between God the Father and His Son Jesus Christ! It would be impossible to summarize the concept of **Super Power Change** any better than the prophet Joseph Smith did: when he said: "...**Jesus treads in the tracks of His Father...**" and "...I do the things I saw my Father do...and I must do the same...".

Super Power Change Between the Gods and Man

The prophet Joseph Smith, in this same discourse, then expanded this subject to include how this type of progressive relationship between the Father and the Son also applies to us:

> *Here then is eternal life—to know the only wise and true God; and you have got to learn how to be Gods yourselves, and to be kings and priests to God, the same as all Gods have done before you, namely, by going from one small degree to another, and from a small capacity to a great one...When you climb up a ladder, you must begin at the bottom and ascend step by step, until you arrive at the top; and so it is with the principles of the Gospel—you must begin with the first, and go on until you learn all the principles of exaltation. But it will be a great while after you have passed through the veil before you will learn them...* (see reference above, emphasis added).

A Familiar Sound to the Conditions Formulas

These teachings have a familiar sound to them. Do you hear it? When we read of how we are to progress from: "...one small degree to another, and from one small capacity to a great one..." we could easily substitute the word **Condition** for the words "degree" and "capacity."

Also, these teachings from the prophet make it plain that, as far as our potential to improve our spiritual Condition is concerned, *the Lord has placed no limits to our progression*. It is possible for us to even: "*... learn to be Gods...*". Not only is this possible, *this is what the Father* *and the Son want us to do!*

The School of the Gods

The next questions to consider are *how* and *where* can we: "...learn to be Gods...?" We have already addressed this question, at least partially. However, it is important to make certain that each reader knows that *God's Temples are the only places on earth we can receive the training and the priesthood ordinances which are the investiture of knowledge and power that can make it possible for us to eventually become Gods.*

The prophet Joseph also taught this lesson prior to his martyrdom. He declared that:

> ...as soon as the Temple and baptismal font are prepared we calculate to give... their washings and anointings, and to attend to those last and more impressive *ordinances without which we cannot obtain celestial thrones. But there must be a holy place prepared for that purpose...*so that men [meaning both men and women] may receive their endowments and be made kings [and queens]and priests [and priestesses] unto the most high God... (*Teachings*, page 362, emphasis added).

Because of Their Fairness and Their Love, the Father and the Son Have Made Their Gospel Super Power Formula Available to All, Through the Ordinances of the Holy Temple

The quotation above speaks of "...the temple and baptismal font..." What does this mean? The baptismal font is a sacred place within every temple, where baptisms are performed for those who have passed on without the benefit of receiving this necessary ordinance. Just before He ascended into heaven, Jesus Christ gave His apostles this instruction:

> ...Go ye into all the world, and preach the gospel to every creature. He that believeth and is baptized shall be saved..." (New Test. Mark 16:15 and 16), emphasis added).

If faith in Jesus Christ, repenting of our sins and being baptized are essential to salvation, what about all the people who have not believed in Jesus Christ, and who have died without being baptized? Could God be the perfect Being that people believe Him to be, without also being fair? Also, if the Father and the Son are loving and fair, would They not make some provision for those who have died without the opportunities of receiving His gospel **Super Power Formula** and of doing **Super Power Change** with Them? To answer these questions, we will consider the beautiful and the true doctrine of salvation for the dead.

How God's Super Power Formula and the Option and the Opportunity to do Super Power Change with God are Made Available to the Dead

Have you ever wondered: what did the Spirit of Jesus Christ do while His body lay in the tomb for the three days prior to His resurrection? In the book *Jesus The Christ*, apostle James E. Talmage answered this question. He wrote:

Jesus the Christ died in the literal sense in which all men die...His immortal Spirit was separated from His body of flesh and bones, and that body was actually dead. While the corpse laid in Joseph's [Joseph of Arimethia] rock hewn tomb, Christ existed as a disembodied Spirit...He went where the sprits of the dead ordinarily go...

Death has claimed as its own...both the just and the unjust. To them went the Christ, bearing the transcendently glorious tidings of redemption from the bondage of death, and of possible salvation from the effects of individual sin...To the penitent transgressor crucified by His side, who reverently craved remembrance when the Lord should come into His kingdom, Christ had given the comforting assurance: 'Verily I say unto thee, today shalt thou be with me in paradise' (*New Test. John* 5:25-29).

...Paradise is a place where dwell righteous and repentant spirits between bodily death and resurrection. Another division of the spirit world is reserved for those disembodied beings who have lived lives of wickedness and who remain impenitent [unrepentent] even after death...While divested of His body, Christ ministered among the departed, both in Paradise and in the prison realm where dwelt... the spirits of the disobedient. To this effect, testified Peter, nearly three decades after the great event: 'For Christ also once suffered for sins the just for the unjust, that He might bring us to God, being put to death in the flesh but quickened by the Spirit [alive as a Spirit]: by which also *He went and preached unto the spirits in prison...*' (*New Test. 1st Peter* 3:18-20).

...Justice demanded that the gospel be preached among the dead as it had been and was yet to be more widely preached among the living." Peter also taught: 'For *for this cause was the gospel preached also to them that are dead, that they might be judged according to [or like] men in the flesh, but live according to God in the spirit*' (*1st Peter* 4:5,6, emphasis added).

Apostle Talmage also taught that before He died, Jesus Christ knew:

...that His mission as the universal Redeemer and Savior would not be complete when He came to die...," for He said: 'Verily verily [truly truly] I say unto you, the hour is coming and now is, when *the dead shall hear the voice of the Son of God: and they that hear shall live*' (*John* 5:25-29). Old Testament prophets had also foreseen Christ's mission among the spirits of the departed. Isaiah wrote: '*And they shall be gathered together, as prisoners are gathered in the pit, and shall be shut up in the prison, and after many days shall they be visited*' (*Isaiah* 24:21-22)... David, singing the praises of the Redeemer whose dominion should extend even to the souls in hell, shouted in joy at the prospect of deliverance: *'Therefore my heart is glad...For Thou wilt not leave my soul in hell... [the spirit prison]'* (*Psalm* 16:9-11).

The fact that the gospel was preached to the dead necessarily implies the possibility of the dead accepting the same and availing themselves of the saving opportunities thereof. *In the merciful providence of the Almighty, provision has been made for vicarious service of the living for the dead in the ordinances essential for salvation." Paul sites the principle and practice of baptism by the living for the dead as proof of the actuality of the resurrection: "Else what shall they do which are baptized for the dead, if the dead raise not at all? Why are they then baptized for the dead?"* (*1ˢᵗ Corinthians* 15:29).

Free agency. The divine birthright of every human soul, will not be annulled by death. Only as the spirits of the dead become penitent and faithful will they be benefited by the vicarious service rendered in their behalf on the earth. ***Missionary labor among the dead was inaugurated by the Christ...[and it] has been continued by His authorized servants...the faithful apostles and other ministers of the word of God ordained to the Priesthood...They are called to follow in the footsteps of the Master ministering [serving] here among the living, and beyond among the dead.***

*The victory of Christ over death would be incomplete were its effects were confined to the small minority who have heard, accepted, and lived the gospel of salvation in the flesh. Compliance with the laws and ordinances of the gospel is essential to salvation. Nowhere in scripture is a distinction made between the living and dead. The dead are those who have lived in mortality upon the earth. The living are mortals who yet shall pass through ordained change we call death. All are children of the same Father...Christ's atoning sacrifice was offered, not alone for the few who lived upon the earth while He was in the flesh, nor for those who were born in mortality after His death, but for all inhabitants of earth then past, present, and future. He was ordained of the Father to be the judge of both quick [living] and dead...there will be but a single class, for all live unto Him. **While His body reposed in the tomb, Christ was actively engaged in the further accomplishment of His Father's purposes by offering the boon [benefit or blessing] of salvation to the dead, both in paradise and in hell [spirit prison]*** (Apostle James E. Talmage, *Jesus the Christ*, Deseret Book Company, 1915, 1977, Salt Lake City, pages 670-676, emphasis added).

Thus, are God's **Super Power Formula** and the option to do **Super Power Change** with God made available to the dead. Wow! Even though my knowledge of this great plan dates back about one half of a century, it is still amazing to consider the completeness, the fairness and the perfection of the Father and the Son's plan for us! And yet, none of us should be surprised by how wonderful the plan is, for Their plan is but a reflection of the completeness, fairness, and perfection of God the Father, and of His Son, Jesus Christ!

Is God Fair, or Not?

To my understanding, all other religions which profess a belief in Jesus Christ, have no good answer to the question: what provisions has God made to ensure that *all* of His children are given a fair opportunity to learn of, have faith in, and follow His Son? We will illustrate this point with an incident that occurred in the life of a young Latter-day Saint missionary. This missionary, and his more experienced mission president, were engaged in a conversation with a learned minister of another Christian faith. According to the report of this discussion, later provided by this mission president, this is what happened:

> Years ago I presided over a mission head-quartered in the Midwest. One day with a handful of our missionaries, I spoke with an esteemed representative of another Christian faith. This gentle soul spoke of his own religion's history and doctrine, eventually repeating the familiar words: 'By grace ye are saved'. 'Every man and woman must exercise faith in Christ in order to become a saved being'. Among those present was a new missionary who was all together unfamiliar with other religions. He had to ask the question: 'but sir, what happens to the little baby who dies before he is old enough to understand and exercise faith in Christ?' The learned man bowed his head and looked at the floor and said: 'there ought to be an exception, there ought to be a loophole, there ought to be a way, but there isn't'. *The missionary looked at me, and with tears in his eyes said: 'goodness President, we do have the truth, don't we*!' (Elder Douglas L. Callister, Knowing That We Know, *Ensign of The Church of Jesus Christ of Latter-day Saints*, November, 2007, pages 100-101, emphasis added).

Positive Statistical Trend, or "Fruit" Number Six: The Percentage of God's Children Who Have, Had, or Will Have Access to His Super Power Formula, and Thus Have An Opportunity to do Super Power Change With Their Father in Heaven is 100%

In *The Power Formulas, Part Three*, we reviewed five "fruits", or statistics, which testify of the prophetic calling of the prophet Joseph Smith, and of the truthfulness of The Church of Jesus Christ of Latter-day Saints. We will now consider a sixth, or a bonus, "fruit." As noted above, other Christian churches do not believe that God's plan for salvation will be made available to all of His children. In fact, if we consider all of the human family who have lived upon the earth, it is possible, and perhaps even likely, that the majority of them will *not* have learned enough about Jesus Christ while living in mortality to decide if they should follow Him, or not.

Since we don't know what the actual percentage is, we will have to estimate it. Let's suppose that the percentage of those who have a fair opportunity to accept the Savior, and to follow Him is 50%. Or if you wish, you could raise this estimate to 60 or even 70%. Is that enough? What about 99%, or 99.9999999999%? Would that be enough? The honest person would have to answer "no!"

For God to be fair, the opportunity to learn about our Father in Heaven and His Son, Jesus Christ, and the opportunity to follow the Savior, would have to be extended to *everyone.*

100% Get 100%!

Through the restored gospel, and through the re-established Church of Jesus Christ, and through God's temples, all of which came about through the Lord's revelations to the prophet Joseph Smith, 100% of God's children have had, do have, or will have, an opportunity to accept their Savior and to follow Him back into the presence of their Heavenly Father!

Not only will 100% of God's children receive the opportunity to follow Him, all will have had, do now have, or will have the opportunity of receiving 100% of the blessings God has made available to the living who accept His gospel, and who do **Super Power Change** while in mortality.

Here is a Sixth "fruit" to come through the revelations that God has given to the Prophet Joseph Smith. This fruit, like the others stated previously, are sweet to the soul. Also, this fruit, along with the others considered previously, and with *The Book of Mormon* provide ample evidence to the honest seeker of truth, that God has spoken to us through His modern Prophet, Joseph Smith, and that He has restored His true Church upon the earth.

"Every [Temple] Foundation Stone ... Increases the Power of God and Godliness"

Each month, the Church's magazine, *The Ensign*, contains an article from the prophet of the Church or from one of his counselors in the First Presidency. A recent message was written by President F. Uchtdorf, the second counselor in the First Presidency. By way of background, President Uchtdorf was an airline pilot. He was later called by the Lord to serve as one of the Twelve Apostles, and then also as a counselor to the Prophet of the Church, who is Thomas S. Monson.

In this article, titled "Temple Blessings", he wrote:

> I can still remember when my parents took our family to the newly erected Swiss Temple, the first in Europe, to become a forever family. I was 16 then and the youngest of four children. We knelt together at the altar to be sealed on earth by the power of the priesthood, with a wonderful promise that we could be sealed for eternity. I will never forget that magnificent moment.
>
> *As a boy, I was quite impressed that we crossed country borders to be sealed as a family. To me it symbolizes the way temple work crosses worldly boundaries to bring eternal blessings to all the inhabitants of the earth.* **The temples of The Church of Jesus Christ of Latter-day Saints are truly built for the benefit of all the world, irrespective of nationality, culture, or political orientation.**
>
> Temples are unyielding witnesses that goodness will prevail. President George Q. Cannon (1827-1901), First Counselor in the First Presidency, once said, *'Every foundation stone that is laid for a temple, and every temple completed... lessens the power of Satan on the earth, and increases the power of God and Godliness'...There we receive further light and knowledge and make solemn covenants that, if followed, help us walk the path of discipleship.* In short, the temple teaches us about the sacred purpose of life, and helps us get our true physical and spiritual bearings.
>
> We do not attend the temple for ourselves only, however. Each time [after our first

visit, when we receive the ordinances for ourselves] we enter these sacred edifices, we play a role in the hallowed, redemptive work of salvation [for those who have passed on] made available to all of God's children as a result of the Atonement of the Only Begotten of the Father. This is a selfless and holy service and one that allows us as mortals to participate in the glorious work of becoming saviors on Mount Zion assisting in bringing others to the Savior and back to their Father in Heaven, [see *Old Test. Obadiah* 1: 21] (*The Ensign of The Church of Jesus Christ of Latter-day Saints*, August 2010, page 4, emphasis added).

A Second Great Secret: the Source of God's Power

Previously, we have considered a topic that the Prophet Joseph Smith termed: "the great secret." That amazing truth, which was revealed through the prophet Joseph Smith, is about the nature of God. Again, referring to God the Father, the prophet taught that:

He was once a man like us that God Himself, the Father of us all, dwelt on an earth, the same as Jesus Christ Himself did...(*see The Great Secret above for a more complete description of these concepts, and for the reference*).

Now we will consider another 'great secret': What is the source of God's Power? The Father, Himself, answered this question. This information is contained in a revelation He gave to the prophet Joseph Smith. In this revelation, the Lord was describing events that occurred during our pre-earth life. God revealed a conversation He had with Lucifer, who became Satan, by rebelling against God. Lucifer demanded that the Father give him His Power. Please note what the Father then said about what His Power is:

And it came to pass that Adam, being tempted of the devil—for, behold, the devil was before Adam, for he rebelled against me, saying, *Give me **thine honor, which is my power**,* and also a third part of the hosts of heaven turned he away from me because of their agency [freedom to choose good or evil] (*Doctrine and Covenants* 29:36).

To understand what this means, we will look at another revelation. This is a revelation about how we can receive, and how we can keep, God's power:

Let thy bowels be full of charity towards all men...and let virtue garnish thy thoughts unceasingly; then shall thy confidence wax strong in the presence of God...The Holy Ghost shall be thy constant companion, and *thy scepter ["...*royal or *imperial authority..."]* an unchanging scepter of righteousness and truth; and *thy dominion shall be an everlasting dominion, and without compulsory means it shall flow unto thee forever and ever* (*Doctrine and Covenants* 121: 45-46, emphasis added).

The way in which we can eventually receive God's power is but a reflection of how He received His power. **The power to do good in the universe is received "...without compulsory means."** The intelligences that either occupy, or are, the matter and the energy of the universe voluntarily give heed to and obey the will of God. They do so because they hold Him in such high esteem. These intelligences honor the Father and the Son because they recognize in Them the attributes of perfect love and perfect knowledge. They also realize that the Father and the Son are Beings who can, and will help them to progress.

Therefore, if the Father, the Son or Their authorized servants were to say unto a mountain "...Remove hence to yonder place...it shall remove." (*New Test. Matthew* 17:20). This is because the very matter and energy which make up the mountain can hear and obey God. Of course, in order for the Lord's servants to exercise such mighty power, they must be doing it according to His will. Also, those who would exercise God's **Super Power** in such a way must have perfect faith in the Father and the Son and in Their power.

The Consent of the Governed

Just as the power of the government of the United States comes from the consent of its citizens, so God's Power comes from the consent of the intelligences who have voluntarily decided to be governed by the Lord, and by His perfect laws. Thus, the power of God flows to Him: "... without compulsory means...forever and ever" (*Doctrine and Covenants* 121:45).

Why it is Necessary for There to be Power and Super Power Formulas From God?

If we are ever to receive God's Power to do good in the universe, we will need to progress to the point where we also have perfect love, and perfect knowledge, like our Father in Heaven, and like our Savior. How can we progress to this high degree? We can do so by following the plans, and directions, which They have given us.

Their plans and directions are contained in Their Gospel **Power Formulas** and in Their **Super Power Formula**. This is why these formulas are necessary.

Also, having Their **Power** and **Super Power Formulas** is not enough. We must accept, believe and follow these **Formulas**, thus doing **Power Change** and **Super Power Change** with Jesus Christ. Following God's **Power** and **Super Power Formulas** means following Jesus Christ. We can only receive the Father and the Son's power, which is Their honor, by becoming honorable, as They are.

A Third Great Secret: Why Have the Father and the Son Given Us Their POWER AND Super Power Formulas, or, in Other Words, What is Their Purpose?

Have you ever wondered what is the purpose of the Father and the Son for doing all that They do? They have actually also answered this question in modern scriptural revelation to Their "...servants the Prophets...," (see *Old Test. Amos* 3:7). We will now review a revelation that answered this question: what is God the Father and His Son Jesus Christ's purpose?

God's Purpose in Twenty Words

Through the prophets Moses and Joseph Smith, God has given us an amazing insight into His purpose. This revelation is found in a book of scripture titled *The Pearl of Great Price*. From its

Introductory Note, we learn that:

> *The Pearl of Great Price* is a selection of choice materials touching many significant aspects of the faith and doctrine of The Church of Jesus Christ of Latter-day Saints. These items were produced by [revealed through] the Prophet Joseph Smith...Following is a brief introduction to the present contents [of *The Pearl of Great Price*]: Selections from the *Book of Moses*. An extract from the book of *Genesis* of Joseph Smith's Translation of the *The Bible*, which he began in 1830...

The first chapter of *The Book of Moses* contains the great secret of God's purpose. Here are the verses in which this treasure is found:

> And the Lord God spake unto Moses saying: The heavens, they are many, and they cannot be numbered unto man; but they are numbered unto me, for they are mine. And as one earth shall pass away, and the heavens thereof even so shall another come; and there is no end to my works, neither to my words. *FOR BEHOLD, THIS IS MY WORK AND MY GLORY—TO BRING TO PASS THE IMMORTALITY AND ETERNAL LIFE OF MAN* (*The Pearl of Great Price*, The *Book of Moses* 1:37, 39, published by The Church of Jesus Christ of Latter-day Saints, Salt Lake City, 1880, emphasis added).

There it is, in just twenty words! God's Purpose! Wow! The Father and the Son are all about us! Sure, They make worlds, but the reason They do so is so we will have a place to live, develop and progress.

THE FOURTH GREAT SECRET: WE HAVE A HEAVENLY FATHER AND A HEAVENLY MOTHER

In **The Power Formulas**, *Part Two*, *Chapter One*, we considered our relationship to our Heavenly Parents. Here is what this chapter stated:

> Prior to the creation of this earth, God did not exist alone. Jesus Christ and each of one of us existed with our Father in Heaven prior to this earth life. We were all spirit children of our Father in Heaven. This is why He is called our Father in Heaven. Since we are the spirit children or "offspring" of our Heavenly Father, it only makes sense that we also have a Heavenly Mother.

Our Heavenly Mother

A famous Latter-day Saint Hymn teaches this profound truth:

> **In the Heavens, are parents single? No, the thought makes reason stare. Truth is reason, truth eternal, tells me I've a Mother there...When I leave**

this frail existence, when I lay this mortal by, Father, Mother, may I meet you in your royal courts on high?

Then, at length, when I've completed all you sent me forth to do, with your mutual approbation let me come and dwell with you. (*Hymns of The Church of Jesus Christ of Latter-day Saints*, 1985, Deseret Book Company, Salt Lake City, Utah, "Oh My Father", page 292).

"We Know that We Are Spirit Children of Heavenly Parents..."

A modern Apostle has recently taught that we have Heavenly Parents. Elder Boyd K Packer, who is the President of the Quorum of Twelve Apostles, said this:

We Know that we are Spirit Children of Heavenly Parents, here on Earth to receive our mortal body and to be tested" (Elder Boyd K Packer "These Things I Know, *Ensign of The Church of Jesus Christ of Latter-day Saints, May 2012*)

Women can Become Like Our Mother In Heaven

Lorenzo Snow who was the fifth prophet of the Church of Jesus Christ of Latter-day Saints wrote

"You Sisters, I suppose, have read that poem which my Sister [Elisa R Snow] composed years ago, and which is sung quite frequently now in our meetings ["Oh My Father"]. It tells us that we not only have a Father in "that high and glorious place," but that we have a Mother too; and you will become as great as your Mother, if you are faithful. (*Deseret Evening News*, July 20, 1901, 22.)

Our Heavenly Parents' Mark Upon the Universe

In *Part Three*, we considered a concept taught in the movie *Casper*. This was the profound truth that our children are our "mark upon the world". In like manner, we are our Heavenly Parents' 'mark upon the universe'! The greatest accomplishment of all Their creations is not to make worlds or even galaxies. Rather, it is to create Beings like Themselves who can progress to become even as They are.

Our Purpose

The purpose of our Heavenly Parents and Jesus Christ is to promote life, and to help us to become immortal, perfect beings as They are. If Their purpose is help us progress, shouldn't progressing, and helping others to progress also be our purpose?

The FIFTH Great Secret: The Motive Behind God's Purpose Can Be Described in One Word: Love

The Savior Himself revealed the reason why The Father sent Him to live among us:

> For God so loved the world, that He gave His only begotten Son, that whosoever believeth in Him should not perish, but have everlasting life" (*New Test. John* 3:16).

In another revelation, Jesus Christ confirmed that His motivation is the same as our Father in Heaven's. In this revelation, He also taught that our motivation should be the same as Theirs. He said:

> This is my commandment, That ye *love* one another, as I have *loved* you. Greater *love* has no man than this, that a Man lay down His life for His friends (*John* 15:12-13, emphasis added).

What Would, or Better Still, What Does L. Ron Hubbard Think of These Concepts?

Thirty to sixty seconds. Thirty to sixty seconds after his spirit left his body. This is about how long it took for L. Ron Hubbard to realize that some corrections needed to be made. Before we look at what corrections are needed, we will look at some of the good that has been accomplished by L. Ron Hubbard. The ideas he has shared have blessed my life. He has helped many, many people, and he has done much to improve the **Conditions** of men and women on the earth. We, whom he has helped, are grateful for all the good that he has done.

"...Good and Great Men...Have Been Sent by the Almighty..."

Apostle Howard W. Hunter, who later became the prophet and the president of the Church once taught:

> All men share an inheritance of divine light. God operates among his children in all nations, and those who seek God are entitled to further light and knowledge...Elder [apostle] Orson F. Whitney, in a conference address, explained that many great religious leaders were inspired. He said that: *[God] is using not only His covenant people, but other peoples as well, to consummate a work, stupendous, magnificent, and altogether too arduous for this little handful of Saints to accomplish by and of themselves...* All down the ages men bearing the authority of the Holy Priesthood— patriarchs, prophets, apostles and others—have officiated in the name of the Lord, doing the things that He required of them, and...*other good and great men, not bearing the Priesthood, but possessing profundity of thought, great wisdom, and a desire to uplift their fellows, have been sent by the Almighty into many nations to give them... that portion of truth that they were able to receive and wisely use* (In *Conference Report*, April 1921, pages 32-33, *The Ensign of the Church of Jesus Christ of Latter-day Saints*, November 1991, page 19, emphasis added).

L. Ron Hubbard was one of these "...good and great men." With his inquisitive mind, it would not have taken L. Ron Hubbard long to start learning about his new surroundings in Paradise. As noted in the paragraphs above, our Father has provided teachers to assist the spirits of those who have died. Undoubtedly, L. Ron Hubbard would have sought out the best teachers available.

These teachers may have included people like Moses, Isaiah, Abraham, or other Old Testament prophets. Also, he may have been taught by the Apostles of old, such as Peter, James or Paul. He may have also learned from the Lord's chosen prophets and apostles of the Latter-days, such as Joseph Smith, Brigham Young or James E. Talmage, among others. He may have also been taught by some of the great women of the past, such as Mary, Martha, Ruth, Esther, etc.

What would these teachers have taught L. Ron Hubbard? Well, it would be the same things that the Savior taught anciently. L. Ron Hubbard would have been taught the same truths that the Lord's representatives have been teaching, both before and after Jesus Christ's mission upon the earth. It would have been the **Gospel of Jesus Christ**, which contains **God's Power Formula**!

What would have happened after that? One of two things would have happened. First, L. Ron Hubbard may have said thank you, but no thanks. I want to continue thinking and doing what I did in mortality. However, my impression is that he had a different response, and that L. Ron Hubbard accepted the teachings he has received there in the Spirit World. He is now following his Savior, Jesus Christ.

After receiving and accepting **God's Power Formula**, is it not likely that he would want to share what he had learned with his friends, family, and followers? How could this be done? He would have started there to teach those who had followed his teachings while they lived upon the earth. This would be of great benefit to these spirits.

However, what of the many followers of L. Ron Hubbard who are still living upon the earth? How could they be helped to know of and receive **God's Power and Super Power Formulas**? One way would be for a latter-day saint, with some knowledge of L. Ron Hubbard's ideas, to write these books.

Course Corrections

It is my impression that L. Ron Hubbard would want to see at least seven course corrections for those who look to him for direction. These seven are: 1) A correction of Bridges; 2) A correction in the way that the eight dynamics are viewed and ordered; 3) A correction in the honors we seek, and from whom we should seek honors; 4) A correction in the understanding of what happens to our spirits after this life: i.e., resurrection not reincarnation; 5) A correction in the way that people are cleared and healed; 6) A new Conditions List for our spiritual progression, and 7) A correction in which the Church is recognized by L. Ron Hubbard's followers as the senior repository of truth on the earth. We will now consider these seven, one at a time.

Course Correction One: A Correction in the Bridge to Eternal Life

The Power Formulas, Part One contains a chapter titled *Bridges*. Please see that chapter for more complete information about why a change of bridges is necessary for those who follow the directions of L. Ron Hubbard. However, the short answer is that the bridge to eternal life with our Father in Heaven has to take Jesus Christ, and His sacrifice for us, into account.

"What Think Ye of Christ..."

Jesus asked this question. This is the most important question we will ever have to consider. How we answer this question will determine which path, and which bridge we take in life. Life offers us almost unlimited options of paths we can take. However, only one of these paths will lead us to our highest potential. This is the path of faith, love, service and obedience to His Father's will. This is the path that Jesus Christ walked.

What happens if we decide to go another way and travel a different path than the one our Savior has blazed? Thomas S. Monson, the President and Prophet of the Church of Jesus Christ of Latter-day Saints has written recently about our freedom to choose the path we will take in life, and about the consequences of our choices.

> Although in our journey we will encounter forks and turnings in the road, we simply cannot afford the luxury of a detour from which we may never return...
>
> When faced with significant choices, how do we decide? Do we succumb to the promise of momentary pleasure? To our urges and passions? To the pressure of our peers?
>
> Let us not find ourselves as indecisive as is Alice in Lewis Carroll's classic *Alice's Adventures in Wonderland.* You will remember that she comes to a crossroads with two paths before her, each stretching onward but in opposite directions. She is confronted by the Cheshire cat, of whom Alice asks, "Which path shall I follow?"
>
> The cat answers, "That depends where you want to go. If you do not know where you want to go, it doesn't matter which path you take."
>
> Unlike Alice, we all know where we want to go, and *it does matter which way we go, for by choosing our path, we choose our destination...*
>
> I plead with you to make a determination right here, right now, not to deviate from the path which will lead to our goal: eternal life with our Father in Heaven (*Ensign of the Church of Jesus Christ of Latter-day Saints*, November 2010, pages 67 and 68, emphasis added).

His Hand is Reaching Out to Us

In *Part Two*, we reviewed the Savior's teachings in *John* chapter eight. Jesus Christ taught, in this chapter, what happens to those who choose to not believe in Him as the Savior and the Redeemer:

...if ye believe not that I am He, ye shall die in your sins (*John* 8:24).

What did the Savior mean when He said "...ye shall die in your sins"? This means you will have failed to fulfill the purpose of your life, for you will not be with your Father in Heaven in the next life. This is because, as Nephi taught us in *The Book of Mormon,* that:

> ...no unclean thing can dwell with God...(*Nephi* 10:21)

To some, the Savior's statement, "if ye believe not that I am He, ye shall die in your sins..." may seem to be a blunt, unfeeling or even a harsh statement. However, it is not. Rather, it is a simple statement of fact, and it is a warning.

This statement is equivalent to 'you are drowning—here I am reaching to rescue you. If you don't reach for my hand and then hold on with all your might, mind and strength, you will perish'. Jesus Christ is our Eternal Life Guard. Because of His atoning sacrifice for our sins He is the only One that can forgive us and save us from the effects of our sins. This is why when we reject Him as our Savior, we will also reject forgiveness, and thus we will die in our sins.

"God is [Tough] Love"

Let us step aside for a minute to look at an example of how these books have been written. One morning, a thought occurred in my mind: "...God is love" (*New Test. 1st John* 4:8, 16). Then another thought came to mind, that sometimes, when He needs to be for our benefit, God is *tough love!* Of course this is a metaphor. God is not just Love, He is a Person who has, as one of His attributes, Perfect Love. *To be perfect, love must also, when necessary, be tough.* If we will listen for what He wants to communicate to us, *He will tell us what we need to know and do, and not just what we want to hear.*

Okay, so these ideas came into my consciousness. How should this information be used? Should it be part of these books or not? If so, where should it be placed? Then later that day, while reviewing this manuscript, and specifically this section on "What Think Ye of Christ", and how we will die in our sins if we don't believe in and follow Jesus Christ, it became apparent that *here* is where this idea fits.

When Jesus Christ made this statement, He was speaking to those who were rejecting Him, and who were even trying to find a way to suppress His work and destroy Him. Even though they were doing so, He still loved them. After all, He is their older Brother, as He is ours. Because of His desire to help them, and to help us, He has to say it like it is, and at times, He has to use tough love to get our attention.

Perhaps, all of this is just a coincidence that these ideas came one after another. The reader will have to decide. In my mind, there is no doubt. These ideas, like so many others that have come while writing these books, are coming from Someone greater. Also, it is my belief that these ideas are coming because of His love, and His desire to help you and me.

"...Line Upon Line, Precept Upon Precept, Here a Little, There a Little..."

In continuation of the information above, about God showing tough love, other thoughts also came to mind the next morning. One of these thoughts was something that was brought to my remembrance. This was an explanation, or a primer, on the subject of revelation, taught by the Prophet Joseph Smith:

...A person may profit by noticing the first intimation of the Spirit of revelation: for instance, *when you feel pure intelligence flowing into you, it may give you sudden strokes of ideas, so that by noticing it, you may find it fulfilled that same day, or soon*: (i.e.) those things that were presented unto your mind by the Spirit of God, will come to pass (*Teachings*, page 151, emphasis added).

Another idea that occurred during the same morning was from the scriptures and it is used in the subtitle of this section. It is this: God gives us information gradually and sequentially. He does so by providing His information to us:

...line upon line, precept upon precept, here a little, there a little... (see *The Doctrine and Covenants* 98:12; 128:21, and *Old Testament, Isaiah* 28:10).

Up the Awareness Scale

These next paragraphs are further examples of the "line upon line, precept upon precept" way that the Lord can give us truths. These ideas came about a week after above information, in the early morning hours before arising from my bed.

The thought that came is this: when Jesus Christ warned these scribes and Pharisees that they would die in their sins if they rejected Him, the Savior was actually also trying to bring them up the awareness scale. This scale was described by L. Ron Hubbard (see *What is Scientology, based on the Works of L. Ron Hubbard*, Bridge Publications, Los Angeles, 1993, 1998, pages 180-181).

These leaders of the people, who sought to destroy the Savior had "no clue", that what they were really doing was destroying themselves. The Savior's words, if heeded, could have led them to see that their lives were in "**ruin**". With improved awareness, they could start to see their precarious situation, and they could advance to the "**need of change**", to "**demand for improvement**", "**hope**", and higher. All this was still possible, if they could come to have faith in Jesus Christ as the Son of God, and as their Savior. If they would listen to Jesus Christ, and believed in them, they could have still repented and have been saved from dying in their sins.

The above look at how these books have come to be written is an example of this 'line upon line, precept upon precept' concept. Also, these linked concepts are an example of how the Lord can give us guidance along His path and across His Bridge.

Our Abyss

As described in the first book of this series:

There is simply no 'other way', around the Savior, on the road to reaching our highest potential...the reason that this is so is because our road of life passes over the great abyss of death and sin. Each of us must face the reality that our bodies will die. Also, each of us must face the fact that some of our actions have been harmful to ourselves and to others.

These harmful and counter-survival acts are sins. Our bodies all must die, and our spirits have all been separated from our Father in Heaven because no person whose sins have not been forgiven, can live with God (see The Book of Mormon, 1st Nephi 10:21). **Sin and death are the obstacles—the abyss which block our way.**

Our spirits are eternal, and can never be destroyed or die. However, also from *Part One:*

This separation from God is called spiritual death. It is from this condition of spiritual death that we must be reborn, or 'born of God'. Spiritual rebirth occurs as we have faith in Jesus Christ, repent of our sins, are baptized for the remission of sin, and receive the gift of the Holy Ghost which heals us, and changes our hearts. He is also our guide along the path and the Bridge of life.

God's Bridge

There is a Bridge, which makes it possible for us to overcome physical death and to be forgiven of our sins, thus overcoming spiritual death. **God's Bridge is the resurrection and the atonement provided by our Savior, Jesus Christ! Because of His suffering for our sins, we can be forgiven. Because of the resurrection and His atonement, we can gain the power to cross over the abyss of sin and death, which blocks the path back to our Father in Heaven.**

Even after we have entered the gate, have started upon the path and have begun to cross the Bridge by accepting the Savior and His atonement, we have a long and difficult path ahead of us. We must persist and:

...endure to the end in following the example of the Son of the living God... (*The Book of Mormon 2nd Nephi* 31:16).

It will take our greatest effort to walk the path, and we will need the guidance of the Holy Ghost, which has been promised to those who choose to come to Jesus Christ through spiritual rebirth.

The Bridge

Jesus Christ has overcome
all of our enemies and all of the
obstacles to our being with, and to our being like
Our Heavenly Parents.
This is why
the power of His atonement,
and the power of His resurrection
provide our Bridge across the Abyss
of sin and death.
Jesus Christ is the Way, the Truth
the Life, and He is

the Bridge to our Heavenly Parents.

"…No Other Name Given or Any Other Way…"

In a recent General Conference of the Church, Elder Neil Andersen, of the Quorum of the Twelve Apostles taught:

> We are grateful for the 52, 225 full-time missionaries serving in more than 150 countries. The sun never sets on righteous missionaries testifying of the Savior. Think of the spiritual power of 52,000 missionaries, endowed with the Spirit of the Lord, boldly declaring that there is '*no other name given nor any other way nor means whereby salvation can come…, only in and through the name of Christ*'. (*Book of Mormon*, Mosiah 3:17)

It is my belief that L. Ron Hubbard has now accepted that Jesus Christ is our Savior, and that he sees the need to change to the true Bridge, that only our Savior, the Son of God, can provide.

The question is now put to you:

What think ye of Christ?…(*Matthew* 22:42, emphasis added).

Course Correction Two: A Correction in the Way That the Eight Dynamics are Viewed and Ordered

A dynamic is a:

> '…drive, impulse or urge…' to survive. L. Ron Hubbard identified eight subdivisions of the basic command: "Survive!" (*What Is Scientology?*, Bridge Publications, Los Angeles, 1993, pages 153-155).

Most of us think we understand what the word survive means. However, to survive means more than just the continuing existence of our physical bodies.

Progression—A Requirement for Survival

In his description of the graph of the **Normal Condition**, L. Ron Hubbard described the slant of the statistical trend of those who are in this Condition as:

> "Slightly up" (*The Organization Executive Course, Basic Staff Volume*, Bridge Publications, Los Angeles, 1986, page 521).

The **Normal Condition** is the make/break level for survival. This means that the Conditions below Normal are not conducive to survival, and positive improvements must be made to avoid destruction. With these facts in mind, it then becomes apparent that *survival requires* *progression.* This means our statistical trend must be in an "up" or positive direction for survival to occur. Merely holding ones ground by keeping your statistical trend level is not enough. *A flat trend will eventually lead to "flat lining" of the individual or group who do not make corrections and progress!*

Because survival requires progression, the eight dynamics can be viewed as indicators of one's level of progression, and not just in terms of survival. The dynamics are indicators of the level of our progression in terms of our spiritual condition, meaning our relationship to God, people, other life forms, the earth, and the universe.

When we consider the dynamics as indicators of progression, the order must be corrected. The corrected list, in order of importance is:

8,7,2,3,4,1,5,6

Why should the 8th, or the God dynamic be placed 1st? Why place the 7th, or the spiritual dynamic, 2nd in the list? Why should the 1st, or self, dynamic be moved to the sixth position? Also, each of these questions can be answered in terms of the order that is most beneficial for progression.

In other words, if we place the dynamics in the order which will allow us to eventually do **Super Power Change** with God, then the corrected order is 8 (God); 7 (Spiritual life, meaning our relationship to God); 2 (Family); 3 (People we know and associate with, thus those that we are part of a group with); 4 (Everyone else); 1 (Self); 5 (non-human Life forms); and 6 (The physical universe).

Four Reasons for Changing the Order of the Dynamics:

Reason One, The Meaning of Optimum Survival

At first glance, it seems counterintuitive to not place ourselves first. This is because we have come to view survival as the continuation of the life of our physical body. Granted, this is one of the definitions for survival. However, there is another definition of survival: the progression and growth of our spirits so that we can have not just the greatest quantity, *but also the greatest quality* of life eternally.

As noted earlier, L. Ron Hubbard used the term "optimum survival" while defining ethics (see page 4) It should be noted that 'optimum survival' doesn't mean the longest life span. Optimum survival is "Eternal Life", and eternal in this phrase means more than just living forever. Eternal Life, as defined by God, is a *qualitative* as well as a *quantitative* descriptor. God's definition of Eternal Life is that we will live with Him, and like Him. This is truly optimum survival. Also, "optimum survival" takes other beings, life forms, and God's creations, into account. We are to be concerned with the survival, the progression and the happiness of all beings, and not just ourselves.

The greatest example we have of optimum survival is Jesus Christ. However, in terms of life span, He survived in mortality for only 33 years. Yet when His mission on earth was over, His spirit, and His resurrected and immortal body returned to be with His Father. No doubt, He there received a fullness of joy and eternal glory which started with the embrace of His Father, and which will continue on eternally. This same joy is available to us. We can be with our Savior, our Heavenly Parents and our families, forever. Nothing could be better than this, for this is eternal life, and this is **optimum survival**!

Reason Two for Changing the Order of the Dynamics: 'I Am Sixth'

There is a movie titled *Brian's Song*. Perhaps you may have seen it. This is a very inspirational movie based on a true story about two professional football players. These men, Brian Picole, and Gayle Sayers, started out as competitors for the same position of running back for the Chicago Bears. Later, these two became strong friends. Brian eventually was diagnosed with cancer. Soon, he died from this disease.

Gayle Sayers went on to become a Hall of Fame player. He later wrote a book about Brian and their friendship. He titled his book: "*I am Third.*" The reason he chose this title was to express his conviction that he placed God first in his life, then other people, and then "I am Third." This true concept can be expanded, when considered in relation to the dynamics, to 'I am sixth', for we should place others before ourselves (for more on this, see *Reason Four*).

Reason Three for Changing the Order of the Dynamics: "The First Principle of the Gospel [God's Power and Super Power Formulas] is to Know For a Certainty the Character of God..."

You will recall a previous quotation from the section above titled "The Great Secret." Part of that quotation included these words:

> The First Principle of the gospel is to know for a certainty the character of God, *and to know that we may converse with Him as one converses with another, and that He was once a man like us; yea, that God Himself, the Father of us all, dwelt on an earth, the same as Jesus Christ Himself...*

The Prophet Joseph also taught in this same discourse two reasons why it is the first principle to come to know God:

> [1] *If men do not comprehend the character of God, they do not comprehend themselves,* and [2] *If we start right, it is easy to go right all the time;* but if we start wrong, we may go wrong, and it will be a hard matter to get right *(Teachings* pages 342-362, emphasis added*).*

Until we understand God's true character, and that we are progressive beings as He is, we cannot even consider that there are such things as a **Power Formula** and a **Super Power Formula,** from God, for us to follow.

Reason Four for Changing the Order of the Dynamics: The Survival Paradox

Of course we need to use reason, care and good judgment in regards to keeping ourselves alive. A very important part of becoming an adult is gaining the ability to access risk, and to make correct risk-versus-benefit decisions. At first glance, it would seem that we need to "watch out for number one," and put one's self first. However, this is not true, because there is a survival paradox.

The survival paradox is that by putting God and others first, we actually improve our *optimum survival.* The Savior stated this truth in this way:

> Whosoever shall seek to save his life [by putting himself and his own needs first] shall lose it; and whosoever will lose his life [by putting God and His children's needs before their own] shall preserve it (*New Test. Luke* 17:33).

Course Correction Three: A Correction of the Honors We Should Seek, and From Whom We Should Seek These Honors

"...The Honour That Cometh From God Only..."

Closely related to the concept of The Bridges noted previously, is the concept of from whom we should seek honors. In the current concept accepted by Scientology, individuals move up the bridge as they do auditing and training. With the completion of each of the steps on this bridge, in addition to personal growth, these people receive positive reinforcement in the form of praise, plaques and applause, which constitute honors from their peers.

Many people also seek after other honors, such as Olympic medals, Tony Awards, Oscars, fame, wealth, worldly power, etc. There is a greater honor. It is the highest honor, and it is the one honor that that we should be investing our time, our resources, and our efforts to obtain. The Highest Honor is optimum survival, or eternal life with our families in the presence of our Savior and our Heavenly Parents.

In the fifth chapter of *John*, the Savior taught:

> I receive not honour from men...How can ye believe, which receive honour one of another, and seek not *the honour that cometh from God only*? (*John* 5:41, 44, emphasis added)

In *Part Two*, we reviewed *John* Chapter 5, and asked the question: "What is '...the honour that cometh from God only'?" In answer to this question, the reader was referred to *Matthew* 25:34-40. In these verses, we find the answer to the question:

> Then shall the King say unto them on His right hand, ***Come, ye blessed of the Father, inherit the kingdom prepared for you from the foundation of the world.*** For I was an hungered, and ye gave me meat: I was thirsty, and ye gave me drink: I was a stranger, and ye took me in: Naked, and ye clothed me: I was sick, and ye visited me: I was in prison, and ye came unto me. Then shall the righteous answer him, saying, Lord, when saw we thee an hungered, and fed thee? or thirsty, and gave thee drink? When saw we thee a stranger, and

took thee in? Or naked, and clothed thee? Or when saw we thee sick, or in prison, and came unto thee? And the King shall answer and say unto them, Verily I say unto you, *Inasmuch as ye have done it unto one of the least of these my brethren, ye have done it unto me,* emphasis added.

We receive honour from God by having faith in Jesus Christ, and by following His example, including loving and treating people the way that the Savior loved and treated them. When we do the things that Jesus Christ has done, this is doing **Power Change** with Him.

As we love and serve others, as the Savior did, we will not only receive honour from God but we will be honored by the intelligences, which make up the universe, thus gaining **Power**. For more on this, see The Great Secret #2 above.

If we love and serve others as the Savior did, the day will come when we will hear Him say to us:

Come ye blessed of the Father, inherit the kingdom prepared for you... (New Test. Matthew 5:40).

This is the honour we should seek and obtain! *This is "the honour that cometh from God only...".*

Course Correction Four: A Correction in the Understanding of What Happens to Our Spirits and physical bodies After This Life: Resurrection not Reincarnation

As another consequence of the first course correction above, which requires an acceptance of Jesus Christ as the Son of God, and as our Savior who has created the Bridge back to our Father in Heaven, we also must accept His teachings. One of His most important teachings was about the resurrection of our bodies. Indeed, His very life, including His empty tomb, is a testimony to the truthfulness of the doctrine of the bodily resurrection.

Jesus Christ plainly taught that the resurrection was universal:

Verily, verily the hour is coming, and now is, when the dead shall hear the voice of the Son of God: and they that hear shall live. For as the Father hath life in Himself; so hath He given to the Son to have life in Himself; and hath given Him authority to execute judgment also, ...Marvel not at this: for the hour is coming, in the which *all that are in the graves shall hear His voice, and shall come forth; they that have done good, unto the resurrection of life; and they that have done evil, unto the resurrection of damnation* (*New Test. John* 5:25-29, emphasis added).

Another reason why it has to be resurrection and not reincarnation is because families and marriages are meant to be eternal. As noted in *The Power Formulas Part Three* above, titled 'By Their Fruits [Stats] Ye Shall Know Them', when a couple is sealed in a temple marriage by someone who has been given the priesthood sealing keys to bind on earth and in heaven, their marriage relationship and their relationships to their children are eternal.

If the idea of reincarnation were true, a person could conceivably be married to a great number of different spouses, and be part of a great number of families, in their various incarnations. Which marriage and which family relationship would be the eternal one? In short. it is resurrection, not reincarnation.

How to Continue to Progress

There is a general principle here. Whenever the Savior's doctrines are different than those taught by others, including L. Ron Hubbard, the teachings of Jesus Christ always contain the correct and true data. The Lord's teachings and His ordinances are the ones we need to follow. This is what *Afterword #2* means when it states that the correct teachings of the Lord's representatives in His Church are "...senior to all other sources of truth". Failure to understand or accept this essential concept will damn the flow of one's progression.

This occurs if a person refuses to accept revealed truth. If we:

> ...reject the words of the prophets of God...the words which have been spoken concerning Christ..., [this will] ...quench the Holy Spirit...(*The Book of Mormon, Jacob* 6:8).

Without the Lord's help, or Grace, we cannot return to, or become like, Him (see *The Book of Mormon, 2 Nephi* 25:23).

Course Correction Five: A Correction in the Way That people Are Cleared and Healed

It also makes sense that if the Bridge is corrected, then the way one gets across the Bridge is going to change. Although class work and auditing can provide gains in people's lives, the Lord has a much faster, and a more complete way to clear us, to instruct us, and to heal us.

"...He Hath Sent Me to Heal the Broken Hearted..."

Luke's gospel records one of the first things that Jesus Christ did when He started His ministry. This event occurred in a Jewish synagogue on the Sabbath day. The Savior stood and read a prophecy from the Old Testament prophet, Isaiah. He then declared that He was the fulfillment of this prophecy:

> The Spirit of the Lord is upon me, because he hath anointed me to preach the gospel to the poor; he hath sent me *to heal the broken-hearted*, to *preach deliverance to the captives*, and the recovering of sight to the blind, *to set at liberty them that are bruised*... (*New Test. Luke* 4:18 emphasis added).

We might ask: what did the Lord mean in this verse when He stated: "...He hath sent me to heal the broken hearted...[and] ...to set at liberty them that are bruised?" In the scriptures, the word heart does not mean the organ in our chest that pumps our blood. Rather, *heart in the scriptures means our emotions, or the feeling part of our personality.*

Also, implied in these words is the fact that painful experiences which 'leave a mark', or have caused us to be "bruised", can actually effect our ability to be free, thus necessitating that we be "... set at liberty...".

This last sentence above is an apt description of what L. Ron Hubbard described as engrams. A definition of an engram is:

> ...a complete recording, down to the last detail, of every perception present in a moment of partial or full 'unconsciousness'. Also, "When a person is 'unconscious,' the reactive mind exactly records all the perception of that incident, including what happens or is said around the person. It also records all pain and stores this mental image in its own banks, unavailable to the individual's conscious recall and not under his direct control...(*What is Scientology — Based on the works of L. Ron Hubbard*, Bridge Publications, Los Angeles, 1993, 1998, page 147).

Healing Minds and Bodies and Bringing Life From Death

When Jesus described two aspects of His mission as healing the broken hearted and setting at liberty those who have been bruised, what these phrases really mean is healing the emotional part, and the thinking part of our minds. The healing of our minds includes the freeing or clearing of all engrams. Of course Jesus Christ is able to do this. He can heal us, both mind and body.

The Savior's earthly mission included many miracles of healing. During His three-year mission, the Savior restored sight to the blind (see *John* chapter 9); He caused the lame to walk (*Matthew* 11:5, *Luke* 7:22); He cured leprosy many times (*Matthew* 8:2, *Luke* 7:22); He cured a medical condition which caused chronic bleeding (*Matthew* 8:43-48); He cast out evil spirits, thus curing the mental and the behavioral problems that these evil spirits were causing (*Matthew* 8:16, *Mark* 5:8). Also, Jesus Christ actually restored a person from death to life. In fact, He did so on *three* separate occasions! (see *New Test. Mark* 5:22-43, *Luke* 7:11-15, and *John* 11:1-45).

Jesus Christ's Healing Power Continued with His Apostles and His Ancient American Disciples After the Savior Ascended into Heaven

The Savior's ancient apostles also gave blessings of healing for both the bodies and the minds of the people of their time (see *New Test. Acts* chapter 9, and 20:7-12).

In addition, *The Book of Mormon* teaches that the Savior's 12 disciples, who led His ancient American Church also had the power to heal (see *3rd Nephi* 19:4)

A *Book of Mormon* prophet named Alma, also prophesied, before the Savior's birth, of how the Savior would gain the knowledge and experience to know how to heal us. Here is what Alma taught:

> And *He shall go forth, suffering pains and affliction and temptations of every*

kind...and will take upon him the pains and sicknesses of His people. And He will take upon Him their infirmities, that His bowels may be filled with mercy...*that He might know according to the flesh how to succor [meaning how to come to the aid of] His people...*" (*Alma* 7:11-12, emphasis added).

Later, in *The Book of Mormon,* the Savior explained how this healing is brought about. Jesus Christ taught that when people:

...return and repent, and come unto Me with full purpose of heart, and I will heal them... (*3 Nephi* 18:32, emphasis added).

Here is how this spiritual healing happens:

God sent His Beloved Son, Jesus Christ, into the world so that all of God's children would have the possibility of returning to live in His presence after they die. Only through the Savior's grace and mercy can we become clean from sin so that we can live in our Heavenly Father's presence. *Becoming clean from sin is being healed spiritually* (*Preach My Gospel,* The Church of Jesus Christ of Latter-day Saints, Salt Lake City, 2004, page 60, emphasis added).

What clearing and healing could be better than that which comes from the Lord Himself?

We Can Also Participate in the Healing Process for Ourselves and for Others

A modern apostle has taught of this truth with these words:

As we extend our hands and hearts towards others in Christ-like love, something wonderful happens to us. *Our own spirits become healed,* more refined, and stronger. We become happier [our emotional tone level improves], more peaceful, and more receptive to the whisperings of the Holy Spirit...as we contemplate, with reverence and awe how *our Savior embraces us, comforts us, and heals us, let us commit to become His hands, that others, through us, may feel His loving embrace* (President Dieter F. Uchtdorf, "You Are My Hands", *The Ensign of The Church of Jesus Christ of Latter-day Saints,* May 2010, page 75, emphasis added).

Course Correction Six: God's SPIRITUAL Conditions List

The Introduction to *The Power Formulas Part Two* included a list of the **Conditions** described by L. Ron Hubbard. As explained in the beginning of this section, because God's power supersedes all other powers, His power is really **Super Power**. Also, as we move up the Spiritual Conditions to become like our Father in Heaven, we will eventually arrive at **Super Power Change**. Therefore, in regards to the **Conditions Formulas** that God has in place for us, this would be the corrected list:

Super Power
Super Power Change
Power
Power Change
Affluence
Normal
Emergency
Danger
Non Existence
Liability
Doubt
Enemy
Treason
Confusion

(Adapted from: L. Ron Hubbard, *Introduction to Scientology Ethics*, Los Angeles, Bridge Publishers, 1989, p. 3)

Definitions Related to the Conditions List Above

Super Power (Eternal Life) means receiving the Power of God, by actually becoming a God ourselves. This can occur, but only "...in the far future..." according to apostle James E. Talmage (as quoted in *Super Power*, see The Great Secret, #1).

Super Power Change is what we do with the rest of our lives, after receiving God's **Super Power Formula** in one of His Temples.

Power is learning, believing and then living the Gospel of Jesus Christ sufficiently that we are able to receive a Recommend (admission certificate) to God's Temple.

Power Change means, in terms of our relationship to God, receiving the Gospel of Jesus Christ, as taught in the scriptures of The Church of Jesus Christ of Latter-day Saints. We need to accept, and live the Gospel of Jesus Christ by loving and serving others. Also, we need to prepare to receive the Conditions above (see *The Book of Mormon, 3rd Nephi* 26:1-11).

Non Existence means coming out of Spiritual Non Existence in our relationship to God by being born of God through faith in our Father in Heaven and in Jesus Christ, repentance, baptism, and receiving the Gift of the Holy Ghost. This makes us aware that we are God's children, and changes our hearts).

Course Correction Seven: A Correction in Which Church is Recognized, by the Followers of L. Ron Hubbard, as the Senior Repository of Truth on the Earth

This is a biggey! Would L. Ron Hubbard really want this correction to be made? In answer to this question, we will consider the words of two modern apostles and prophets. Howard W. Hunter taught that:

Latter-day Saints have a positive approach toward others who are not of our faith. We believe they are literally our brothers and sisters, that we are sons and daughters of the same Heavenly Father. We have a common genealogy leading back to God, but more than that, we also seek the true and beautiful wherever it may be found. And we know that God has blessed all His children with goodness and light.

This modern apostle, Howard W. Hunter also quoted a previous prophet:

President George Albert Smith so lovingly suggested: 'We have come not to take away from the truth and virtue you possess. We have come not to find fault with you nor to criticize you. We have not come to berate you because of things you have not done; but we have come here as your brethren...and say to you keep all the good that you have, and let us bring you more good, in order that you may be happier and in order that you may be prepared to enter into the presence of our Heavenly Father' (Howard W. Hunter, The Gospel a Global Faith. *The Ensign of The Church of Jesus Christ of Latter-day Saints*, November 1991, page 10).

The Gospel of Jesus Christ is "A Divine Gift" and "The Ultimate Formula for Happiness and Success"

How does God's Gospel, including His **Super Power Formula**, which is found in The Church of Jesus Christ of Latter-day Saints change us so that we are prepared "...to enter into the presence of our Father in Heaven"? In answer to this question, we will refer to the words of another modern apostle, President Deiter Uchtdorf of the Church's First Presidency. In a recent General Conference of the Church, President Uchtdorf taught that the Gospel is:

...not someone's theory or proposition. It does not come from man at all. It springs from the pure and everlasting waters of the Creator of the universe, who knows truths we cannot even begin to comprehend. And with that knowledge He has given us the Gospel, a Divine gift, the ultimate formula [or **Super Power Formula**] for happiness and success.

President Uchtdorf also taught that as we accept Jesus Christ, and start to follow Him, we will:

...reach out in merciful acts of kindness, forgiveness, grace, and long suffering patience...this is the peaceable way of the followers of Jesus Christ... (The Way of the Disciple, President Deiter Uchtdorf, *The Ensign of the Church of Jesus Christ of Latter-day Saints*, May 2009, pages 75-78)

When we follow **God's Gospel Power and Super Power Formulas,** as they are taught in The Church of Jesus Christ of Latter-day Saints, we start to think and act like Him. This is how we are eventually prepared to be with Him, and to be like Him. This is also how we will eventually receive His Honor, which is His **Power**. This is why the world needs *God's* Church, His Gospel **Power Formula**, and His **Super Power Formula** which is taught only in His Temples.

The Lord's Church

Some people become upset and offended when we refer to The Church of Jesus Christ of Latter-day Saints as the Lord's Church, or as the true Church. Many subscribe to the *'all', or 'the none'* theories, when it comes to the idea of their being a true Church on the earth. What this means is that some people believe that *all* Churches are good and true. Others believe that *none* are true, and that there is no such thing as God's true Church on the earth. Some people even refuse to believe in God at all.

However, probably everyone who has even a passing familiarity with *The Holy Bible* will agree that when Jesus Christ was on the earth, He organized His followers into a Church, or as the apostle Paul described it: "...one body..." (see *New Test. Ephesians* 4:1-14). Also there is no evidence that Jesus started more than one Church. Therefore, Jesus did establish His one true Church anciently. His Church was built upon "...the foundation of apostles and prophets, Jesus Christ, Himself being the chief cornerstone" (see *Ephesians* 2:19-21).

You will recall the reason that the 14-year-old Joseph Smith went into the grove of trees to pray. He wanted to know which church was *the* true church so he could join it. In answer to his prayer, the Father and the Son appeared and instructed Joseph to join none of the existing churches for none of them was God's Church.

Joseph Smith entered that grove of trees as a boy, but he left it as a prophet of God. It would be through His prophet, Joseph, that the Lord would once again established His true Church upon the earth. The Lord's Church would be again founded upon living apostles and prophets, through whom the Savior directs the Church by revelation. *Without a living prophet, no church can be God's Church, because it necessary that God have someone He can communicate with, so He can provide direction for His Church!*

Please Don't Choose to Become Angry When We Describe The Church of Jesus Christ of Latter-day Saints As 'The Only True Church'

In a relatively recent Conference of the Church, one of the Church leaders described an incident when he was asked by someone if it was not egoistical for the members of our Church to describe it as 'the only true Church'. This Church leader was inspired to answer that it is not, because it is not the members of the Church who make this claim. Rather it is the Lord, Himself! The Savior has revealed:

> For thus shall *my Church be called in the last days, even The Church of Jesus Christ of Latter-day Saints...".* [Also, the Lord has described The Church of Jesus Christ of Latter-day Saints as:] *"... the only true and living Church upon the face of the whole earth...* (*The Doctrine and Covenants* 115:4, and

1:30, emphasis added).

Our Progression in Our Relationship with Each Member of the Godhead

If our desired destination is to arrive back with our Heavenly Parents, and with Jesus Christ, then it is certain that we will have to travel the road that leads back to Them. The Savior gave us the directions to the path when He said:

> I am the way, the truth, and the life: no man cometh unto the Father, but by Me (*New Test. John* 14:6, emphasis added).

Each of us need to be born of the Spirit, so we can receive and follow the consistent guidance of the Holy Ghost.

This occurs as we learn of Jesus Christ, develop faith in Him, repent of our sins and are baptized. We are then confirmed a member of The Church of Jesus Christ of Latter-day Saints, and receive the Gift of the Holy Ghost, by the laying on of hands of a priesthood holder of the Church. As we follow the inspiration we receive from the Holy Ghost, and as we keep God's commandments, love God, and His children, we will eventually be lead by the Holy Ghost to Jesus Christ. The Savior will then take us into the presence of our Heavenly Parents.

Thus, there is a progression in our relationships with each member of the Godhead. First we associate with the Holy Ghost.

Thus, in review, as we come into The Church of Jesus Christ, we receive the Gift of the Holy Ghost. We can then live our lives in association with the Holy Ghost, who is the third member of the Godhead. By following the guidance of the Holy Ghost, we will one day see our Savior, Jesus Christ, face to face, when we are sufficiently prepared. Only our Savior will then reunite us with our Heavenly Parents. Jesus Christ taught:

> ...I am the way, the truth and the life; *No man cometh unto the Father, but by Me* (*John* 14:6).

This progression is represented in the diagram that follows:

Two More Lessons From England

Lesson One: Earlier, we briefly reviewed the great success of the work performed by early Latter-day Saint missionaries in England. Here is another story from that period:

> In March 1840, Elder Wilford Woodruff of the Quorum of the Twelve Apostles arrived in Hanley, England where he met recent converts William and Ann Benbow. Elder Woodruff [who, also, later became the prophet and president of the Church] and Brother Benbow traveled to the Herefordshire area to teach William's brother, John, and his family. The Benbow brothers then invited their neighbors to join them in hearing what the missionary had to say. They introduced Elder Woodruff to their former congregation: over

600 people who had formed their own church, the United Brethren. All but one was eventually baptized... (*The Ensign of the Church of Jesus Christ of latter-day Saints*, July 2010, inside front cover).

Just as the conversion of a few people led to nearly an entire church coming into God's Kingdom, as described in this amazing episode from history, the acceptance of **God's Power Formula** by L. Ron Hubbard, and one or more of his influential followers upon the earth, could lead to a great infusion of strong, committed members into God's Kingdom, which is The Church of Jesus Christ of Latter-day Saints.

Lesson Two: As you may imagine, when so many people joined the Church and migrated to America, it created quite a stir in English society. An English newspaper sent a reporter to the ship docks in Liverpool to find out about these "Mormons" before they sailed for the United States to be with the main body of the Church. This reporter admitted that prior to meeting these emigrants, he expected to expose these people as an undesirable group. However, as he interviewed and came to know these people, he was greatly surprised by the quality of these converts. He described them as:

> '...the pick and flower of England'. This reporter was Charles Dickens, the English novelist (Our Father's Plan—Big Enough for All His Children, [apostle] Quentin L. Cook, *The Ensign of the Church of Jesus Christ of Latter-day Saints*, May 2009, pages 34-38).

Just as these early Latter-day Saints were impressive to those of their day, Scientologists are very impressive. It has been my privilege to get to know many members of the Church of Scientology, International. They are positive, ethical, honest, hard working and committed to helping people. They could do much good by joining and serving in the Lord's Church! They could accelerate the growth of the Lord's Kingdom, and help to prepare the world for the Savior's glorious return.

The Source of Salvation

Recently, *The Flag Land Base News* contained an article by L. Ron Hubbard titled: "An Invitation to Freedom, Man Can Save His Soul." In this article, L. Ron Hubbard paraphrased a teaching of Jesus Christ in this way:

> As Christ said, the innocent can first be saved in a little time, in minutes, the child can be saved. But the rich and the mighty, the enslaver and destroyer would lag behind for years—but they too can be saved...
>
> ...Man's soul can be saved. We know how. If Man does not want to be saved, that is a decision Man must make, each one for himself. You have been invited. You will be accepted. If you do not care to be accepted, that too is your freedom. Heaven waits. At least we have shut, for some, the yawning jaws of Hell.

At the time he presented this material, L. Ron Hubbard referred to a teaching of Jesus Christ. However, he was not teaching that people had to believe in Jesus Christ as their Savior and follow Him in order to be saved. Instead, he taught that "…man can save his soul…" How does L. Ron Hubbard feel about this extremely important issue now? In answer to this question, here is my impression of how he would teach these concepts now:

> [Because of Jesus Christ,] man can be saved, [but not without man's own consent, and not without his complete participation and effort.] We now know how. If Man does not want to be saved, that is a decision Man must make, each one for himself. You have been invited. You will be accepted. If you do not care to be accepted, that too is your freedom. Heaven waits. At least [Jesus Christ] has shut the yawning jaws of Hell [for those who have faith in Him and who will follow Him]. (Adapted from L Ron Hubbard, "An Invitation to Freedom, Man Can Save His Soul," as quoted in *The Flag Land Base News*).

Plain Words About L. Ron Hubbard, The Power Formulas, Time and Lives

L. Ron Hubbard would not want us to beat around the bush. He would want it said in the most clear and direct way possible: He wants every Scientologist to become a Latter-day Saint. Also, if L. Ron Hubbard were asked why, my impression is that he would say: 'I discovered and made the principles of the **Power Change Formula**, and of **Power Formula** known, but the Latter-day Saints actually *have* **God's Power and Super Power Formulas**. Only they can show you how to do **Power Change and Super Power Change** with God! If you want to follow me, then follow Jesus Christ and His authorized servants, the apostles and prophets, for that is what I am now doing. It is that simple. Now that you know this, do something about it! Time is a wasting. More importantly, lives are a wasting!'

A Summary of The Power and Super Power Formulas

In conclusion, we are coming to the end of *The Power Formulas* and **Super Power**. In these books, we have looked at a number of reasons and evidences why God the Father, and His Son Jesus Christ have given us Their **Gospel** which is Their **Power Formula** and Their **Super Power Formula**. These reasons and evidences are summarized below.

1. *The Book of Mormon* is a series of **Power Formulas** and **Power Change** between inspired ancient American prophet record keepers, and these add up to a **Power Formula** from God to us.

2. *The Holy Bible* is a record that shows how the Father has done a **Power Formula** for His Son Jesus Christ, and how Jesus Christ has done **Power Change** with His Father.

3. *The New Testament* is also a record of how Jesus Christ established His Church upon the earth and did a **Power Formula** for the ancient apostles and prophets to prepare them to lead His Church after His departure.

4. *The Holy Bible* is also a record of how Jesus Christ taught a spiritual **Non Existence** and a spiritual **Power Formula** for all of His followers: the members of His ancient Church.

5. *The Holy Bible* is also a record of how the Savior's apostles and prophets did **Power**

Change with the Savior and carried on as Jesus Christ had done in teaching **God's Gospel Non Existence and Power Formulas** to others.

6. *The Doctrine and Covenants* and *The Pearl of Great Price* are records of how that, after the truth had been lost during the dark ages which followed the death of the ancient apostles and prophets, the Savior repeated the **Power Formula/ Power Change Cycle of Action** by re-establishing His Church through first calling new apostles and prophets, and restoring His Church to the earth.

7. Through these scriptural **Power Formulas** and through modern apostles, prophets and of His other representatives, God has been, and will continue, sharing His **Spiritual Non Existence and Gospel Power Formulas** with the people of the world, including you.

8. Because we have been given **God's Spiritual Non Existence and Power Formulas**, it is possible for us to do **Power Change** with God.

9. Those who receive and accept and live by **God's Spiritual Non Existence and Power Change Formulas** receive rich blessings in this life, including: opportunities to help in the rapid growth of the Church, have more successful marriages, the blessing of having more descendants, the blessings which come from doing service, and improved survival, as evidenced by longer life spans.

10. True **Super Power** is God's Power, and is obtained by doing **Super Power Change** with God.

11. God has established His temples as the only places on earth where His children can receive His **Super Power Formula**, and be endowed with His **Super Power**, which is also the **Condition of Eternal Life**.

12) Because God is both loving and fair, all these blessings, which are available to the living, are also made available to those who are on the other side of the veil. These blessings include eternal marriage and eternal families for those who did not receive these opportunities during their mortal lives.

Knowing the Truth

If you really, *really* want to know if all of this is true, you can find out for certain, because God has promised you a revelation:

> ...by the Power of the Holy Ghost, and by the Power of the Holy Ghost you may know the truth of all things..." (*The Book of Mormon, Moroni* 10:4-5).

The way you can find out is to study, "...ponder..." and then to "...ask God."

We Must Be Willing to Know the Truth

In a PBS Masterpiece Theater program, a wise older man gave this counsel to a younger man:

> Before a man can know, he must be willing to know (from *Lark Rise to Candleford*).

This is the answer to the question of what does the Lord mean when He taught that as we pray to learn truth, we must do so with "real intent" (see *The Book of Mormon, Moroni* 10:3-5).

Also, praying with real intent means having the intent to, and the will to act upon, the revealed truth which we receive from God.

Our Destination

What is the destination of this path? It is a Condition called "Eternal Life." What is Eternal Life? It is more than just living eternally. All of the Father's children will live forever because the resurrection is a free gift to us all from God the Father, and from Jesus Christ. Eternal life has to do with the *quality* of the life, and not just its duration or *quantity*. To have Eternal Life means to *live with*, and to *live like our Heavenly Parents, and Jesus Christ. This includes having their Power*, which is **Super Power**.

How to Get Up to the Condition of Super Power Change

*We start this process by being born again, which equals doing a spiritual **Non Existence Formula**. In review, this occurs as we develop Faith in Jesus Christ, repent of our sins, are baptized, and receive the Gift of the Holy Ghost. When these changes take place in our lives:*

> *...our view of ourselves and the world changes... [and] ...we recognize that we are children of God...*
>
> *Once we have entered the strait and narrow path by our faith in Jesus Christ, repentance, and by the ordinances of baptism and receiving the Holy Ghost, we must exert every effort to stay on the path. We do so by continually exercising faith in Jesus Christ, repenting, and making commitments [by renewing our baptism commitments weekly as we partake of the sacrament at Church, and by following the direction of the Holy Ghost]...we promise to do good works, serve others, and follow the Savior's example...this life-long commitment is often called 'enduring to the end'. By following the gospel path [and bridge], we can draw closer to God, conquer temptation and sin, and enjoy the gift of the Holy Ghost more abundantly. As we patiently, faithfully, and consistently follow this path throughout our lives, we qualify for eternal life (Preach My Gospel, The Church of Jesus Christ of Latter-day Saints, Salt Lake City, 2004, pages 62 and 66).*

The process of growth and development described above is analogous to moving up the **Spiritual Conditions** from **Non Existence** to **Super Power Change**.

Personal Course Correction and Quality Control

Prior to partaking of the bread and water of the sacrament, we can reflect upon our attitudes and actions during the week we just experienced. In this way, we can do quality control as we review our personal statistics and determine, with the Lord's help, what our **Spiritual Condition** is at that moment. We can also, with His inspiration and help, decide upon, and take the needed corrections and improvements in our lives to raise our **Spiritual Condition**.

As we are faithful in our following the Savior's example, the time will come when we are prepared to go to the Lord's House, the Temple. It is there that we receive knowledge and sacred ordinances, including eternal marriage sealing, which give us the power to become like Jesus Christ, and our Heavenly Parents.

OUR PROGRESSION IN OUR REGAINING RELATIONSHIPS
WITH EACH MEMBER OF THE GODHEAD

We Lived With Them and Knew Them in our Pre-Mortal Existence, But We Have Forgotten This Due to a Veil of Forgetfulness Which Occurred When We Were Born into Mortality (Job 38:7 and Jeremiah 1:5).

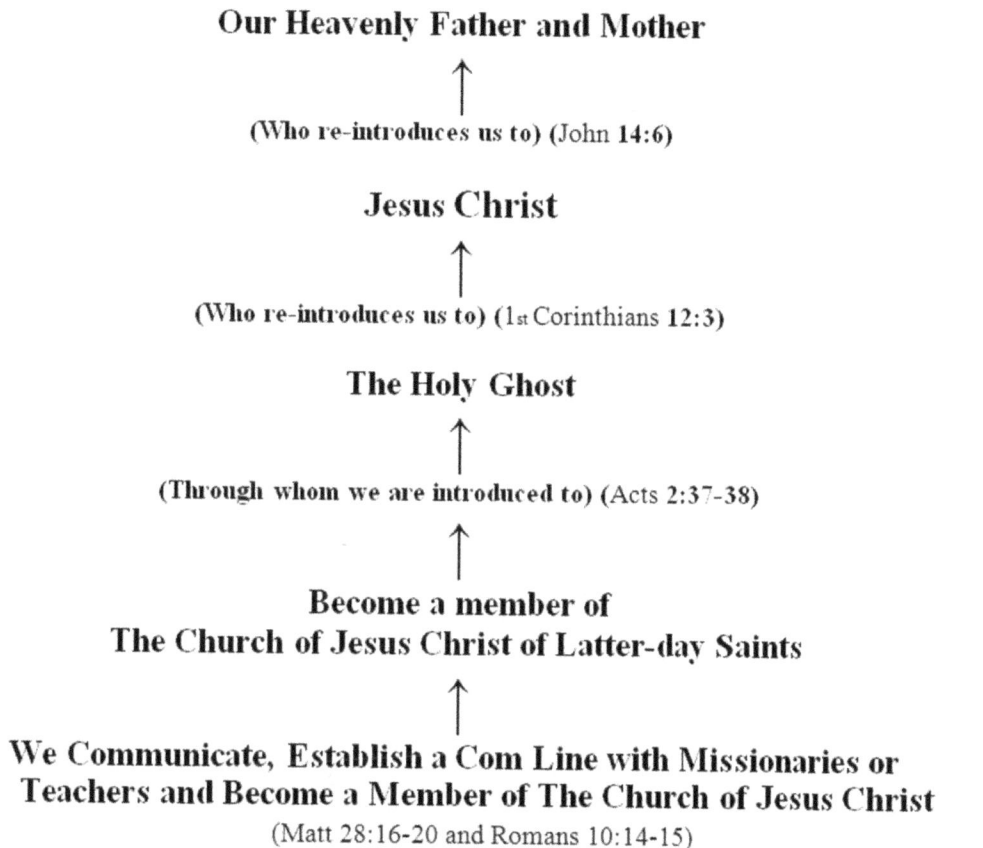

Our Heavenly Father and Mother

↑

(Who re-introduces us to) (John 14:6)

Jesus Christ

↑

(Who re-introduces us to) (1st Corinthians 12:3)

The Holy Ghost

↑

(Through whom we are introduced to) (Acts 2:37-38)

↑

Become a member of
The Church of Jesus Christ of Latter-day Saints

↑

We Communicate, Establish a Com Line with Missionaries or Teachers and Become a Member of The Church of Jesus Christ

(Matt 28:16-20 and Romans 10:14-15)

To "Overcome" is to Do Power and Super Power Change with God

The terms: "Overcome", or "overcometh [overcomes]" were used in the revelations recorded by the apostle John, at least 12 times. These references are found in 1 John 2:13, 14; 4:4; 5:4, 5; Revelation 2:7, 11, 17; 3:5, 12, 21 and 21:7.

These oft repeated themes in John's writings must be very important to him, and to God. As we carefully review these references, we can learn about three related themes. These are: One, *what is it that we are to overcome. Two, how do we overcome*; and three, *what rewards or blessings await those who do overcome.* We will now consider these three concepts individually.

What Are We to Overcome?

In 1 John 2:13, John wrote:

> …ye have overcome the wicked one [Satan]….

Later in this epistle, or letter, John wrote about those who:

> …overcometh the world…

John also defined "the world" in this way:

> …the lust of the flesh, the lust of the eyes, and the pride of life (1 *John* 2:16).

How Do We Overcome the World and Satan?

In the 5th chapter of his first epistle, the Apostle John wrote that:

> Whosoever believeth that Jesus is the Christ is born of God… [and]
> For whatsoever [whosoever] is born of God… *overcometh* the world:
> and this is the victory that *overcometh* the world, *even* our faith (1
> *John* 5:1, 4).

Also, John wrote that we are to:

> …love God… [and] love the children of God (1 *John* 5:2).

The way we love God is to:

> …keep His commandments… (1 *John* 5:1,4)

The way we love God's children is by serving them. In a recent General Conference of the Church, one of the apostles, M. Russell Ballard taught how loving and serving others is the way to receive the mighty change of heart, and as we do so, we are born of God.

This is the way that we can overcome the obstacles to our returning to be with our Savior and our Heavenly Parents.

> How do we make this change? How do we ingrain this love of Christ into our hearts? There is one simple daily practice that can make a difference for every member of the Church [and others], including you boys and girls, you young men and you young women, you single adults, and you fathers and mothers.
>
> That simple practice is: In your morning prayer each new day, ask Heavenly Father to guide you to recognize an opportunity to serve one of His precious children. Then go throughout the day with your heart full of faith and love, looking for someone to help. Stay focused… If you do this, your spiritual sensitivities will be enlarged and you will discover opportunities to serve that you never before realized were possible…

I know that if you do this—at home, at school, at work, and at church—the Spirit will guide you, and you will be able to discern those in need of a particular service that only you may be able to give. You will be prompted by the Spirit and magnificently motivated to help pollinate the world with the pure love of Christ and His gospel ("Be Anxiously Engaged", Elder M. Russell Ballard of the Quorum of the Twelve Apostles, *Ensign* of the Church of Jesus Christ of Latter-day Saints, November, 2012).

When We "Overcome", by Successfully Completing Power and Super Power Change with God, What Blessings and Rewards Await Us?

We will not review all of the blessings and rewards listed by the apostle John. You can do so yourself by reading all the verses listed above. Many of these verses describe what it will be like to be in Heaven, with God. For our purposes, we will focus on what **our Condition will be and Who will we be like.**

In the Book of Revelation, which was also recorded by the apostle John, we are taught:

And he that overcometh and keepeth my works [follows Me, thereby doing **Super Power Change**] unto the end, **to him will I give power over the nations...even as I received of my Father** (*Revelation* 2:26, 27,emphasis added).

Also, as noted previously:

To him that overcometh will I grant to sit with me in my throne, even as I also overcame, and am set down with my Father in his throne (*Revelation* 3:21, emphasis added).

In addition, John recorded this revelation from "Alpha and Omega" who is Jesus Christ:

He that overcometh shall inherit all things; and I will be his God, and he [or she] shall be my son [or daughter] (*Revelation* 21:7).

What kind of beings are these verses describing? This is left to the reader to determine. However, it's obvious that a being who has power over the nations, who inherits "all things" and who sits with the Savior in His throne, can only be described with the same title we use for our Savior and our Heavenly Parents. You know what the term is.

The following quotes are from *Our Identity and Our Destiny*, a talk by Tad R. Callister, a member of the Presidency of the Seventy of The Church of Jesus Christ of Latter-day Saints, 14 August 2012, during Campus Education Week and is available online at speeches@byu.edu.

First, our identity. There is a sentiment among many in the world that we are the spirit creations of God, just as a building is the creation of its architect or a painting the creation of its painter or an invention the creation of its inventor. The scriptures teach, however, a much different doctrine. They teach that we are more than creations of God; they teach that we are the literal spirit offspring or children of God our Father. What difference does this doctrinal distinction make? The difference is monumental in its consequence because our identity determines in large measure our destiny. For example, can a mere creation ever become like its creator? Can a building ever become an architect? A painting a painter? Or an invention an inventor? If not, then those who believe we are creations of God, rather than His spirit offspring, reach the inevitable conclusion that we do not have the capacity to become like our creator, God. In essence, their doctrine of identity has defined and dictated a diminished destiny...

C. S. Lewis, as a rampant advocate of this simple but glorious truth, wrote:

The command Be ye perfect *is not idealistic gas. Nor is it a command to do the impossible. He is going to make us into creatures that can obey that command. He said (in the Bible) that we were "gods" and He is going to make good His words. . . . The process will be long and in parts very painful; but that is what we are in for. Nothing less. He meant what He said.*

Could our potential to progress be stated with any more clarity than C.S. Lewis has done?

It was C. S. Lewis who again and again reaffirmed this divine proposition:

It is a serious thing to live in a society of possible gods and goddesses, to remember that the dullest and most uninteresting person you talk to may one day be a creature which . . . you would be strongly tempted to worship. . . . There are no ordinary people.

The True Goodness and Beauty of God's Power and Super Power formulas

What is the true goodness and beauty of the principles contained in God's **Power and Super Power Formulas**? Is it not that the Godhead, who are in a **Condition of Super Power**, and thus above others, do not try to keep others down, and in subjection to Themselves. Rather, the Father, the Son, and the Holy Ghost want to elevate us to Their own level. Thus, They do not hoard Their power. Instead, they want to share Their power with all those who are willing to do what is necessary to obtain it. What is necessary is to follow Their example, thus doing a **Super Power Change** with them.

The Father has done **Power and Super Power Formulas** for His Son, and His Son, Jesus Christ, has done a **Super Power Change** with His Father. Jesus Christ has also provided **Power and Super Power Formulas** for us. The question is this: what will we do? Are we willing to do a **Power and Super Power Change** with God? Will we get on the path, and to stay on it *no matter what*?

It is my hope and prayer that you will decide to receive God's Gospel **Power Formula** and His **Super Power Formula**, so you can do **Power** and then **Super Power Change** with God. May God bless you as you make this journey. My testimony is that our Father in Heaven and His son Jesus Christ live! They love you! Because of His great love for you, the Father sent His Son Jesus Christ to rescue you, and to bring you home safely to your Heavenly Parents.

Also, because of the Son's great love, He was willing to "...descend from His throne Divine..." and "...He suffered, He bled, and died..." in my place, and in yours. ("I Stand All Amazed", *Hymns of The Church of Jesus Christ of Latter-day Saints*, page 193).

Jesus Christ did these things so that we could have a Bridge back to our Heavenly home. To get there, we need to walk the path and cross over His Bridge. The Third Member of the Godhead, the Holy Ghost, will guide us along the path. This is the promise we receive as we thoughtfully and worthily review our lives, repent and covenant to follow the Savior's example each week, while receiving the sacrament. This is a weekly recommitment to do **Super Power Change** with the Savior (see *The Book of Mormon, Moroni* 4:3 and 5:2).

The Savior wants you to receive:

> ...all that My Father hath... (*Doctrine and Covenants* 84:38).

This means that He and the Father want you to also have Their Power, which is Their Honor. To do so, we must become like Them. This is why They have given us Their **Power** and Their **Super Power Formulas**, which are contained in Their scriptures, in the teachings of Their living apostles and prophets, in Their temple instructions and ordinances, and in Their guidance through the Holy Ghost.

If we will do as our Savior taught when He said: "...Follow me", we will eventually overcome and be able, as He taught:

> ...sit with Me in My throne even as I also overcame,
> and am set down with My Father in His throne
> (see New Testament, Book of Revelation 3:20-21).

When we "overcome" our **Spiritual Condition**, we will be like our Savior, and like our Heavenly Parents, and we will have Their

Super Power

AFTERWORD

1) To start this process, please call 1-801-240-1000 for the Church's Headquarters. Ask them to put you in touch with the Church's missionaries in your area, or contact http://mormon.org/missionaries.

2) As you are taught God's **Non Existence** and the gospel **Power** and **Power Change Formulas**, remember that they are teaching you data that is senior to all other sources of truth.

3) Our journey won't be easy, but it will be exciting and joyful! This will be especially true when we hear the Savior say, "...sit with me in my throne..." (see *New Testament Revelation* 3:20-21).

4) *A wise man once said: "You can have eternal life if you want it, but only if there is nothing else you want more."*

5) ***God's commandments and His teachings are His Power Formula to us, and keeping His Commandments and following His teachings is doing Power Change with God.***

6) *Two words.* God's **Power Formula** and **Power Change Formula** can both be summarized with just two words:

  God's **Power Formula** = Provide Direction

  God's **Power Change Formula** = "Follow Me". Also,

  God's **Power Change Formula** = "Complete Compliance"

(Thanks to my wife, Karla, for this insight). Please remember "Complete Compliance" when you start to feel a desire to rebel. Not only will this help you, it will also help those who will, in turn, look to you to "provide direction".

7) *"Table it":* It is almost certain that as you keep learning more, you will come across information, or data, that you don't understand. At first, **Doubt** may start to occur. People may also try to turn you aside from the path. *Don't let what you don't know destroy what you do know to be true.* Eventually from further study, instruction or from inspiration, you will clear the misunderstood words or concepts and receive the answers you are looking for. Until that time, don't be forced into making a decision about your faith, without having all the data. Simply do as Robert's Rules of Order would suggest and 'lay the matter on the table' or 'table it' until the Lord has shown you the answer. Stay on the *Way,* even if you don't yet know the *Why!*

8) *Enough said and enough read. Now it is time to decide and to do! (see #1 above)*

with all my love — Craig.

www.ingramcontent.com/pod-product-compliance
Lightning Source LLC
Chambersburg PA
CBHW081630040426

42449CB00014B/3251